Contents

Acknowledgments — *vii*

Introduction: Walking Between the Lines
Marilisa Jiménez García and Sonia Alejandra Rodríguez — *1*

Opening Poem: My Curriculum
Alissa Alina Flores — *19*

Section 1: Youth as Intellectuals and Storytellers

Chapter 1 — Out of Empire's Shadow: Confronting US Imperialism through Randy Ribay's *The Patron Saints of Nothing*
Lara Saguisag — *23*

Chapter 2 — Becoming a Girl: Girlhood, Child Marriage, and Widowhood in Kashmira Sheth's *Keeping Corner*
Blessy Sharon Samjose — *41*

Chapter 3 — "Let Me Tell You a Story": Healing, Environmental Justice, and Resistance in Mark Oshiro's *Each of Us a Desert*
Sonia Alejandra Rodríguez — *59*

Section 2: Intersectionality and Counternarratives

Chapter 4 — Representations of Asian American Girlhood in Contemporary Young Adult Literature
Jung E. Kim — *77*

Chapter 5	In the Spirit: Womanist Notions of Blackness, Indigeneity, Gender, and Dis/ability in Children's Literature *Reanae McNeal*	99
Chapter 6	The Power of Story, Images, and Policy in Native Studies: An Interview with Traci Sorell and Alia Jones *Marilisa Jiménez García and Sonia Alejandra Rodríguez*	119

SECTION 3: COMMUNITY FRAMEWORKS

Chapter 7	African American Children's Literature: The First 100 Years (reprint) *Violet J. Harris*	135
Chapter 8	Critical Indigenous Literacies: Selecting and Using Children's Books about Indigenous Peoples (reprint) *Debbie Reese*	153
Chapter 9	The Mirror, the Matrix, the Movement: Intellectual Legacies of the Council on Interracial Books for Children *Marilisa Jiménez García*	161
Coda:	Reflections on Struggle, Freedom, and Storytelling *Marilisa Jiménez García and Sonia Alejandra Rodríguez*	179

List of Contributors   187
Index   191

Ethnic Studies and Youth Literature

SUNY series in Multiethnic Literatures
Mary Jo Bona, editor

Ethnic Studies and Youth Literature

A Critical Reader

Edited by Marilisa Jiménez García and

Sonia Alejandra Rodríguez

SUNY PRESS

Published by State University of New York Press, Albany
© 2025 State University of New York
All rights reserved
Printed in the United States of America

No part of this book may be used or reproduced in any manner whatsoever without written permission. No part of this book may be stored in a retrieval system or transmitted in any form or by any means including electronic, electrostatic, magnetic tape, mechanical, photocopying, recording, or otherwise without the prior permission in writing of the publisher.

Links to third-party websites are provided as a convenience and for informational purposes only. They do not constitute an endorsement or an approval of any of the products, services, or opinions of the organization, companies, or individuals. SUNY Press bears no responsibility for the accuracy, legality, or content of a URL, the external website, or for that of subsequent websites.

EU GPSR Authorised Representative:
Logos Europe, 9 rue Nicolas Poussin, 17000, La Rochelle, France
contact@logoseurope.eu

For information, contact State University of New York Press, Albany, NY
www.sunypress.edu

Library of Congress Cataloging-in-Publication Data
Names: Jiménez García, Marilisa, editor | Alejandra Rodríguez, Sonia Alejandra, editor
Title: Ethnic studies and youth literature : A critical reader / Marilisa Jiménez García and
    Sonia Alejandra Rodríguez, editors.
Description: Albany : State University of New York Press, [2025] | Series:
SUNY series in Multiethnic Literature | Includes bibliographical references and index.
Identifiers: ISBN 9798855802986 (hardcover : alk. paper) | ISBN 9798855802962 (ebook)
    | ISBN 9798855802979 (paperback : alk. paper)
Further information is available at the Library of Congress.

Acknowledgments

An earlier version of chapter 7, "African American Children's Literature: The First One Hundred Years" by Violet J. Harris, was originally published in the *Journal of Negro Education*, vol. 59, no. 4, 1990, pp. 540-55, htttps://doi.org/10.2307/2295311.

An earlier version of chapter 8, "Critical Indigenous Literacies: Selecting and Using Children's Books about Indigenous Peoples" by Debbie Reese, was originally published in *Language Arts* (2016).

Marilisa

I would like to thank my family and friends for supporting me during the various institutional battles and victories she participated in during the writing of this book. An immense thank-you to Sonia Alejandra Rodriguez for bringing her truth and critical eye every day to our many meetings, and her colleagueship and support in making this project better. I want to honor my students and colleagues at the Institute of Critical Race and Ethnic Studies at Lehigh — Sirry Alang, Mary Mitzdarfer, Ruben Rosas, Alex Gonzalez, Kevelis Matthews-Alvarado, Faith Roncoroni, Jimmy Hamill, Paige Pagan, and Sam Sorenson — for their amazing creativity and work even when people thought we were all crazy. We were crazy good. At Simmons, while writing this book, Alex Smith, Amber Weinstock, Betty Thompson, Renee Runge, James Smith, Elifgul Buyakora, Kat Keyser, and Natalie Shroud helped me think about the ways kid lit needs to expand to accommodate the next generation. Thank you to the Hazel Dick Leonard Public Scholars Seminar at Simmons, especially Jyoti Puri, for their readings of drafts and comments. To all the educators, who get up early to love our kids and help them see themselves winning.

Sonia Alejandra

I would like to thank my husband for his invaluable support. I'd also like to thank Marilisa for inviting me to be part of this project. Marilisa, your faith in me and your trust in my expertise, has meant the world to me. Thank you to all my teachers and to my fellow educators, librarians, and practitioners. Also, thank you to Rebecca Colesworthy, Mary Jo Bona, Derrick Brooms, Ivory A. Toldson, and Sandra L. Osorio. Finally, thank you to our amazing contributors: Alissa, Lara, Blessy, Jung, Reanae, Traci, and Alia!

Introduction

WALKING BETWEEN THE LINES

*Marilisa Jiménez García and
Sonia Alejandra Rodríguez*

Ethnic Studies and Youth Literature: A Critical Reader represents a generation of scholars bridging the fields of ethnic studies and youth literature. We began this project by asking scholars and practitioners to consider the last ten years of youth literature and the field's reckoning with its role in systemic racism and oppression. We build on generations of scholars of color whose collective and individual publishing of anthologies and monographs (Sims Bishop 1992; Harris 1993; Thomas 2018, Saguisag 2019; Jiménez García 2021) argue that study of children, youth, and their literatures needs an epistemological shift. We also build on more than fifteen years in the field of youth literature as writers, mentors, and editors advocating for the creation of spaces for underrepresented literatures and scholars. Terms such as diversity and racial justice have become important to how the fields of youth literature and childhood/youth studies have organized themselves in the last five to ten years. Some landmarks we want to recognize include the We Need Diverse Books social media movement (2014); the founding of the *Research on the Diversity in Youth Literature* journal (2018), where Sonia Alejandra has served as co-editor for three years; the "We Need Diverse Scholars" (2016) Forum in *The Lion and the Unicorn,* where Marilisa authored a piece; and the Rutgers University-Camden's Childhood Studies department's Mellon-funded "Racial Justice" grant program and conference (2018). Our volume turns to ethnic studies as a path for understanding how racial justice might work in youth literature. We believe ethnic studies demands we go beyond seeing race, ethnicity, culture, and even diversity as a conversation about identity and difference into how marginalized positionalities create epistemologies that shape our understanding of craft, genre, youth, and knowledge production (Rodríguez 2018; Jiménez García 2018). In particular, this volume expands the call to examine the role of youth literature and culture in the study of the United States empire and vice versa through ethnic studies (Jiménez García 2021). Generations before We Need Diverse Books, writers and scholars of color have countered how whiteness shapes the telling, historicizing, and even imagining of childhood and youth and texts and media for young audiences.

Ethnic studies is a path for examining the underutilized lens of the US empire in youth literature studies, and indeed the larger realm of literary and cultural studies. Clearly postcolonial theory has provided a rich framework for considering the relationship between subjectivity, language, childhood, and the nation-state in youth literature, as the work of Clare Bradford and Ann Gonzalez demonstrates. Yet an emphasis on postcolonial theory often emphasizes British imperial case studies, which shift scholarly analysis from ongoing US colonialism in its past and present occupations. In 2024, scholar Lara Saguisag organized a panel for the Modern Language Association stemming from Daniel Immerwahr's *How to Hide an Empire* (2022), which brought public and academic attention to the literal invisibility of past and current US imperialism, and Marilisa's book *Side by Side* (2021), which was the first monograph in youth literature studies to analyze the US empire vis-à-vis Puerto Rico. A focus on the US empire allows us to see the impact race has had on national identity beyond traditional national borders. As Marilisa asks in *Side by Side:* "How would our study of US literature change if we approached the US as a conglomeration of competing settler colonial projects — on Indigenous land — through race, class, gender, and language?" (19).

Lara, whose chapter on Filipino youth and police violence in youth literature opens this volume; Marilisa; Gabriela Lee (University of the Philippines); Edcel Cintron-Gonzalez (Illinois State University); and Ayantika Mukherjee (University of Alberta, Canada) presented their research on US imperialism at MLA. We mark this as an evolving conversation in US literary and cultural studies that can no longer be ignored, especially as more scholars, descending from US colonized peoples, enter public and academic conversations on US imperial practices such as historical erasure, foreign and domestic aid for climate crisis, arms support, and refugee policies.

Often in literary and cultural studies, talking about race becomes fashionable, yet few want to discuss the US academy's position as a settler colonial institution and its role in the erasure and control of our local histories, schools, and repositories in places like the Philippines and Puerto Rico. Ethnic studies, founded by US colonized peoples, helps unravel how race, language, culture, nationality, immigration, migration, and settler colonialism collide in the US. The US itself is a layered empire of multiple European remnants — including French, Dutch, Spanish, English — on Indigenous lands marked by the Transatlantic slave trade. We also use the term "youth literature" in concert with Marilisa's project in *Side by Side* (2021) to delineate our work from terms such as children's literature, which are often uncritically encoded as Anglo British and Anglo American ways of writing about and for children. The authors in this volume use youth literature — art forms such as the picture book, the middle grade novel, and the young adult novel — as ways of tracking cultural norms about childhood and youth, such as age appropriateness and audience, but also as a means of analyzing how youth are imagined in the community, the family, and the nation through notions of literacy, reading cultures, and storytelling.

Vivian Yenika-Agbaw, whose passing in 2022 was felt and honored by the youth literature community, wrote in 1997 that children's literature must be "taken seriously." Her call emphasizes youth literature as both a rigorous artistic medium and a project of social justice. Young adult novels, picture books, and school reading lists are the nexus of culture war battles and national book bans, yet in many ethnic studies conferences and anthologies, children's and young adult literature is absent from the scholarly and political purview. Beyond individual scholars, we wanted a collection that critically examined the need, creativity, and rigorous processes of joining the scholarly fields of ethnic studies and youth literature. Many of our contributors know the work of presenting their research at venues such as the American Studies Association, Latinx Studies Association, Critical Ethnic Studies Association, Association for Asian American Studies, and National Women's Studies Association and being on perhaps the only panel on youth texts. Simultaneously, many of our contributors also know the dissonance of attending panels at the Children's Literature Association and American Library Association on BIPOC authors and literature and noticing the absence of Asian American studies, Latinx studies, and Black studies scholars in the audience and in citations.

The practice of walking between these liminal fields while also engaging multiple audiences has created a rigorous and exciting area of scholarship that joins with the past intellectual labor of communities of color in youth literature and opens up new avenues and intentional visibility for BIPOC scholars, writers, and practitioners. We wanted an anthology where interdisciplinary training was valued and centered; therefore, contributors come from the multidisciplinary and professional fields of library science, creative writing, literary criticism, and education.

Marilisa is a working-class Puerto Rican woman researcher, writer, and educator with schooling experiences in Florida, New Jersey, and New York — areas where multilingual Latinx communities comprise large portions of the population — yet she never read a book in class about her community until she began grad school. Going to high school, college, and graduate school in Florida shaped Marilisa's ideas about race and racialization in the 1990s — growing and studying in the Old South meant Puerto Ricans faced anti-Black and anti-immigrant racism from whites and even other Latinxs. Her career in youth literature was ignited through her examination of Puerto Ricans and ethnic studies movements in materials published for young people. After graduating, Marilisa continued to search for ways that communities of color recover literacies and histories through youth literature, and she also participated in the creation of research spaces in higher education that center ethnic studies methods. Marilisa's time in English departments, Latin American studies programs, ethnic studies institutes, and children's literature programs has led her to write and speak in ways that support building pathways, especially in community with students of color going into multiple careers who find her classes on youth literature to be a space to discuss law, policy, childhoods of color, and art.

Sonia Alejandra is a Mexican American, queer educator and writer from Chicago living in Queens, New York. Their experiences as a formerly undocumented immigrant, the oldest daughter of a mixed-status household, a first-generation college student, and now a first-generation faculty member influence their approaches to teaching and writing about literature. As an undergrad, Sonia Alejandra found answers to questions about the systemic oppression plaguing them and their family in ethnic studies courses. Sonia Alejandra also found a community of student activists in ethnic studies courses with whom to organize against racism and discrimination on campus. They were introduced to youth literature in graduate school, and the connection between youth literature and ethnic studies has been a significant part of their research since then. Sonia Alejandra's research focuses on representations of healing practices in books with Latinx protagonists written by Latinx authors. At the heart of Sonia Alejandra's work with youth literature is a desire to empower young people through storytelling. Throughout their academic career, Sonia Alejandra has been active in the communities outside the university or college campuses they attended. This community involvement has always included storytelling in some form or another.

We met through our collective work at the historic Library and Archives, Center for Puerto Rican Studies (Centro), Hunter College, CUNY, in 2014. Sonia Alejandra was completing their doctoral dissertation and conducting archival research while Marilisa was a Research Associate at Centro, her first academic position after receiving her PhD. Over the years, Marilisa and Sonia Alejandra's work in Latinx youth literature in particular forged a necessary bond over the disparities in their multiple fields, and they continued to work as co-mentors and researchers. We often talked about the importance of anthologies such as *This Bridge Called My Back: Writings by Radical Women of Color* (1979) for how it gathered the experiences, approaches, and solidarities of women of color in the academy and represented an epistemic shift. Like *Bridge,* this volume represents an account of our coming to consciousness with our community's histories in youth literature as a tool for liberation and healing (Moraga and Anzaldua xix). We also note that this volume "is less about each one of us and much more about the pending promise inscribed in all of us who believe that revolution — physical and metaphysical at once — is possible" (xxi)." We wondered what it would mean for a similar work to exist in the field of youth literature studies, especially from perspectives that challenged colonial logics of the US Empire and communities of color as a monolithic category.

In preparing for this book, we talked about previous important anthologies such as Laura Alamillo, Larissa M. Mercado-López and Cristina Herrera's *Voices of Resistance: Interdisciplinary Approaches to Chicano/a Children's Literature* (2018) — which Sonia Alejandra also wrote a chapter for — and how it foregrounded important issues in children's literature tied to social movements and ethnic studies bans. *Voices of Resistance*, in particular, reminds us that book challenges around ethnic studies and racial justice curriculum materials are nothing new. Indeed, while both Marilisa and Sonia Alejandra were in graduate school and on the job market for the first time, Chicanx/Latinx

Studies was banned in Arizona, an important moment *Voices of Resistance* lists as a catalyst for the anthology. Then as now, youth literature, played an important part of the ban for how it "created both counterstories that forged spaces of curricular inclusion for students who were a minoritized majority in their state, but exposed them to histories of Chican@ activism." This exposure to activist histories, Alamillo et al notes, "ignited their political and activist consciousness … resulting in collective student efforts to oppose a measure that had permitted state authorities to confiscate books while students sat in class" (ix). As Latinx grad students, our consciousness and our work was also shaped by the constant undermining of our literatures and ways of knowing in academic spaces — but more specifically, the understanding that we were entering the job market at a moment when few academic institutions were interested in supporting "contraband" literatures, even as phrases like "diversity in children's literature" were becoming more popular. For this project we wanted to assemble writers and literatures which represented racial and ethnic solidarities in the study of US imperialism. We also found ourselves drawn to scholars who challenged ideas about communities of color and scholars of color as monolithic identities. In tandem with our way of organizing this volume via Christine Sleeter and Miguel Zavala's hallmarks of ethnic studies, our authors represent, in some cases, marginal fields and marginal positionalities within marginal communities, and we believe this adds to the depth of our project, while still inviting further work and research.

In the last ten years of our scholar journeys, we have witnessed and also participated in the productive and problematic transformations of ethnic studies, youth literature, and the publishing industry. We witnessed how diversity in the field has become a profitable commodity while industries and the academy still leave out communities of color by erasing their scholarship and/or lived experiences. We have been invited by faculty members to speak on diversity panels and to mentor future scholars of color, even while we were still graduate students or researchers outside of traditional faculty positions struggling to mentor ourselves. Although we have had gracious mentors and supporters, some white and some of color, in many ways we had to imagine ourselves as models of success even when there were few positions in academia waiting to hire us, especially between 2011 and 2016. During the MLA panel in 2024 in Philadelphia, Saguisag asked panelists to consider how empire continues to haunt the work they do. Marilisa responded by saying that even though there was time when she felt haunted by imperial erasure and academic silence, in tandem with Eve Tuck's 2013 essay "A Glossary of Haunting," she was now "ready to be the ghost." As Tuck writes:

> Settler colonialism is the management of those who have been made killable, once and future ghosts — those that had been destroyed, but also those that are generated in every generation. Settler horror, then, comes about as part of this management, of

the anxiety, the looming but never arriving guilt, the impossibility of forgiveness, the inescapability of retribution.

Haunting, by contrast, is the relentless remembering and reminding that will not be appeased by settler society's assurances of innocence and reconciliation. Haunting is both acute and general; individuals are haunted, but so are societies. The United States is permanently haunted by the slavery, genocide, and violence entwined in its first, present and future days. Haunting doesn't hope to change people's perceptions, nor does it hope for reconciliation. Haunting lies precisely in its refusal to stop. Alien (to settlers) and generative for (ghosts), this refusal to stop is its own form of resolving. For ghosts, the haunting is the resolving, it is not what needs to be resolved. (642)

A haunting like the one Tuck describes might seem harsh in the somewhat nice world of children's literature, but it's perhaps even more important when writing from inside an empire that — as Immerwahr suggests — chooses to hide its imperial tendencies, and its imperial subjects — in plain sight. We have been the ghosts and we will continue to haunt fields of studies that insist on the erasure, silence, and marginalization of literature by people of color.

Ethnic Studies and Youth Literature is a result of years of struggle and conversation. As we write in 2024, we are aware of this volume's timely message as critical race theory, ethnic studies, and youth literature are at the forefront of political legislation after the Black Lives Matter uprisings in 2020. In the summer of 2020, after the brutal murder of Breonna Taylor and George Floyd at the hands of law enforcement, many corporations, universities and school boards "came to the altar" with promises of committing to antiracist initiatives and curriculum (Alang 2022). Yet many anti-racism initiatives, such as the one in York, Pennsylvania, were met with legislative banning in the name of "patriotic education" such as the kind of education outlined in Donald Trump's administration's 2020 *1776 Report*. In particular, critical race theory has become synonymous with any kind of teaching exposing the US's racist past and present, in many battleground states, such as Florida, Pennsylvania, and Texas (Jiménez and Pagan 2022). For example, the Institute on Critical Race and Ethnic Studies at Lehigh University, which Marilisa helped found and directed, was placed on a watch list by a conservative group with the project of creating a "resource for parents and students concerned about how Critical Race Theory, and implementation of Critical Race Training, impacts education. We have compiled the most comprehensive database to empower parents and students" (Critical Race Training in Education). Of course, proponents of ethnic studies know that this is just the latest in a long legacy of criminalization ascribed to BIPOC frameworks and resources that expose US imperialism, including racism and its legal and political systems. The fight for the College Board African American history Advanced Placement exam in particular highlights how it's not so much the *content* but the *context, framework,* and *theory* of how histories are taught and who they are allowed to center in the classroom, especially intersectional lives of BIPOC. As Sonia Alejandra later reflects in the coda, it's storytelling — not books — that is under attack.

Ethnic Studies as a Framework for Youth Literature Studies

Many times in our work we have found it necessary to define what we mean by ethnic studies. Ethnic studies disrupts the additive approaches to diversity in youth literature studies in the US because it does not allow the field to continue seeing itself as solely in conversation with the British empire and exposes the US as a product of several settler colonies, including Spanish, French, Dutch, and so forth. We are not saying it is the only way to examine the US empire; however, we are saying it is a productive way to get at issues of racial and social justice in US-based literatures. Ethnic studies grows out of working-class student movements in the late 1960s and is an intellectual project different from area or regional studies often preferred by university departments/programs for organizing othered faculty, students, and literatures, such as global studies, Africana studies, Asian studies, or Latin American studies, all of which began as projects supporting US foreign policy and surveillance (Davila 2022). In *Critical Ethnic Studies: A Reader*, Nadia Elia, David Hernandez, Jodi Kim, and Shana L. Redmond write that they "hope to enlarge the origin stories of ethnic studies, to blur the demarcation that prejudicially separates scholar from activist, and to further collective knowledge production" (217). This volume, in part, seeks to show how ethnic studies movements and youth literature intertwine, influencing how scholars and practitioners in these fields apply activism as both a theory and practice toward social change.

Reflecting on ethnic studies as a history and framework requires us, as Dan Berger writes, to consider "how academic knowledge and movement knowledge are negotiated in the academy" (215). Academic programs, spaces, and archives dedicated to ethnic studies research and pedagogy continue to fight for space in the US academy. Often university administrations have a difficult time seeing how critical race theory and ethnic studies models differ from area studies or programs focusing on geographical regions, such as Asian studies, Latin American studies, and global studies. Even terms such as the Global South and the Global North demarcate racial and cultural differences without much specificity to power analysis and histories of oppression in and as a result of US imperialism.

The creation of spaces in which to house ethnic studies and critical race research in predominantly white institutions also inspired this volume. Marilisa's work as a professor of youth literature and Latinx studies demanded ways to support her students and research at her previous institution — the lack of interdisciplinary cohabitation and participation led to her work as the principal investigator and founding director of the Institute on Critical Race and Ethnic Studies (ICRES) at Lehigh University. Marilisa and her colleagues, including Professor Sirry Alang, doctoral student Sam Sorensen, undergraduate student Alissa Flores, and graduate fellow Kevelis Matthews-Alvarado, created a proposal for funding, in conversation with past student activism around gender and racial justice, in which they had to state why a new research institute on ethnic studies differed from major existing and funded programs such as Africana studies and Latin American studies. In that proposal, Marilisa and Sirry Alang wrote about how ethnic studies, as a model, "is a form of knowledge production that centers anti-racism, anti-sexism and anti-colonialism. It also brings frameworks implemented by communities of color, in relation to the world-wide struggles for rights and liberation, in the forefront of learning and inquiry." Students centered as key intellectual workers and creators speak to what is meant. The ICRES included two main research projects, the Health Justice Collaborative through Alang's research in public health, and the Education Justice Initiative through Marilisa's work with teacher education and curriculum. Ultimately, ethnic studies disrupts the narrative of the US as a benevolent conqueror and the US academy as a site for the study of diplomacy and democracy. This lens centers the knowledge systems of US colonized peoples and brings issues of land occupation, transnational humanitarian struggle, and rights violations within US imagined borders. The experience of articulating the nuances of an ethnic studies and/or critical race studies model in the creation of university research spaces, including how such models come from working class students of color demand, shaped the conversations leading to this volume. Sonia Alejandra's work in ethnic studies at a community college in New York City looks different because the needs of community college students are different from those at traditional four-year universities. As of 2024, the creation of an ethnic studies option at LaGuardia Community College (CUNY) is fairly new. Students majoring in liberal arts now have the option to focus their associates degree in ethnic studies. For Sonia Alejandra, ethnic studies frameworks have always been central to their pedagogy in the composition, literature, and creative writing classroom. Without a required introductory course in ethnic studies for all students, Sonia Alejandra finds it important that their students leave courses with basic understandings of the differences between race and ethnicity, with an understanding of intersectionality, of race as a social construct, and of the importance of community knowledge as a tool for liberation. As co-director of Casa de las Américas, a new cultural hub at LaGuardia Community College, Sonia Alejandra leads initiatives like the First Generation Student Support Circles, a student-led community space dedicated to supporting first-generation students and centering their experiences as sites of knowledge. Through Casa de las Americas, Sonia Alejandra frequently invites BIPOC and LGBTQIA authors to campus to speak to students about the importance of storytelling and telling our communities' stories.

Ethnic studies grows out of underserved and invisibilized communities of color in the US who became part of the American experience through colonialism and displacement, including Indigenous, African American, Latinx, and Asian American studies. Native author Traci Sorell, in her interview in this collection, "The Power of Story, Images, and Policy in Native Studies," reflects on her undergraduate studies in the 1990s at the University of California, Berkeley, Native American Studies program, a program born out of student demand. The program, along with ethnic studies, African American studies, Asian American studies, and Chicano studies, formed part of the historic Third World College at UC Berkeley, which is now, through various reiterations and university politics, the Ethnic Studies Department in the College of Letters and Sciences.

The traditional groups represented by the post–Civil Rights student struggles in K-12 and higher education include populations directly impacted by US empire vis-à-vis land occupation, economic, political exploitation, and upheaval, including Native, African American, Chicanx, Puerto Rican, and Asian American students. Such student struggles saw themselves as participating and in solidarity with the Third World Peoples and transnational struggles for liberation in areas such as Vietnam. In *Transformative Ethnic Studies in Schools: Curriculum, Pedagogy and Research*, Christine Sleeter and Wayne Miguel Zavala write, "Precisely because of the ongoing colonization and struggle against it, the movement (or movements) for Ethnic Studies can be characterized as generative, as developing in nonlinear and nonunitary ways, and as unfinished" (3). For this reason, newer diasporas produced through US occupation such as in Central America and the Middle East, often among the least represented in youth literature, provide rich histories and legacies for reconsidering ideas of who has a stake in the US and ongoing discussions about Americanness, citizenship, and belonging.

Ethnic studies and critical race theory are not dogmas or formulas, and we recognize the limitations of any theoretical framework and any one volume. However, we believe that critical ethnic studies and critical race studies provide ways to recover the intellectual histories of communities of color and support the work of racial justice past and future by marking important differences between corporate diversity and inclusion models and the work of political and intellectual liberation for colonized peoples. We also believe the legal battles surrounding ethnic studies and critical race theory today reinforce how these frameworks challenge the white status quo and invert racial justice language for its purposes. For example, proponents of 2022 Florida's "Stop Woke" (HB 7), which forbids the teaching of critical race theory — broadly defined by legislation as "discussing racism" — in schools and corporations have said the act protects employees from a "hostile work environment due to critical race theory training" (Florida, Office of Governor Desantis).

The Hallmarks of Ethnic Studies and Youth Literature

It is also important to define what we mean by youth in this collection. As scholars interested in childhood as a site for understanding multiple forms of subjectivity, agency, and resistance, we engage with literature written for young people as a means of teasing out how authors and creators imagine young people participating in community and knowledge-making. Karen Sanchez-Eppler writes, "Books for children remain one of the best gauges for a particular society's views of childhood and one that we know that children themselves engaged with directly. The books written for children instruct the young in how their particular culture understands their role" (37). Ethnic studies models emphasize young people as integral to intellectual inquiry, labor, and leadership that counter deficit discourses about students of color in the academy. This volume features contributors reflecting on the work of faculty and students of color in the classroom, bookstores, and libraries. Through an analysis of mostly young adult novels, picture books, and activist organizations, our authors also consider the role of youth activism, agency, and youth of color as participants in their own stories. Traditional modes of children's literature in the academy have at times driven a wedge between how writers and practitioners think of texts for youth as completely separate from young people or from "the child." While we believe it is limiting for literary critics and practitioners to presuppose, romanticize, or ventriloquize what they believe a young person of color sees in a book, we also believe it is impossible to dismiss the impact that stories and particularly historical erasure have had on youth of color. The research in ethnic studies is clear on how affirming representations of communities of color impact positive school performance, including high school and college retention rates (Amy Sueyoshi, Sutee Sujitparapitaya). This interdisciplinary volume contains approaches for considering texts and their impact as socially engaged art without separating the reality of youth as both within and without books.

Christine Sleeter and Miguel Zavala introduce "The Hallmarks of Ethnic Studies" in *Transformative Ethnic Studies in Schools*. The hallmarks are listed as curriculum as counternarrative, criticality, reclaiming cultural identities, intersectionality and multiplicity, community engagement, pedagogy that is culturally responsive and mediated, and students as intellectuals (8). These hallmarks inspired the work of this volume in at least three ways. First, in the preliminary phases of planning this volume, Marilisa used these hallmarks as a way of grounding the Education Justice Initiative branch of the ICRES. The Education Justice Initiative at ICRES, from 2019 to 2022, carried as part of its mission the study and implementation of ethnic studies pedagogies in K-12 through the use of youth literature. The hallmarks were a guide for determining how texts and lesson plans supported racial justice through countering racial and gender stereotypes and engaging in students of color empowerment in the classroom. All teacher training workshops began with the Hallmarks of Ethnic

Studies infographic made by a student-researcher, Alissa Flores. Teachers in Pennsylvania reflected on how their district's curriculum and/or talking points were or were not following the Hallmarks, some even sending the infographic to their principals, district leaders, and school counselors. Second, the contributors of this volume were provided a list of suggested resources as they revised chapters, including *Transformative Ethnic Studies in Schools* and the Hallmarks infographic. Third, our organization of this volume relates to how we saw contributors working with and responding to specific Hallmarks we revised to reflect the work of youth literature in ethnic studies.

Youth As Intellectuals and Storytellers: While the audience for youth literature is young people, it often seems that the literature is used to inform young people how to be, how to behave, and how to become active citizens in their society without actual input from young people. Though our volume does not emphasize young readers' responses to literature or young writers themselves, we searched for chapter contributions where young characters were centered as intellectuals and storytellers in their own right: How are youth portrayed in the stories? Are they centered as carrying knowledge? Are they complicit in systems of oppression, and how do they navigate that complicity? How do youth participate in telling their own stories? The chapters in this section highlight protagonists who use knowledge and storytelling to challenge the status quo and push for liberation in their communities.

In chapter 1, "Out of Empire's Shadow: Confronting US Imperialism through Randy Ribay's *The Patron Saints of Nothing*," Lara Saguisag argues that Randy Ribay's young adult novel reveals and confronts the entanglements between US imperialism and practices of coercive policing in the Philippines. Further, Saguisag insists that Filipino Americans must envision themselves as global citizens who contest national and political borders and commit themselves to decolonial and de-imperializing projects.

In chapter 2, "Becoming a Girl: Girlhood, Child Marriage, and Widowhood in Kashmira Sheth's *Keeping Corner*," Blessy Sharon Samjose examines girlhoods in the South Asian context as a negotiated state of existence through a critical close reading of Kashmira Sheth's historical young adult novel *Keeping Corner*. This chapter challenges reading girlhood as an impending initiation into womanhood, defined by marriage, motherhood, and a daughter-in-law's responsibilities.

In chapter 3, "Let Me Tell You a Story": Healing, Environmental Justice, and Resistance in Mark Oshiro's *Each of Us a Desert*," Sonia Alejandra Rodríguez explores the multivalent role of storytelling. Through an analysis of Mark Oshiro's *Each of Us a Desert*, Rodríguez demonstrates how centering young people as intellectuals and storytellers can lead to community liberation. Storytelling can be used as a tool for healing and resistance against prescriptive gendered roles and environmental injustice and lead to a queer future.

Intersectionality and Counternarratives: Data and data visualization have become an important way that the youth literature community discusses the area of racial justice in the last ten years. For example, the Cooperative Children's Book Center's statistics on books published by, on, and about communities of color and its racial categories tend to influence how we talk about race in the field and how we further imagine what change might look like to see those numbers grow or dim perennially. Lee and Low's Diversity Baseline Survey also importantly allowed the public to see the unbearable whiteness of children's publishing. Yet ethnicity, nationality, sexuality, and race, especially when discussing US-based racial and ethnic categories, are often conflated in youth literature discussions when we consider what and who counts as a text by, for example, a Black author. Categories such as African American and Black are often seen as synonymous, while Latinx and Black are often seen as separate, veiling Afro Latinx authorship, among others. The rise of multiethnic families and school populations in the US, not only as children of past and present diasporas, but also as those identifying outside Black and white binaries, and even gender binaries, makes intersectional youth literature a necessity in our reading lists (Duran and Jimenez Garcia 2018). How complicit are characters, plots, and theories in the colonial project? Are stories countering colonial tropes? One way we advocated for intersectionality and counterstories in this volume was by choosing not to organize chapters by race and ethnicity and instead allowing for conversations to form among chapters that engage with ethnic studies as a model. We need to grow beyond our understanding of traditional racialized categories, many of which parallel colonial logics of the US empire. We call for more nuanced understanding and critique of diversity within diversity. US colonized peoples are not a monolith, and neither are their frameworks. For example, the authors and contributors in this section represent stories from the margins, such as Afro-Indigenous storytelling (chapter 5) and Queer Asian American girlhood and the lack of forums and data that would support the visibility of such narratives (chapter 4).

In chapter 4, "Representations of Asian American Girlhood in Contemporary Young Adult Literature," Jung E. Kim analyzes a number of young adult books from the last several years with Asian American female protagonists. While the model minority myth is still very much an active part of many of these books, there are several books, such as Lyla Lee's *I'll Be the One*, that depict Asian American young women who defy the norms — whether by being fat, interested in the arts, or queer. Kim's chapter also represents recent data collection on recent Asian American stories and challenges the US monolith on these communities.

In chapter 5, "In the Spirit: Womanist Notions of Blackness, Indigeneity, Gender, and Dis/ability in Children's Literature," Reanae McNeal demonstrates how Black women activist-writers highlight socially engaged spirituality through Youth Literature that delves into diversity, equity, inclusion, justice, and spiritual principles. While spirituality has been a central component of Black social justice movements historically, varied Black women activists across social locations throughout time have grounded themselves in a socially engaged spirituality that accompanies their activism for justice. Applying an Afro-Indigenous, womanist lens, McNeal also offers a rereading and reframing of Harriet Tubman through Carole Boston Weatherford's *Moses: When Harriet Tubman Led Her People to Freedom* (2006).

In chapter 6, "The Power of Story, Images, and Policy in Native Studies: An Interview with Traci Sorell and Alia Jones," Sorell and Jones reflect on the monolithic ways that stories about Native kids, children's literature medals, and library spaces are organized. Both Sorell and Jones represent different perspectives in education, creating stories, and working with youth as Indigenous creators and practitioners. This chapter offers practical ideas for how to move the conversation forward in terms of youth literature and change-making policy in publishing and lawmaking.

Community Frameworks: When considering the role of literature in social movements, we have to wonder how often literature itself has played a part in oppression, dehumanization, and erasure. For example, authors and activists often point out the ways publishing, education systems and library programs failed to represent their communities as complex, active agents with their own solutions to societal problems. Scholars working at the intersections of ethnic studies and youth literature often have to gauge harm done while also looking for ways communities have created pathways for empowering through texts and story. However, how often are community legacies and frameworks left out of intellectual debates or even seen as part of an intellectual legacy? Often we see how texts form part of community healing, reclaiming, and recentering intellectual and activist legacies, with young people frequently playing an important role. Are youth imagined as integral to their communities as opposed to separate? Are communities seen as possessing intellectual legacies? Do potential solutions involve the community?

In chapter 7, Violet Harris's seminal "African American Children's Literature: The First One Hundred Years" casts the net for how critical historiography and civil rights and social justice movements intersected with African American traditions. The chapter serves as a means of looking back on the ways scholars of color broke ground for merging together Black studies and children's literature to multiple audiences in education, Africana studies, history, and youth literature.

In chapter 8, "Critical Indigenous Literacies: Selecting and Using Children's Books about Indigenous Peoples," Debbie Reese makes the case for "indigenizing" youth literature and really seeing the field, especially in library science, through Indigenous histories and literacies. This chapter models what we mean by forcing scholars and practitioners to adopt Native frameworks to understand youth literature, rather than simply adding Native books to their classrooms and home libraries. It also serves as a way to train non-Natives to read through this lens.

Finally, in chapter 9, "The Mirror, the Matrix, the Movement: Intellectual Legacies of the Council on Interracial Books for Children," Marilisa Jiménez

García argues for recovering the intellectual legacies of the Council on Interracial Books for Children, including their work in documenting ethnic studies movements in the late 1960s, specifically their turn to racial solidarity and global freedom struggles in contrast to today's corporate-led DEI initiatives in youth literature. This chapter offers a reading of the CIBC textbook *Human and Anti-Human Values in Children's Books* (1976) as containing a model for families, scholars, and practitioners for unearthing racism as tied to imperialism and colonialism in the US.

Ethnic studies and critical race theory are fields of training and study that we argue shape the world of youth literature past, present, and future. An author or scholar of color's positionality as a person of color does not mean their work participates in the project of ethnic studies. Not all books written by ethnic people are ethnic studies books. Ethnic studies is a field of study, and assumptions that ethnic scholars are automatically ethnic studies experts is not true. Ethnic studies requires growth and revision — it's not a stagnant field.

The Limits of Empathy

Often communities of color are included in all-white spaces simply as material for aspiring writers, librarians, and scholars. There is a tendency, especially in literature classrooms, to teach our literatures as supporting the project of empathy for social justice. In other words, often literature by people of color is included in syllabi as a means to learn about the "other" and as a push to recognize the humanity of the "other." But in many cases the project of being a student of color, or a new faculty member of color hired as a change agent, is that existing in those same spaces becomes a project of constantly countering deep-seated theories and narratives. We run into profound problems of equity when structural and epistemic differences are treated as interpersonal problems or when the proficiency of a kind of literature or group of writers of color means that a group believes they are beyond structural inequities. As Richard Delgado and Jean Stephanic write in *Critical Race Theory: An Introduction* (1995), working in those environments and "trying to" constantly counter narratives "makes one come across as humorless or touchy" (Delgado and Stephanic 33). More specifically, they reflect on the limits of empathy, and indeed, the project of empathy as an agent of any sort of social change: "The idea that one can use words to undo the meanings that others attach to these very same words is to commit the empathic fallacy — the belief that one can change a narrative by merely offering another, better one — that the reader's or listener's empathy will quickly and reliably take over. Unfortunately, empathy is in shorter supply than we think" (34).

And yet, coming out of the summer of 2020, so many of us in K-12 and higher education saw the drafting of countless statements on antiracism and professed commitments to equity. However, none of these statements ever deals with the failure to fund ethnic studies, to support faculty of color when they are maligned by the media, or to commit to structural reconsiderations of police in classrooms and campuses. By uniting this project to critical race theory and ethnic studies, we are asking the field of youth literature to truly take stock of its basic structural inequities, its failure to acknowledge our knowledge systems in the field, its inability to provide spaces and opportunities for graduate students of color, its rigidity at recruiting and retaining scholars of color as leaders in spaces like the Children's Literature Association, and its complicity in an abusive system through its constant faith in books alone to undue systemic racism. At the same time, we do not claim that this or any one volume can bear the burden of undoing systemic oppression and harm. Instead, with this volume, we imagine a pathway where scholars of color and ethnic studies frameworks are central to the study of youth literature and culture. In our coda, we come back to this issue of storytelling and empathy as a means of reflecting on the volume and suggesting more productive engagements with texts and stories.

Conclusion

Ethnic Studies and Youth Literature: A Critical Reader is part of an ongoing conversation that we believe has the potential to lead to transformative change. We believe that Ethnic Studies methodologies are no longer a choice, but instead are a necessity if the intellectual project of youth literature within the larger humanities hopes to survive. As we urge for the centering of ethnic studies, it's important to also center the communities ethnic studies was created for to begin with. Ethnic studies as a practice requires that we question who is at the table, who is getting the research awards, who is being invited to diversity panels, who is hired at our institutions, who are we citing, and who are we leaving out by taking up this work ourselves.

As we worked on this collection, the study of writing craft was also something we kept in mind as we asked who is telling our stories and which stories are making it into the public. While the majority of the chapters in this collection are literary criticism, how stories are told and who gets to tell those stories is a fundamental argument in all of them. Matthew Salesses reminds us that "Craft is never neutral" (22). As scholars who study youth literature and youth culture, it's difficult to separate discussions of the book from how the book is made. In the time since we started putting this collection together, the publishing industry in the United States has undergone a reckoning demanding more diversity in the stories that are told, diversity in writers telling those stories, and diversity in the people working behind the scenes. Lee & Low Books' 2023 Diversity Baseline Survey Results showed that the publishing industry was 73% white, 71% cis woman, 69% heterosexual, and 84% non-disabled. The University of Wisconsin-Madison's Cooperative Children's Book Center (CCBC) reported that in 2019, 41.8% of the total books received featured white characters, and 29% of total books featured animals. In other words, it's not surprising that if the majority of the people working in the US publishing industry are white, the majority of the books published also feature white characters. The CCBC also reports that of the books that include BIPOC characters, not all of those representations are written by BIPOC authors — in fact, a significant percentage of books with BIPOC characters are about them but not by them. The state of the publishing industry in the US and who is telling these stories is something that we can't ignore as we, as scholars, engage critically with the literature for young people. Despite the blatant whiteness of the industry and of the books being published, there are those who believe that it is a difficult time to be a white person writing books. Such sentiments extend from critiques of the publishing industry wherein it's more likely that a white person will get published for writing diverse characters than a BIPOC who is also writing diverse characters. The practice of "writing the other" has created debates about who can write what, with people on one side asking that educating oneself be a part of writing the other, while people on another side claim restraint on their creative freedom and that they should be allowed to write whatever they want.

Once again, Salesses reminds us, "Make no mistake — writing is power. What this fact should prompt us to ask is: What kind of power is it, where does it come from, and what does it mean?" (xviii). Our consideration for the craft of children's books is grounded in our investigation of power. The chapters in *Ethnic Studies and Youth Literature* ask readers to question, examine, and acknowledge power in all facets of youth literature, youth culture, and the study of youth literature. As Salesses reminds us, "Craft is the history of which kind of stories have typically held power — and for whom — so it also is the history of which stories have typically been omitted. That we have certain expectations for what a story is or should include means we also have certain expectations for what a story isn't or shouldn't include" (19).

We believe that it is also time to center scholars and writers of color in the pursuit of racial justice in our various fields, and we believe that in itself is impossible without understanding and committing to ethnic studies models. As scholars of color, we also understand the importance of examining our own privilege within our communities of color so that we do not enable the same kinds of sexism, racism, ableism, and homophobia as legacies of imperialism and colonialism in the US. This collection is a celebration of the work that is being done by scholars and creators of color in ethnic studies and youth literature.

Works Cited

Ella, Nadia, et al. *Critical Ethnic Studies: A Reader.* Duke University Press, 2016.

Davila, Arlene. "What My Students Don't Know about their History." *New York Times*, 15 October 2022, https://www.nytimes.com/2022/10/15/opinion/hispanic-heritage-Latinx-studies.html.

Durand, Sybil, and Marilisa Jiménez García. "Unsettling Representations of Identities: A Critical Review of Diverse Youth Literature." *Research in the Diversity of Youth Literature*, vol. 1, no. 1, 2018.

Moraga, Cherrie, and Gloria Anzaldúa. *This Bridge Called My Back: Writings by Radical Women of Color.* State U of New York P, 2015.

Jiménez, Laura M., et al. "Where Is the Diversity in Publishing? The 2023 Diversity Baseline Survey Results." Lee & Low Books The Open Book Blog, 28 February 2024, https://blog.leeandlow.com/2024/02/28/2023diversitybaselinesurvey/. Accessed 1 March 2024.

Jiménez García, Marilisa. *Side by Side: US Empire, Puerto Rico, and the Roots of Youth Literature and Culture.* University Press of Mississippi, 2021.

Jiménez García, Marilisa. "The Lens of Latinx Literature." *Children's Literature*, vol. 47, 2019, pp. 1-8.

Sims Bishop, Rudine. *Shadow and Substance: Afro-American Experience in Contemporary Children's Fiction.* National Council for Teachers of English, 1982.

Harris, Violet. *Teaching Multicultural in Grades K-8.* Christopher Gordon, 1992.

Rodríguez, Sonia Alejandra. "Conocimiento Narratives: Creative Acts and Healing in Latinx and Young Adult Literature." *Children's Literature*, vol. 47, 2019, pp. 9-29.

Saguisag, Lara. *Incorrigibles and Innocents: Constructing Childhood and Innocents in Progressive Era Comics.* Rutgers, 2019.

Saguisag, Lara. "Children's Literature in the Long Shadow of Imperialism." Modern Language Association, 2024.

Sleeter and Zavala. *Transformative Ethnic Studies in Schools: Curriculum, Pedagogy, Research.* Teachers College P, 2020.

Salessas, Matthew. *Craft in the Real World: Rethinking Fiction Writing and Workshopping.* Catapult, 2021.

Tuck, Eve, and C. Ree. "A Glossary of Haunting." *A Handbook of Autoethnography*, edited by Tony E. Adams et al., Routledge, 2013.

Thomas, Ebony Elizabeth. *The Dark Fantastic.* New York UP, 2020.

President's Advisory Committee. The 1776 Report. January 2021. https://trump-whitehouse.archives.gov/wp-content/uploads/2021/01/The-Presidents-Advisory-1776-Commission-Final-Report.pdf.

Yenika-Agbaw, Vivian. "Taking Children's Literature Seriously: Reading for Pleasure and for Social Change." *Language Arts*, vol. 74, no. 6, October 1997, pp. 446-53.

Opening Poem

MY CURRICULUM
Alissa Alina Flores

my curriculum
because *their* curriculum is a little *too* used to the dehumanization of Black and Brown
        bodies
a little *too* comfortable with bleak and unempathetic   so called "conversation"
about the struggles that surround our ancestry

I want to *hear*   about the congos of the Afro-Cuban community
I want to *hear*   about Nuyorican voices   the diaspora
and the woman whose writing is a little *too* intimidating
a little *too* revolutionary for their curriculum

I want to hear about forgotten leaders
      the women of the Young Lords Party,
            The Women's Union of Nigeria
stories of men stripped of their lives in the fight
for a sense of comfort   for protection in their own country
that's what I want in *my* curriculum

their curriculum moves past the conversations that are real and raw and honest
conversations   that paint pictures   outlined with blood of the people
who apparently don't belong on the land stolen from them
moves past the conversations that are a little *too* uncomfortable   *too* political

but *not* in my curriculum
and I didn't learn Shakespeare and Jane Austen the way I learned Gloria Naylor,
        Judith Cofer
in my curriculum, we leave space for people that don't fit your canon
their stories just as valid
      their stories life changing
           their stories representative of a larger struggle

we should learn the origin of the word Boricua
and closely read Audre Lorde   Toni Morrison   Julia De Burgos
the myth of the Latin woman
I'm saying   third   world   women

In my curriculum, I wanna hear the different dialects
the sound of the tongue that seems lost
buried under a facade that deems it insignificant

deems it textbook worthy   not conversation worthy
textbook worthy   not poetry worthy
textbook worthy   not *quite* course work worthy
the songs of a culture I never got to study but could one day *touch* me
change   me

I want them to *fear* my curriculum
fear the way it will hold open their eyes   dissect their preconceived notions
make them overflow with a new found curiosity

In *my* curriculum   stories of furrowed brows and big hoops
            strong curls, red lipstick
a little *too* aggressive for you

spaces where we unpack and we see ourselves
we yearn   and yell   and vent
and I don't know about you, but that's not aggression,
In my curriculum
that's what I call healing   *curación*

with all of these stories to share
diverse in meaning, in color, in tradition
in hair texture, in slang, in dance, and in art
where do we lose?
tell me,   *where* do we lose
in learning about the culture that we never truly lost
but rather   was permitted to this gray area
the culture that serves as background noise
glorified stories of colonization

a history they deemed invaluable   but let me tell you,
in *my* curriculum
we navigate these forgotten stories with a hunger
                              a determination
                                          a plea
to *never*   for a second   undermine the bodies
that can teach us so much about change and struggle,
                        triumph and beauty
not in *my* curriculum.

SECTION 1

Youth as Intellectuals and Storytellers

ONE

Out of Empire's Shadow

CONFRONTING US IMPERIALISM THROUGH RANDY RIBAY'S *THE PATRON SAINTS OF NOTHING*

Lara Saguisag

On the night of August 16, 2017, seventeen-year-old Kian Loyd delos Santos was killed by police in an anti-drug operation in Caloocan, a city in the Metro Manila region of the Philippines. The initial police report stated that Kian was a drug runner. Police alleged that the boy fired at them and attempted to flee, and claimed they only shot back in self-defense. A .45-caliber handgun and two sachets of what appeared to be shabu (methamphetamine) were found near Kian's lifeless body.

Kian's family and friends disputed the accusation that he was armed and involved in drug dealing. CCTV footage refuted the narrative that Kian resisted arrest, showing how he was dragged away by police. Witnesses claimed that police beat the boy and handed him the gun; one attested that he heard the high school student cry out, "Tama na po! May exam pa ako bukas!" ("Please stop! I have an exam tomorrow!"). Three cops were eventually found guilty of murdering Kian, but they were cleared of charges of planting evidence.

The barbaric murder of Kian was not unusual. It had been more than a year since President Rodrigo Roa Duterte, who was sworn into office on June 30, 2016, launched a brutal "war on drugs." During his presidential campaign, Duterte promised to rid the country of illegal drugs in "three to six months," boasting that his drug policy would be one of slaughter (qtd. in Terada). As he put it, "there's no such thing as bloodless cleansing" (qtd. in Terada). Even before he was sworn in, the Philippine National Police (PNP), in tandem with vigilantes, launched what would become a years-long crusade to "clean up" Metro Manila and other urban areas through grisly public executions of suspected drug users and dealers. Human rights groups estimate that these extrajudicial killings have claimed the lives of 20,000 Filipinos. Investigative journalists and human rights advocates have also exposed how Duterte's so-called war on drugs has been, in reality, a war on the poor (Punongbayan and Mandrilla; Wells). This terroristic campaign also resulted in tens of thousands of arrests and surrenders, straining already overcrowded, unsanitary, and mismanaged prisons.

The slaying of Kian catalyzed widespread protest against Duterte's policies. Thousands came out in support of Kian's family during his funeral. #JusticeforKian trended on social media, and celebrities and senators, including some allied with Duterte, called for an investigation into the young man's killing. But even as #JusticeforKian mobilized some Filipinos against police violence, it did little to contain the epidemic of extrajudicial killings (Talabong). While the case of Kian resulted in tremors of outrage, it appears that most objected to the murder of an innocent rather than the practice of extrajudicial killing itself. By and large, majority of Filipinos continued to support Duterte's stringent and vicious law-and-order approach to governance ("Second Quarter 2019"). At the tail end of Duterte's term in 2022, he maintained a high approval rating ("SWS: Rodrigo Duterte").

Whenever I tell my colleagues and students about Duterte's bloody, antipoor crusade against drugs, I often see disbelief register on their faces. For how can one remain impassive when hearing of streets littered with bloodied corpses, some adorned with cardboard signs that read "Pusher ako, wag tularan" ("I'm a pusher, don't be like me")? But whenever I share my distress about extrajudicial killings in the Philippines, I worry that I participate in othering my homeland, inadvertently depicting it as a uniquely brutal and backward country under the thumb of a despotic leader. Once, a student asked me, "How do Filipinos feel about living out a dystopian narrative?" It was a question that stunned me. On the one hand, I concede my student was engaging in truth-telling, as they named the Duterte administration's cruel, unjust, and *popular* policies as symptoms of an ailing and broken-down society. But what gnawed at me was the way their query framed the Philippines as some sort of elseworld prone to dysfunction and breakdown, a country that is geographically, politically, economically, and morally antipodal to the United States. My student's question was expressive of a US tendency to view the Philippines as fundamentally less than, as incomprehensibly foreign.

Yet a few students also apprehend these atrocious killings as all too familiar. Sometimes a student would draw connections between the Duterte administration and the corrupt, destructive governments that their families fled from. For others, the story of Kian was troublingly evocative of police brutalities against Black youth in the US. Kian reminded them of Trayvon, Mike, and Tamir. I appreciate these parallels that my students draw; their stories illuminate for me how the specter of US empire reveals itself in violent ways around the world. While it is crucial to refrain from collapsing the unique contexts of Gaza, Iguala, Lagos, and Manila, to remain attentive to the nuances between #BlackLivesMatter and #JusticeforKian, the connections that my students make offer pathways for recommitting to internationalist anticolonial movements and building deep solidarity across borders.

In trying to work through this mixture of responses to the extrajudicial killings in the Philippines, I began thinking about how the 2019 young adult novel *The Patron Saints of Nothing* by Filipino American author Randy Ribay not only lays bare injustice and violence in the Philippines but also lays out the complex contexts of such injustice and violence. By contextualizing and historicizing the extrajudicial killings under Duterte's regime, the novel urges readers to recognize the Philippines not as antithetical to the US, but as a nation that has been profoundly shaped by US imperialism. The novel opens a space for students and educators to discuss the history of US colonialism and evaluate how such history casts a shadow on postcolonial institutions and systems in the Philippines. Thus, *Patron Saints* counters the propensity of educational spaces — including publishing for young people — to elide the fact of US empire. As Marilisa Jiménez García elucidates, "the contemporary US academy, including its pipeline of K-12 curriculum, which includes youth literature, tends to resist the notion of the US as an empire in ways which other colonial powers, such as England, France, and even Spain, make much more plain to young readers" (19). *Patron Saints* strives to make things plain, calling attention to the debilitating impact of US expansionism, militarism, and intervention on peoples and communities around the world. The novel can potentially encourage students and educators to critique and revamp curricula that are often evacuated of lessons on historical and current expressions of US imperialism.

Through the close examinations of two characters, this chapter illustrates how the novel can enable discussions of the legacy of US imperial rule in the Philippines. It probes the contradictions of Jay's uncle Maning, a police chief who declares himself anticolonial yet is an ardent defender of oppressive, hierarchical, and colonial structures. It also pays attention to the character of Jay, a child of an immigrant parent who endeavors to understand his roles and responsibilities as one who is at once Filipino and American. Jay's interactions with his uncle are discomfiting, full of interrogations and provocations. But these exchanges are what, in part, spur Jay to excavate familial and cultural histories that others seem intent on burying. He also observes and names his uncle's incongruities, signaling his rising political consciousness. These two characters express the complex ways Filipinos — in both the Philippines and the United States — contend with the Philippines' enduring entanglements with its former colonizer.

In the novel, Jay encounters the vital decolonial work already pursued by Filipinos in the Philippines, and he comprehends why it is imperative to center their knowledges and experiences. In this vein, US readers could work to decenter *Patron Saints* itself: Rather that turning to a novel originating in the US as the definitive text for young people to learn about extrajudicial killings in the Philippines, we could deliberately take steps to amplify and defend the work of the authors and artists in the Philippines who risk their livelihoods and lives by writing against the government's assault on human rights. In juxtaposing *Patron Saints* with Philippine-published texts critical of extrajudicial killings, we may create starting points for imagining and enacting solidarity across communities and borders, among Filipinos in the homeland and the diaspora.

Empire's Presence and Persistence

In an interview with the Philippine news site *Rappler*, Ribay discusses how he and his friends in the US felt compelled to respond to Duterte's anti-drug campaign. As he puts it, "we wanted to create art that would bring attention to some of these things, to keep the conversations going, in the hopes of doing something with our writing" (qtd. in Paris). Ribay's response came in the form of the young adult novel *Patron Saints*. In the novel, the protagonist, Jay Reguero, a high school senior, learns that his cousin Jun became a casualty of the so-called war on drugs. Jay travels to the Philippines to mourn his cousin as well as cut through the stifling secrecy surrounding Jun's murder. During his trip, Jay confronts his ignorance about the linked histories of the Philippines and the US and the ways that Philippine politics, economics, and cultures express colonial trauma.

In one scene, Jay fathoms how very little he knows about the US colonization of the Philippines. With his uncle taking on the role of a rather inimical guide, Jay tours the National Museums district in Manila. As they make their way through various buildings, Maning lectures and grills his nephew on Philippine history. It dawns on Jay that "this trip is less about educating me and more about exposing my ignorance" (151). In the Museum of Fine Art, they pass through galleries filled with religious iconography from the Spanish colonial period; paintings of rural life; an exhibit devoted to the national hero Jose Rizal, who was charged with inciting rebellion by the Spanish colonial government and executed in 1896; and visual depictions of the Japanese Occupation during World War II. Maning asks Jay, "Do you notice what is not emphasized here?" (153). Reflecting on the gap between the exhibits on Rizal and the Japanese Occupation, Jay tentatively offers a response that turns out to be correct: "American colonialism?" (153).

The museum's minimal engagement with the Philippines' US colonial period (1898-1946) could be taken as expressive of Filipinos' hesitation to process how their nation's past — as well as present and future — is inextricably tied to the trajectories of the US. But Maning is not keen on reflecting on this point. Rather, the lacuna gives him the opportunity to upbraid his nephew, whom he bitterly addresses as a proxy for the US: "Yes. We had declared ourselves free, and then your country ignored that, stepping in where Spain left off" (153). He references how, in the Spanish-American War, two empires — one waning and the other on the rise — disregarded and derailed a powerful anticolonial movement in the Philippines. While Filipino revolutionaries fought for independence from Spain, Spain sold its colony to the US for $20 million. Maning also alludes to how Indigenous peoples from the Philippines were displayed in "human zoos" in the US, most infamously in the "Igorrote Villages" that were set up in the 1904 St. Louis World's Fair and in Coney Island in the summer of 1905. These displays served to cement the notion that Filipinos were so-called primitives and shore up the argument that through colonization, the US could shepherd a purportedly backward nation into the modern, civilized world.[1]

The omission in the Philippines' Museum of Fine Art mirrors a void in Jay's education in the US. As Jay listens to his uncle, he thinks, "I don't know any of this — what does he expect? They never taught us the specifics in school. I think there was, like, a paragraph of the Philippine American War in my US History textbook" (153). Jay becomes defensive, but it seems crucial to recognize that his obliviousness to critical — and appalling — moments in US history is not necessarily an individual failing. Rather, he ends up naming the institutionalized inclination in the US to minimize or erase its imperial history and identity. As historian Daniel Immerwahr writes, "one of the truly distinctive features of the United States' empire is how persistently ignored it has been" (18). The US's perception of itself as a republic — one that arose through staunch anti-imperial resistance, one that prides itself for obstructing other nations' fantasies of expansion — works to conceal its dominant (and destructive) presence in various regions around the world (Immerwahr 19).

Immerwahr, writing in 2019, is not presenting a new argument. He echoes the observation that Amy Kaplan made in her introduction to the edited collection *Cultures of United States Imperialism* in 1994. Kaplan points to tendencies in American Studies to obscure the US's imperial legacies and projects, noting that "United States continental expansion is often treated as an entirely separate phenomenon from European colonialism of the nineteenth century, rather than as an interrelated form of imperial expansion" (17). Kaplan writes how the essays in *Cultures* build on Richard Drinnon and emphasize how violent tactics that dispossessed and attempted to annihilate Indigenous peoples in the United States were exported to lands outside the continental US. The contributors to *Cultures* thus clarify how "United States nation-building and empire-building [are] historically coterminous and mutually defining" (Kaplan 17). Oscar Campomanes, in his 1997 essay "New Formations of Asian American Studies and the Question of U.S. Imperialism," identifies a similar evasion regarding US empire in Asian American Studies. He states that "the major problem […] is the tendency of Asian American studies to 'domesticate' the question of U.S. nationality and nation building, leaving untouched their imperialist moorings" (530). While Kaplan, Campomanes, and many others have provided key interventions that visibilize US imperialism, Immerwahr reminds us of how difficult it is to undo habits of denial that have become systemic and culturally ingrained. In *Patron Saints*, Jay's lack of knowledge about US presence and actions in many parts of the world speaks to how educational systems fail to foster critical engagement with the nation's imperial identity and face the horrific costs of empire-building. Masking the US's status as an empire is a disavowal of the violences it committed and continues to commit against peoples, lands, and cultures around the world.

Maning: In Duterte's Image

In the scene that I discuss in the previous section, Maning directs his ire at his nephew, whom he regards to be more American than Filipino. Throughout the novel, he associates Jay with imperial power and ascribes to his nephew what he deems typical American traits: ignorance, wastefulness, insolence, and entitlement. When Jay challenges his uncle by mentioning that he read articles denouncing Duterte's drug war, Maning scoffs at him. "I am guessing they were written by your Western media?" he replies. "Do you think they know what is happening in this country?" (155). For Maning, foreign journalists — particularly those from the West — misunderstand and even deliberately misrepresent Duterte.[2] He expresses disdain for the foreign press for their omissions: "Have they said nothing about how [the US] government has propped up corrupt officials in the Philippines for years simply because they agreed to support US interests? Nothing about those officials taking money from foreign drug cartels to look the other way as they peddle their poison to our sisters and brothers, our daughters and sons?" (156). Maning also emphasizes Western media's tendency to ignore Duterte's accomplishments: "Have they said anything about President Duterte making the museums free? Building bridges and repairing roads that have lay crumbling for decades? Making contraceptives free for all women, regardless of income? Banning cigarettes so we can breathe cleaner air? Reducing crime to its lowest rates ever so that people finally feel safe walking around their own barangay at night?" (156-57). Maning's praise of Duterte's achievements — which sounds very much like the words of Duterte's real-life supporters — papers over the reality that the president's records on infrastructure, environment, women's rights, and crime reduction are abysmal. "Build Build Build," his flagship infrastructure program, primarily served the interests of foreign investors and Filipino oligarchs (Guzman). Under his administration, land defenders were criminalized and assassinated (Dumalag). Duterte is shameless about his sexual objectification of and misogynistic attacks on women. While he claims his strong-arm methods reduced crime, members of his administration were involved in corruption scandals.

It is striking how Maning's diatribes recall the infamous blustery tirades of Duterte. Compare Maning's retorts to Duterte's response at a 2016 press conference, when a reporter asked him how he would defend extrajudicial killings to foreign leaders like US President Barack Obama. After cursing the reporter, Duterte railed: "Who is [Obama] to confront me? America has one too many to answer for the misdeeds in this country […] As a matter of fact, we inherited this problem from the United States. Why? Because they invaded this country and made us their subjugated people. Everybody has a terrible record of extrajudicial killings [...] Look at the human rights of America along that line, the way they treat the migrants there" ("Transcript"). One might be tempted to applaud Duterte for his anticolonial position and his efforts to lay bare US hypocrisy. But, as Adele Webb reminds us, Duterte deliberately turns to underscoring the "hypocrisy of American intervention in the Philippines to appeal for popular support" (128). His is a strategic stance that bolsters his image as a champion of Filipinos as well as redirects criticism of his own brutal policies. In Maning, we hear echoes of Duterte's contempt for foreign critics and use of deflection when faced with criticism.

Webb also makes the critical observation that "populist leaders such as Duterte, in claiming a radical mandate, might be able to dislocate from power those who would normally occupy it [...] Yet such leaders, time and again, instead of opening up the space of contest that democracy requires, appropriate that central place of power for themselves" (140). In other words, while Duterte positions himself as a critic of US imperialism, in actuality, he reproduces the oppressive, hierarchical, and undemocratic practices of colonial regimes. In *Patron Saints*, Maning's character parallels Duterte in rejecting foreign domination while practicing and believing in absolutism. Perhaps it is not surprising that Maning considers the autocrat Ferdinand Marcos "our greatest president" (147) and "a true hero" (148) despite Marcos's atrocious record of human rights violations and plunder.[3] In his own household, Maning is an exacting patriarch. He attempts to dictate and surveil the activities of his children, dismisses what he perceives to be dissent, and asserts control through silencing and humiliation. He evaluates their household servant Maria, who migrated from a rural town, through an elitist, ethnocentrist lens. He comments to Jay that "she is not very smart and barely speaks Tagalog" (97). Ironically, Maning's estimation of Maria is expressive of the economic, cultural, and linguistic imperialism of Metro Manila over the rest of the nation: the positioning of the urban center as the seat of power and heart of progress often entices residents from rural, impoverished, and often non-Tagalog-speaking areas to leave their families, forgo education, and seek work in the capital.

Patron Saints also implies how Maning does not hesitate to flaunt the political and economic power he has accrued. He uses his privileges as police chief to monitor his son, indicating that he uses public resources for his own needs and interests. Jay is struck by how his uncle's home has transformed since his last visit to the Philippines. He notes how "[it] looks like it was teleported here from one of the billboard advertisements along the highway [...] it's all tall windows and modern angles, accent stones and terra cotta roof tiles, strategically placed mini-palm trees and walkway lights. Plus, this place seems to take up at least twice the space of the other lots and rises an extra level above the surrounding houses" (81). What Ami, Maning's wife, calls "some remodeling" (81) appears more like a public display of accumulated wealth and growing influence. While the novel does not explicitly state that Maning engages in illegal profiteering activities, it implies that, as regional police chief, he has increased access to wealth.

Empire's Legacy: Policing in the Philippines

As an officer in the Philippine National Police, Maning actively participates in a system that maintains, through coercive means, unequal distribution of power. He refuses to acknowledge that those who are criminalized as addicts and pushers often lack political and economic capital. Maning conceives of force and aggression as necessary defenses against so-called enemies of the state. In other words, he takes a page from Duterte's strongman playbook and is rewarded for doing so: Ami boasts to Jay that "[President Duterte] awarded your tito a medal just last month for the excellent work he is doing to protect the people in our region from drugs" (146).

It is easy to label Maning as one of the "bad apples" who undermine a policing system that is supposedly designed to be fair and just. His character, in a sense, speaks to how a culture of misconduct and intimidation are woven into the fabric of the PNP. As Sheila S. Coronel elucidates, "the police routinely violate procedures and just as routinely get away with it. In their pursuit of criminals, policemen resort to criminal methods, justifying this as the only way they can realistically curb criminality in the face of a dysfunctional justice system" (183-84). But Maning also needs to be understood as following through, rather than working against, the objectives of policing: to protect the interests of the state and the privileged rather than serve the needs of the disenfranchised. Police brutality under Duterte's presidency is often apprehended as aberrant, but the fact is that the institution of policing in the Philippines has long functioned to silence and eradicate those who are deemed threats to the nation.

Indeed, the PNP is a vestige of US imperial rule. Allan Severino outlines how the PNP emerged from the Philippine Constabulary, a US-controlled army of Filipinos established in 1901 to stifle so-called insurrections. Severino describes the Constabulary as a "component of [the US] security apparatus [...] involved in episodes wherein the Philippine independence movement was put to heel." The Constabulary endured even decades after the US granted the Philippines independence. It carried out arrests, tortures, and murders under the Marcos regime (1965-1986) and was involved in the 1987 Mendiola Massacre during Corazon Aquino's administration. Because of its notoriety, the Constabulary was disbanded and replaced by the PNP. However, as Severino notes, "the PNP is hardly an improvement over the Constabulary. Large cadres of personnel of the PNP still came from the tumultuous years of the 1970s and 1980s Constabulary, which imbibed a notion of siege mentality in their conduct and habits." As an institution that reproduces techniques of domination developed by a colonizing force, the PNP, as Alfred McCoy puts it, performs "imperial mimesis": "The American colonial regime, by creating the constabulary as a political and paramilitary force, embedded a powerful security apparatus within the Philippine executive that has been employed by almost every Filipino president [...] moreover, the covert doctrines developed under U.S. rule persisted in the Philippines [sic] Constabulary and its successor, the Philippine National Police, allowing state control over a volatile society through clandestine methods of surveillance, infiltration, disinformation, and assassination" (36). In reading the character of Maning through the lens of PNP history, we can see his character's contradictions: Despite declaring himself to be anticolonial, anti-imperialist, and anti-American, he is part of and supports an institution that replicates US colonial practices.

Through an attentive study of Maning, readers of *Patron Saints* have an opportunity to reflect on the link between US imperialism and practices of policing in the Philippines. This is not to suggest that we should no longer consider the culpability of Maning (and his real-life counterparts). Rather, we can widen the lens to see how Maning's harmful beliefs and actions have been institutionalized and normalized and are part of the terrible legacy of US colonization of the Philippines. Through Maning's character, we can examine how citizens of a former colony remain haunted by the ghosts of empire, with some recruited into re-creating and maintaining the very systems established and practiced by former colonizers. Put another way, Maning can be taken as an expression of coloniality, which Nelson Maldonado-Torres explicates as the "long-standing patterns of power that emerged as a result of colonialism, but that define culture, labor, intersubjective relations, and knowledge production well beyond the strict limits of colonial administrations" (243). The tensions that mark Maning's character exemplifies coloniality at work: He rails against US imperial tyranny while replicating the tyrannical practices he derides. *Patron Saints*, through Maning, illustrates how imperialism's cruelties can impact peoples for generations, even after the exodus of formal colonial institutions. In doing so, the novel points to the need for deep, steadfast, and transformative work to dismantle structures of oppression.

Jay's Coming of Age:
Intersections of Identity, Immigration, and Imperialism

Patron Saints invites readers to pay attention to the nuances of Maning's character and see him as more than just the narrative's villain. In a similar vein, the novel encourages us to see the complexities of Jay, the protagonist. Through his character, *Patron Saints* poses the question of what it might mean to grow up under empire's shadow.

Throughout the novel, Jay feels constrained by the ways others define him. He feels as if he is always in between: a child born of a Filipino father and a White American mother, born in the Philippines but raised in the US, an Asian

American expected to assimilate into White culture. Maning derides Jay as too American to be a "real" Filipino and constantly catalogs Jay's so-called deficiencies — his lack of fluency in a Philippine language, his meager knowledge of Philippine history, and his purported indifference to local customs. Yet Jay also feels that he is not a "real" American: A casual comment by Seth, Jay's White best friend, makes clear to Jay that Americanness is habitually associated with Whiteness. "I forgot you're Filipino […] You're basically white," Seth says to Jay (37). When Jay challenges Seth to explain what he means, Seth states, "I just meant you act like everyone else at school" (38). Jay understands whom Seth means by "everyone else": "white kids" (38). Jay grasps how, in a dominant White culture, to become American means to efface parts of himself that diverge from Whiteness.

His parents repeatedly remind Jay to embrace his Americanness. When Jay tells his mother that she has "Filipino children," she quickly corrects him by saying "Filipino *American* children" (26). Jay's Filipino father insists that being an American is a privilege to be embraced. He tells Jay that "I wanted you […] to be American." (53) Speaking of his decision to move the family from the Philippines to the US when Jay was only a year old, the senior Reguero asserts how their settlement in the US led to access to a good education, financial stability, and a healthier, happier, and more prosperous life. As he tells Jay, "I moved us here to give you and your brother and sister a better life" (316). Noting his son's lack of clarity regarding his career, he presses Jay to not waste the opportunities made available to him. Jay's father understands himself as embodying the narrative that the American dream is available to all, and he wishes his son to live out this narrative as well. But, as Campomanes notes, "immigration (or more broadly, migration) and modern imperialism as two sides of a single global phenomenon" (534). More specifically, as Robyn Magalit Rodriguez argues, the neocolonial entanglements between the Philippines and the US have turned the Philippines into "a 'labor brokerage' state [that] plays a crucial role in producing Filipino labor for the United States today" (33). She points to how "recently arrived im/migrants from the Philippines in the United States, many of whom are professionally trained, might appear to be more privileged than their early twentieth-century counterparts. Yet as a labor brokerage state, the Philippines engages in what amounts to nothing less than legal human trafficking" (34). Jay's father imagines the US as a meritocracy that provides opportunities to all, but sustaining this fantasy means occluding the fact that much of immigrant labor is exploited. As Rodriguez clarifies, the Philippines has long served as a source of US labor — and such extraction of labor has become normalized, even idealized. In the Philippines, migrant workers are hailed as "mga bagong bayani" — "modern-day heroes." In the US, immigrants are upheld, at least in liberal circles, as the ones who get the job done, who make America great.

Jay's ambivalence about his Americanness arguably deepen when he hears his uncle Maning contesting the American dream. Maning seems to apprehend, though in arguably ham-fisted fashion, how narratives of US immigration bolster the myth of American exceptionalism. The persistent image of the US as a zenith that many immigrants aspire to reach supports what Campomanes calls "the commonplace that the United States is the highest expression and final terminus of historical progress" (531). Unfortunately, instead of engaging his nephew in a critical discussion about the relationship of the Philippines and the US, Maning takes to airing his grievances about Jay's father. For him, his younger brother's decision to leave the Philippines was a selfish act, a prioritization of self-interest over family, nation, and heritage. He does not take into account that migrations are often responses to systemic political and economic inequalities — inequalities that are often formed and exacerbated by colonial/neocolonial relationships. Ironically, Maning has no issue with the relocation of Maria from the rural "periphery" to metropolitan Manila. Still, in unpacking Maning's ire for his brother, we can find strands of critique that trouble the construction of the US as a nation of unparalleled bounty, a place uniquely attractive to immigrants. The discussions about identity and immigration in *Patron Saints* bring to light how, as Moon-Ho Jung puts it, the act of "[commemorating] the United States as a 'nation of immigrants' — so habitual, so toxic — is to be complicit in its racial and imperial project" (11). Jay has a fraught relationship with his uncle, but it is a relationship that pushes him to grapple with his identity and confront the tension that Campomanes identifies: "the country with which Asian Americans seek to affiliate by birth and circumstance has been, and continues to be, a major imperialist player on the global scene" (533).

Notably, during his trip to the Philippines, Jay comes to the realization that he must refuse the impulse to play the benevolent foreigner who purportedly is in a special position to educate and liberate. When he wonders about "something he could do" to resist Duterte's autocracy and demand justice for Jun, Jun's sister Grace tells him, "No offense, cousin, but even though you are from here, you are also not. I know you want to help, but you have only recently learned about this. You are not going to be the one to save us" (291-92). While this statement wounds Jay, he also accepts that "Grace is right" (292). Indeed, his visit enables Jay to recognize that Filipinos in the Philippines have long been involved in movements for justice and dignity. He sees this in his Tita Chato's work against human trafficking; in the investigative reporting of Mia and Professor Santos; and in Jun's, and later Grace's, documentation of Duterte's violent drug war through a blog titled GISING NA PH! The site's name — which translates to "Wake up, Philippines!" — records the brutalities of Duterte's anti-drug crusade, with the aim of rousing Filipinos to stand up against injustice and police impunity. The title of the blog, however, might also hint at Jay's rising political consciousness: In wrestling with the meaning of belonging and citizenship as a Filipino American, gumigising na siya — he is waking up.

The novel concludes with Jay committing to spending a gap year in the Philippines. Undoubtedly, he is able to make such a decision with relative ease because he comes from an affluent American family. Meanwhile, many

Filipinos in the Philippines do not have the means to pursue higher education, with many forced to drop out of elementary or high school to eke out a living and support their families. To them, Jay's choice may feel extravagant and incomprehensible. And while Jay, with disposable income and a blue passport, can express a desire to travel to the Philippines and, within a few days, arrive in Manila, the majority of Filipinos lack the economic and cultural capital that help facilitate their entry into the US.

As Rick Bonus observes, there is an "ease by which [Filipino Americans'] US identities enable them to define the Philippines as their home as if it were simply a choice (staying or leaving) borne out of convenience, not out of necessity or limitation" (397). Jay, however, comes to understand that the Philippines is not (yet) home, and he seeks to use his privileges to engage productively with Filipinos. He wants to learn more about local languages and histories, support his Tita Chato's work, and deepen his understanding of decolonial projects — not as a tourist or a benevolent liberator but as a person with a transnational identity. His desire to return to the Philippines — the "boondocks" that his father left — may be his way of turning his back on the American dream, and envisioning and experiencing an alternative to the "better life" promised to immigrants.[4]

Conclusion: Decentering US Perspectives and Narratives

In his interview with *Rappler*, Ribay shares how writing *Patron Saints* was a way for him to work through the question "what right do I have to voice out my opinions about what is happening in the Philippines right now?" (qtd. in Paris). Through the character of Jay, the novel deliberates the role Filipino Americans play when responding to injustices taking place in the Philippines. Ultimately, *Patron Saints* suggests Filipino Americans have an obligation to learn about US imperialism — its histories, current manifestations, and consequences — and attend to the ways the US's expansionist and extractive projects have determined the experiences of Filipinos in the Philippines and abroad. Moreover, the novel cautions Filipino Americans against constructing Filipinos in the Philippines as incapable of resisting injustice; rather, it exhorts them to pay attention to how US imperialism has shaped Filipino and Filipino American values and experiences, as well as learn from the knowledges and labors of those in the Philippines.

One way to start learning from Philippine-based Filipinos is by acknowledging and amplifying their work. *Patron Saints* is not the only text for young people that tackles extrajudicial killings under Duterte's regime. There are titles such as Weng D. Cahiles and Aldy C. Aguirre's 2017 *Si Kian* (*This is Kian*) (2017), which was written in the wake of Kian's murder and distributed, for free, by the Philippine Center for Investigative Journalism through the web and limited print editions; Mon Sy and Faye Abantao's *Kakatok-katok sa Bahay ni Benok*

(*Knocking on Benok's House*) (Canvas, 2021), a storybook on police drug operations; and *Triggered: Creative Responses to the Extrajudicial Killings in the Philippines* (Chamber Shell, 2021), a collaboration between college freshmen and authors edited by Jocelyn S. Martin and Cyan Abad-Jugo. *Patron Saints* must be read alongside these texts. However, given the immense influence of US publishing in the global market, *Patron Saints* is likely more accessible to readers in many parts of the world. Philippine publishers do not have the means to compete with US publishers, even if many of their children's and young adult books are translated into or originally written in English. In the ostensible vacuum of books on Duterte's "war on drugs," *Patron Saints* — a novel written in English, printed and distributed by a US-based publisher, authored by a Filipino American, and focused on the political awakening of a Filipino American teen — easily can be held up as *the* essential text for teaching young people about, and mobilizing them against, injustices in the Philippines. Such commemoration of the novel may have the consequence of further marginalizing the important work of creators and activists in the Philippines. We need to work more vigorously to dismantle barriers to distribution. These barriers are expressive of the colonial ordering of the world, buttressed by the myth that texts and narratives from the Global South are less important. A commitment to decolonial pedagogy means a sustained effort at centering narratives that are systematically made peripheral.

Even though Duterte stepped down from the presidency in 2022, it is as vital as ever to foreground the narratives of resistance by Filipinos in the Philippines. Decades after the kleptocratic Marcos was overthrown in the 1986 People Power Revolution, his son and namesake, Ferdinand "Bongbong" Marcos Jr., was elected president by a landslide, owing, in part, to his alliance with the Dutertes. Under Marcos Jr.'s regime, drug-related killings, as well as the harassment of and violent attacks against activists, journalists, and labor leaders, continue (Conde). The Marcos family and their allies have also actively participated in historical revisionism, peddling false narratives that glorify and romanticize the Marcos dictatorship. Their supporters have taken to branding children's book authors and publishers who tell the truth about the Marcos dictatorship as terrorists and communists. Sara Duterte, Duterte's daughter, is now the nation's vice president. She also served as secretary of education, but was forced to stepped down in 2024 because of corruption allegations and the erosion of the relationship between the Marcoses and Dutertes. But the year before her resignation from the Department of Education, she spearheaded the launch of a new K-10 curriculum that, as she put it, "will integrate peace competencies — highlighting the promotion of nonviolent actions and the development of conflict-resolution skills in learners. For after all, [if] there is security, there is peace" (qtd. in Bautista). It is not difficult to see how the statement associates "peace competencies" with conformity and obedience. I am also quite certain that "promotion of nonviolent actions" translates to the prohibition and criminalization of nonviolent civil resistance. In an ecosystem of misinformation and suppression, it remains crucial to support Filipino creatives, activists, and youth who are exercising their right to free expression and pushing back against state harassment and violence.

Literature for young people can play a key role in teaching readers about the long reach of US empire. Unfortunately, those of us who are committed to teaching about and against colonialism and imperialism know that we are teaching under difficult, even dangerous, conditions; speaking truth to power in classrooms can mean facing censorship and censure. But we must not turn away from creating spaces and communities — perhaps outside formal education systems — that allow young people to engage critically with Ribay's novel and other narratives of resistance. Reading *Patron Saints* through the lens of empire can help bring into focus the intertwined histories and politics of the Philippines and the US; enable critical conversations about the mythification of the US as a nation of immigrants; and challenge us to think about how we can practice centering the experiences and activisms of peoples who are pushed to the margins. Reading and studying *Patron Saints* with young people may also spur us to identify the ways we are inevitably marked by empire, perhaps as settlers, as carriers of colonial trauma, or as citizens of a nation that is also an empire. For Filipino readers in the US, reading books such as *Patron Saints* alongside narratives from the Philippines can facilitate critical reflection about their relationship to both the US and the Philippines. *Patron Saints* makes the fact of US empire visible. In doing so, the novel not only allows us to grasp the violent and vile ways that imperial configurations have shaped the lives of many around the world; it can also embolden us to commit to the disassembly of imperial structures.

Works Cited

Allen, Greg. "'Living Exhibits' at 1904 World's Fair Revisited." *Morning Edition*. NPR, May 31, 2004, https://www.npr.org/2004/05/31/1909651/living-exhibits-at-1904-worlds-fair-revisited. Accessed 6 Dec. 2023.

Bautista, Jane. "New Curriculum Adds Sara's Focus on 'Peace.'" *Philippine Daily Inquirer*, Inquirer.net, 11 Aug. 2023, https://newsinfo.inquirer.net/1815131/new-curriculum-adds-saras-focus-on-peace. Accessed 22 Dec. 2023.

Bonus, Rick. "'Come Back Home Soon': The Pleasure and Agonies of 'Homeland' Visits. Manalansan and Espiritu, pp. 388-410.

Breitbart, Eric. *A World on Display: Photographs from the St. Louis World's Fair, 1904*. U of New Mexico P, 1997.

Cahiles, Weng D., and Aldy C. Aguirre. *Si Kian*. Philippine Center for Investigative Journalism, 2017.

Campomanes, Oscar V. "New Formations of Asian American Studies and the Question of U.S. Imperialism." *positions*, vol. 5, no. 2, 1997, pp. 523-50.

Conde, Carlos. "Continuing Human Rights Violations Under President Marcos." Transcript of Opening Statement to European Parliament's Subcommittee on Human Rights. *Human Rights Watch*, 7 Sept. 2023, https://www.hrw.org/news/2023/09/07/continuing-human-rights-violations-under-president-marcos. Accessed 22 Dec. 2023.

Coronel, Sheila S. "Murder as Enterprise: Police Profiteering in Duterte's War on Drugs." Curato, pp. 167-98.

Curato, Nicole, editor. *A Duterte Reader: Critical Essays on Rodrigo Duterte's Early Presidency*. Bughaw, 2017.

Dumalag, Gabryelle. "Duterte's Five Years: Deadliest for Environmental Defenders." *Bulatlat*, 1 Aug. 2021, https://www.bulatlat.com/2021/08/01/dutertes-five-years-deadliest-for-environmental-defenders/. Accessed 8 Feb. 2022.

Guzman, Rosario. "What Build Build Build Has Delivered." *Ibon*, 25 July 2021, https://www.ibon.org/what-build-build-build-has-delivered/. Accessed 8 Feb. 2022.

Immerwahr, Daniel. *How to Hide an Empire: A History of the Greater United States*. Picador, 2019.

Jiménez García, Marilisa. *Side by Side: US Empire, Puerto Rico, and the Roots of American Youth Literature and Culture*. UP of Mississippi, 2021.

Jung, Moon-ho. *Menace to Empire: Anticolonial Solidarities and the Transpacific Origins of the US Security State*. University of California P, 2022.

Kaplan, Amy. "'Left Alone with America': The Absence of Empire in the Study of American Culture." *Cultures of United States Imperialism*, edited by Amy Kaplan and Donald E. Pease, Duke UP, 1993, pp. 3-21.

Manalansan, Martin F. IV, and Augusto F. Espiritu, editors. *Filipino Studies: Palimpsests of Nation and Diaspora*. New York UP, 2016.

Maldonado-Torres, Nelson. "On the Coloniality of Being." *Cultural Studies*, vol. 21, no. 2-3, 2007, pp. 240-70.

Martin, Jocelyn S., and Cyan Abad-Jugo, editors. *Triggered: Creative Responses to the Extrajudicial Killings in the Philippines*. Chamber Shell, 2021.

McCoy, Alfred W. *Policing America's Empire: The United States, the Philippines, and the Rise of the Surveillance State*. U of Wisconsin P, 2009.

Parezo, Nancy J., and Don D. Fowler. *Anthropology Goes to the Fair: The 1904 Louisiana Purchase Exposition*. U of Nebraska P, 2007.

Paris, Janella. "A Young Filipino-American Comes of Age as Duterte's Drug War Rages On." *Rappler*, Nov. 19, 2019, https://www.*Rappler*.com/life-and-style/literature/245078-patron-saints-of-nothing-randy-ribay-review/. Accessed 6 Dec. 2023.

The Nobel Peace Prize 2021. NobelPrize.org. Nobel Prize Outreach AB 2023, 14 Dec. 2023, https://www.nobelprize.org/prizes/peace/2021/summary/.

Prentice, Claire. *The Lost Tribe of Coney Island: Headhunters, Luna Park, the Man Who Pulled Off the Spectacle of the Century*. New Harvest, 2014.

Punongbayan, J. C., and Kevin Mandrilla. "Why the Drug War Thwarts Our Pursuit of Inclusive Growth." *Rappler*, 25 March 2017, https://r3.rappler.com/thought-leaders/165143-drug-war-inclusive-growth. Accessed 31 Jan. 2022.

Ribay, Randy. *The Patron Saints of Nothing*. Kokila, 2019.

Rodriguez, Robyn Magalit. "Toward a Critical Filipino Studies Approach to Philippine Migration." Manalansan and Espiritu, pp. 33-55.

Rydell, Robert W. *All the World's a Fair: Visions of Empire at American International Expositions, 1876–1916*. U of Chicago P, 1984.

Severino, Allan. "Stamped in Blood: A Complicated History of Philippine Policing." *Esquire Philippines*, 21 Dec. 2020, https://www.esquiremag.ph/long-reads/features/stamped-in-blood-a-complicated-history-of-philippine-policing-a2416-20201221-lfrm. Accessed 15 Feb. 2022.

Social Weather Stations. "Second Quarter 2019 Social Weather Survey: Net Satisfaction with Anti-illegal Drugs Campaign at 'Excellent' +70," 22 Sept. 2019, https://www.sws.org.ph/swsmain/artcldisppage/?artcsyscode=ART-20190922154614. Accessed 14 Dec. 2023.

"SWS: Rodrigo Duterte Leaves Office with 'Excellent' Satisfaction Rating." *CNN Philippines*, 23 Sept. 2022, https://www.cnnphilippines.com/news/2022/9/23/Duterte-leaves-office-with-excellent-satisfaction-rating.html. Accessed 14 Dec. 2023.

Sy, Mon, and Faye Abantao. *Kakatok-katok sa Bahay ni Benok* (*Knocking on Benok's House*). Canvas, 2021.

Talabong, Rambo. "3 Years after Kian's Death, Killings Continue after Duterte." *Rappler*, 16 Aug. 2021, https://www.*Rappler*.com/nation/third-death-anniversary-kian-delos-santos-killings-continue/. Accessed 14 Dec. 2023.

Terada, Triciah. "Five Vows, Five Years Later: A Lookback into Duterte's Major Campaign Promises." *CNN Philippines*, 22 July 2021, https://www.cnnphilippines.com/news/2021/7/22/SONA-2021-Duterte-presidential-campaign-promises.html. Accessed 31 Jan. 2022.

"Transcript: Duterte on Obama." *Rappler*, 16 Sept. 2016, https://www.*Rappler*.com/nation/145337-transcript-duterte-obama-human-rights/. Accessed 22 Feb. 2022.

Webb, Adele. "Hide the Looking Glass: Duterte and the Legacy of American Imperialism." Curato, pp. 127-44.

Wells, Matt. "War on Drugs, War against the Poor." *Rappler*, Feb. 5, 2017, https://r3.*Rappler*.com/thought-leaders/160492-war-on-drugs-war-against-poor. Accessed 31 Jan. 2022.

Notes

1. For more on these "living exhibitions" of Indigenous Filipinos in the United States, see Greg Allen, "'Living Exhibits' at 1904 World's Fair Revisited," *Morning Edition*, NPR, 31 May 2004, https://www.npr.org/2004/05/31/1909651/living-exhibits-at-1904-worlds-fair-revisited, accessed 6 Dec. 2023; and Claire Prentice, *The Lost Tribe of Coney Island: Headhunters, Luna Park, the Man Who Pulled Off the Spectacle of the Century* (New Harvest, 2014). These racist, colonialist displays proclaimed and enabled fantasies about US expansionism and exceptionalism. Also see Eric Breitbart, *A World on Display: Photographs from the St. Louis World's Fair, 1904* (U of New Mexico P, 1997); Nancy J. Parezo and Don D. Fowler, *Anthropology Goes to the Fair: The 1904 Louisiana Purchase Exposition* (U of Nebraska P, 2007); Robert W. Rydell, *All the World's a Fair: Visions of Empire at American International Expositions, 1876–1916* (U of Chicago P, 1984).

2. Maning's ire for foreign journalists recalls Duterte's contempt of the press, both local and foreign. The Duterte administration eroded press freedom by denying reporters access to press junkets and subjecting journalists to harassment and lawsuits. Duterte and his supporters specifically targeted *Rappler*, the news site founded by Maria Ressa, claiming that the site peddled fake news. The government sued *Rappler* on the preposterous charge of cyberlibel. In 2021, Ressa and Russian journalist Dmitry Muratov received the Nobel Peace Prize for "their efforts to safeguard freedom of expression" (Nobel Peace Prize, 2021).

3. Maning's categorization of Marcos as a "hero" alludes not only to the disinformation campaigns that sanitized and romanticized the history of the Marcos regime; it also references Duterte's alliance with the Marcos family. Despite protests, the former allowed the burial of the dictator in Libingan ng Mga Bayani (Cemetery of Heroes).

4. The etymology of "boondocks" is the Tagalog word "bundok," meaning "mountain." US forces that occupied the Philippines used the term to refer to remote and wild areas. "Boondocks" (or "boonies") has come to connote rural America or places considered backward. Perhaps owing to the popularity of Aaron McGruder's comic strip "The Boondocks," the term may also be used to refer to insular White enclaves.

Two

Becoming a Girl

Girlhood, Child Marriage, and Widowhood in Kashmira Sheth's *Keeping Corner*

Blessy Sharon Samjose

South Asia brings up contrasting images of oriental mystique and splendor (left over from the colonial era), explosive colors and sounds of Bollywood, and, finally, poverty, gender disparity, and corruption, as depicted in liberal journalism. In this chapter, I bring Kashmira Sheth's young adult historical novel *Keeping Corner* (2007) to this collage to explore complex contradictions in South Asian history that defy the expected nostalgia and exoticism anticipated in South Asian diasporic writing. *Keeping Corner* stands out because it targets a young adult audience and sheds careful light on the intersection of caste and gender in colonial India. In a study of South Asian historical fiction for children and young adults in the US, editor and writer Sandhya Nankani (2009) remarked on the relative unpopularity of historical fiction until recently.[1] Her essay alluded to the need for historical fiction stories that can approach South Asian history realistically while providing spaces to critically engage casteism, patriarchy, and religious fundamentalism.

Across political upheavals and social transformations, casteism and patriarchy in South Asia have evolved to match the times. The presence of a significant South Asian diaspora makes the US an interesting space to trace the mutual influence of the caste system and patriarchy transnationally. Stories like *Keeping Corner*, which are from South Asia or are written by authors of South Asian heritage, are considered postcolonial literature because they "emerged in their present form out of the experience of colonization and asserted themselves foregrounding the tension with the imperial power" (Ashcroft et al. 2). John Marx observed that postcolonial literature and writing, when studied side by side, repudiate and revise imperial and oriental tendencies in the Western literary canon. Many visible and renowned contemporary South Asian diasporic writers achieved recognition and success on account of their ability to engage in reverse orientalism or "re-Orientalism" (Lau and Mendes 2), whereby they renegotiate the oriental exotism ascribed to the East during the colonial era. The writings traverse a wide range of approaches, from postcolonial literature that revives oriental intrigue to those that counter colonial narratives.

Nevertheless, the power of literature does not end there. Literature can also be a "site of resistance" (hooks) to confront oppression. Readers can unleash the power of stories to challenge and transform real worlds (hooks). Historical fiction in classrooms brings new possibilities to poking at gaps in history and shedding light on historical injustices and their contemporary repercussions (Rangachari; Gómez). Building on counter-narratives and cultural literacies, ethnic studies' goal of empowering students by cultivating awareness, empathy, and social justice action shows great promise in revitalizing education (Cuauhtin et al. 3). Although misconceptions question the relevance of ethnic studies approaches to a broad range of students, studies show that these are spaces where all students' lived experiences are recognized and integrated into academic literacies to support visions of change (Acosta 274; Tolbert-Mbatha 95; Riechel 112). Therefore, spaces for critical thinking emerge when young people are presented with stories exploring counter-histories and cultural traditions. Such spaces occur in young people's engagement with South Asian literature. Rather than passively parroting caste and gender inequities in South Asian history and mythology, there are evident efforts to reclaim agency and embrace social justice action. An example of this is seen in the oral storytelling tradition, a staple in many South Asian childhoods.

One of the first places South Asian American children encounter culture and history is through mythology stories. Many diasporic South Asian parents teach mythology stories and religious scriptures to their children to prevent younger generations from losing connection to ethnic and cultural roots (Rayaprol). Women (first-generation South Asian mothers and their second-generation South Asian–American daughters) feel the disproportional and gendered burden of upholding and transmitting ethnic culture and traditions (Rayaprol 142; Pandey, *South Asians in the Mid-South* 115). In dissecting the application of this gendered burden, Aparna Rayaprol points out two intersecting layers of patriarchy: from the parents' host culture and from American society (142). While some young women submit to patriarchal norms to show allegiance to "Indianness," others find ways of resisting dominant patriarchal structures. One such resistance is recorded in Iswari Pandey's ethnographic study of South Asian women teachers at Hindu community centers in the mid-South US. The women took an unconventional path when approaching patriarchy and casteism in the scriptures. Instead of "simply reproducing an imagined past or perpetuating the status quo," they created a "space from which they can challenge the gendered social hierarchy and assert their agency," stimulating critical thinking in their young students (*South Asians in the mid-South* 14).

A similar effort to critically explore casteism and patriarchy in South Asian mythology and folklore is evident in Roshani Choksi's *Aru Shah* series for a middle-grade audience. The series is a modern-day adaptation of stories and characters from the Hindu epics *Mahabharatha* and *Ramayana*. However, the author uses "genderbending" to restore social justice (Thomas and Stornaiuolo) in the story world. A crucial application pertains to the gender of the Pandava brothers in the original epic. When Choksi genderbends them into Pandava sisters, she facilitates readers' critique of patriarchy and caste privileges normalized in the original epic.

I add my reading of *Keeping Corner* to this trend of critical engagement through stories and mythology. Although *Keeping Corner* is fictional, the story is set in real historical events and cultural norms. This intersection of history and fiction allows Sheth to challenge accepted oppressive norms and seek justice. Thus, this chapter examines oppression and resistance at the intersections of caste and gender in South Asian girlhood while considering the overall relevance for young adult audiences in the US, where the story was published in 2007.

There are four main sections in this chapter. Beginning with a brief synopsis of *Keeping Corner*, listing the characters and events readers can expect to encounter, I contextualize the story within the cultural and historical milieu. In the second section, I trace the influences of colonization and the caste system in patriarchy to understand the simultaneity of privilege and oppression and their transnational implications. In the third section, I explore the protagonist, Leela, and her dual struggle opposing colonization and brahmanical patriarchy, arriving at her unique version of satyagraha. In the fourth and final section, I discuss my findings on the impact of Leela's satyagraha in *Keeping Corner* and the interventions anticipated through stories like *Keeping Corner* in ethnic studies curriculums.

Contextualizing Keeping Corner

Keeping Corner is a South Asian young adult historical novel written by Kashmira Sheth. The story follows ten-year-old Leela, an upper-caste Hindu brahmin girl living in 1940s India amid the struggle for independence from British colonization. After her husband dies, Leela is forced into "keeping corner," an oppressive widowhood custom practiced in her upper-caste community. The custom blames the widow, no matter her age, for her husband's death, labels her a "bringer of misfortune," and confines her within her home. Saviben, a college-educated liberal feminist and one of Leela's earliest allies, homeschools Leela while she is keeping corner. Alongside regular lessons and schoolwork, Saviben brings access to news articles and pamphlets articulating the need for freedom from the British. Under Saviben's tutelage, Leela learns about the anticolonial struggle and relates it to her own struggle against brahmanical patriarchy as an upper-caste child widow. Since remarriage is not available to upper-caste widows, Leela negotiates a different path to freedom and opts to become a teacher like Saviben and work toward uplifting other girls and women. Leela's conservative natal family, consisting of her father (bapuji), mother (ba), paternal uncle (kaka), and paternal aunt (kaki), pose varying degrees of impediments to her course of action. Nevertheless, she advocates for her freedom by drawing on the ideas and methods of Gandhian satyagraha from the anticolonial freedom struggle. In addition to Saviben, she also finds allies in her older brother, Kanubhai, and her cousin, Jaya. Thus, *Keeping Corner* addresses the intersections of caste, gender, and widowhood amid the ideas and energies of an anticolonial freedom struggle.

The Myriad Shapes of Patriarchy

While many women supported the anticolonial movement, seeing the chance for their own freedom, historian Suruchi Thapar-Björkert notes that the word "feminism" and its associated meanings were not strongly expressed in the anticolonial struggle (45). Furthermore, the clashes between colonizers and colonized men over control of colonized women resulted in women's doubled oppression. South Asian girls and women were forced to choose between colonization and patriarchy when they needed freedom from both oppressions. Like the gaps between white and women of color feminisms in the US, the feminist movement in South Asia splintered along caste differences. While the upper-caste women aligned with the anticolonial nationalist movement submitting to brahmanical patriarchy, the lower-caste women aspired to a dynamic feminist movement that tackled their caste and class oppressions (Omvedt 35). In the following sections, I trace the impact of colonization and caste norms in shaping the gendered oppression of South Asian girls and women to contextualize Leela's identities and experiences in *Keeping Corner*.

Unlike feminist movements in Europe and the US that fought to secure voting rights, South Asian women directly achieved suffrage upon independence from Britain (Sunder Rajan, *Scandal of the State* 17). However, these rights did not ensure freedom from patriarchal norms. In the introduction to a collection of South Asian women's writings, Annie Zaidi writes, "Many activists now openly say that the 'freedom' we won in 1947 was a political transfer of power, and that women must struggle for their freedom again" (xiii) from patriarchy and the caste system. South Asian feminist Uma Chakravarti uses the term "brahmanical patriarchy" to capture the intersection of patriarchal and casteist oppression in women's lives. Accordingly, brahmanical patriarchy indicates "a set of rules and institutions in which caste and gender are linked, each shaping the other and where women are crucial in maintaining the boundaries between castes" (33). The caste system in South Asia is a hereditary social structure segregating diverse communities into distinct caste groups and subgroups (varnas and jatis). The caste system is hierarchized to secure privileges (access to education, social mobility, material resources, and sociopolitical power) at the top with the upper castes, such as brahmins and kshatriyas (Chakravarti 11-12; Omvedt 26). The caste boundaries between upper and lower castes are maintained through endogamy marriage laws. Since upper-caste girls and women are the "gateways" and "points of entrance into the caste system," severe controls are imposed on their sexuality to prevent breaches between upper and lower castes (Chakravarti 64-65). The controls find expression through oppressive traditions, such as child marriage and compulsory widowhood. Although the practice of child marriage remains consistent across many castes, widowhood and widow remarriage customs greatly vary between upper and lower castes. While the upper-caste widow is forced into isolated widowhood, the lower-caste widow is expected to remarry, rejoin society, and supply productive and reproductive labor (Chakravarti 51, 78; Omvedt 27).

The practice of widowhood over remarriage was traditional among upper castes stemming from upper-caste women's alienation from reproduction and sexuality upon the death of a husband.[2] Because upper-caste girls and women were defined by their purpose in maintaining caste boundaries through reproductive labor, "once she ceased to be a wife, especially a childless wife, she ceased to be a person; she was then neither a daughter nor a daughter-in-law" and became a widow (Chakravarti 78). Traditionally, widowhood took two forms to detach sexuality and reproduction from an upper-caste widow: Sati[3] and keeping corner. Although sati was not a widespread practice, it gained disproportionate attention resulting from the colonial attitude toward a perceived savage native custom (Sinha 5). In sanctioning a widow's death, the custom of sati eliminated the widow and the threat she posed to the caste system's hierarchy. Meanwhile, practices such as keeping corner allowed upper-caste widows to survive but live in a state of perpetual widowhood. In *Keeping Corner,* Leela uses the term "living death" to describe the ostracization and alienation marking an upper-caste widow's life. In the author's note, Kashmira Sheth discloses that she chose to address "keeping corner" because of admiration toward her great-aunt Maniba, who had been a child widow. Therein the author becomes a "quintessential social critic" (Davis-Undiano 14), helping young readers navigate the complexities of the past through its continuity in the present.

The clash of colonization and patriarchy in South Asia greatly exacerbated women's oppression in South Asian society. In her essay "From Patriarchy to Intersectionality," Vrushali Patil draws on Kimberlé Crenshaw's definition of intersectionality to trace the influence of racism and patriarchy in colonization and their impact on localized patriarchies in the colonized lands. Because the colonizers feminized and infantilized the colonized natives, the latter adopted hypermasculinity into anticolonial nationalism to reclaim a subjecthood denied during colonization (Patil 860). However, the hypermasculinity within nationalism also aggravated existing gendered oppression in South Asian society.

Although the British followed a policy of noninterference in local cultural and religious practices in their early years, their policies devolved to active intervention in the later years, especially as the colonized mobilized to achieve freedom (Bose and Jalal 58). When the violent[4] and nonviolent freedom struggles disturbed the image of peace and order in the colonies, the British justified their authoritative presence in colonial India by citing the "white man's burden." They positioned themselves as saviors tasked with the civilizing mission of restraining barbaric customs and traditions, such as sati. They were "white men saving brown women from brown men" (Spivak 48). Accordingly, they introduced social reforms to address child marriage, sati, and the oppression of widows (Ghosh 84-86; Sinha 8). Nonetheless, these reforms were also supported by social reformers among the colonized, who challenged oppressive traditions and favored modernization (Bose and Jalal 65). However, some nationalists opposed these reforms because they challenged existing caste and gender hierarchies and resulting privileges. In *Real and Imagined Woman*, Rajeswari Sunder Rajan explained that the sudden changes accompanying these social reforms produced "effects of alienation in the Hindu male," who advocated a defense of sati and other oppressive practices in an "attempt to recover their identity by enforcing traditional patriarchal norms" (49). As British colonizers and colonized nationalists sought to attract colonized women to their respective sides, the "women question" became a highly politicized space to configure the colonizer/colonized power struggle. It is important to note that neither side allowed women to speak for themselves and express their independent views while negotiating reforms.

The silence imposed on women in the colonial era continues to haunt women via other global and local oppressive power structures, such as racism, neoliberalism, and sexism. The stereotypes defining Third World women in Western feminist writings originate from stereotyped images of colonized native women, such as "the veiled woman, the powerful mother, the chaste virgin, the obedient wife" in colonial writings (Mohanty 41). Thus, many studies of Third World women still locate them as "victims of multinational capital as well as of their own 'traditional' sexist cultures" (Mohanty 72), mirroring women's preexisting victimization at the intersections of colonization and brahmanical patriarchy. However, Third World women express agency and subjecthood by rejecting Western feminism's notions of purely gendered oppression in favor of building holistic feminist movements that tackle the "simultaneity of oppressions" across casteism, racism, imperialism, and colonialism, in addition to patriarchy and sexism (Mohanty 52). Similarly, in *Keeping Corner*, Leela's upper-caste widowhood and her expression of resistance reflect the simultaneity of oppression across colonization, casteism, and sexism.

Therefore, the following questions scaffold the contradictions shaping South Asian girls' and women's oppression and resistance. Should they choose the benefits of colonial feminist reforms at the cost of renouncing anticolonial nationalism? Or should they submit to patriarchal oppression and stand in solidarity with the anticolonial freedom struggle? While the colonizers supported feminist reforms in the colonies, Leila Ahmed us reminds that they were actively fighting to suppress the women's suffrage movements in their own lands. Colonial feminism was "used against other cultures in the service of colonialism, [it] was shaped into a variety of similar constructs, each tailored to fit the particular culture that was the immediate target of domination" (Ahmed 151). On the other hand, unchallenged support of anticolonial nationalism meant submitting to the oppressions of the caste system, patriarchy, and Hindu nationalism. Therefore, the final question is: Can freedom reach the intersections of gender, caste, and widowhood beyond binaries designed to oppress upper-caste widows infinitely? Through Leela, an upper-caste child widow in *Keeping Corner*, I sketch the contradictions and the possibilities for resistance and change.

Privilege and Oppression within Brahmanical Patriarchy

The oppression defining upper-caste widowhood is distinct because of its origins at the intersection of upper caste, sex, and widowhood. However, sexist oppression does not rule out caste privileges such as elevated class status. Access to education is a valuable privilege for upper-caste girls and women because knowledge and education were historically monopolized by upper castes in South Asian society. Nevertheless, Thapar-Björkert cautions that access to education was not uniformly available to all upper-caste girls. Patriarchs and heads of families played a significant role in restricting girls' and women's access to education. *Keeping Corner* provides a valuable example to explore the contradiction. Although girls from Leela's upper-caste community are enrolled in the local girls' school, many drop out because of child marriage practices. After the ceremony of "anu," "a ceremony performed for a bride before she goes to live with her husband" (*Keeping Corner* 273), girls dropped out of school to begin their lives as wives, daughters-in-law, and mothers. Therefore, there were fewer and fewer girls in the higher grades. Even so, Leela's early reading and writing literacy laid the groundwork for critical thinking and her later desire to become a teacher. In addition to access to education, she also benefited from the brahmin caste's upper economic and social class status. Leela's well-to-do family employs Lakha, a manservant from the lower caste of Rabari,[5] to mind the family's cattle. In addition to minding the cattle, he and his wife, Shani, are often seen helping with other chores around the house. Shani provides an interesting contrast to Leela's upper-caste widowhood as a child widow from a lower caste.

While upper-caste women face severe control over sexuality (Chakravarti 2018), some lower-caste women from lower-caste and tribal communities may already experience gender egalitarianism (Sunder Rajan, *Scandal of the State* 32). The latters' relative freedom is also tied to the exploitation of lower-caste women's labor and sexuality. Therefore, unlike Leela, Shani's lower-caste identity permitted her to remarry and reenter society after her first husband's death. Accordingly, Shani has remarried, and her second husband is Lakha, a manservant at Leela's household. Without considering their caste differences and her upper-caste privileges, Leela asks, "If I were Shani's sister, I wouldn't be wearing a chidri and have a bald head. What good was it to belong to the highest caste if I had to suffer?" (167). However, if Leela were Shani's sister, she would not have reading and writing skills and would be a servant in an upper-caste household. The contrasts in privileges and oppressions mark the variations within South Asian womanhood. Because "the most stringent control over sexuality is reserved as a privilege for the highest castes" (Chakravarti 33), oppressive practices such as child marriage, widowhood, and internalized sexism are read as upper-caste privileges although they spelled the opposite of privilege for Leela and others like her. As such, the caste system and brahmanical patriarchy afford privileges to a select few men at the top of the hierarchy. Leela's engagement at age two, child marriage at age nine, and widowhood at age twelve upon her husband's death demonstrate the stringent control over her sexuality.[6] When Shani hears about social reformers' ideas supporting upper-caste widow remarriage from Leela, she exclaims, "How can people of high caste like you even think about it? If you married again, then you'd be like us [lower-caste]" (*Keeping Corner* 166), alluding to widowhood as an exclusive privilege of upper-castes. Both widows show an understanding of widowhood, unaware of the double standards designed to oppress women of all castes.

Another contrast is provided through Fat Soma, a young man from the same caste as Leela. Despite being widowed twice, Fat Soma is unaffected by the stigma of being a widower because he is an upper-caste man. Leela's Ba's comment "Not yet nineteen, and this will be his third wedding. Poor boy!" (226) shows the biased sympathy extended to widowers, but not widows. He continues to be a valued member because a wife's death does not result in misfortune and living death for a man. Feeling trapped by caste rules requiring upper-caste men to remarry upon a wife's death, Fat Soma chooses to renounce his caste privileges and escape the trappings of brahmanical patriarchy. Leela's life as a widow and Fat Soma's life as a widower differ drastically because of their sex. Furthermore, upper-caste girls' and women's oppression is complicated by their own complicity, whereby they align with the anticolonial struggle while submitting to patriarchal and caste norms. At several points in *Keeping Corner,* the expressions of internalized sexism prove upper-caste women's complicity.

In practice, brahmanical patriarchy coerced upper-caste women into the complicity of internalized sexism where they "themselves controlled their own sexuality and believed that they gained power and respect through the codes they adopted" (Chakravarti 70-71). Leela's Masi (maternal aunt) reveals the damages of internalized sexism in *Keeping Corner*. She constantly doubts Leela's adherence to keeping corner and widowhood. In the early weeks of Leela's widowhood, she bemoans: "who knows what will happen when Leela's older? […] She's the youngest, so she's more than a little spoiled […] She won't listen to her Ba [mother], and she'll disgrace the family […] When Leela's beauty blossoms, what will happen? She'll be as wild as a kothimda vine in monsoon" (*Keeping Corner* 65). Later in the story, Masi undermines Leela again by comparing her to Kaveri, a child widow who had run away. She exclaims in outrage, "a brahman widow running away with a lower-caste boy.

Such a stain! Not only for her family, but for the whole caste" (185). Masi is a firm believer in the rules of her society and takes it upon herself to monitor other women. Referring to Saviben's[7] involvement in the anticolonial freedom struggle, Masi asks: "Don't you see Saviben is smitten by politics? Is this a woman's concern?" (187). In saying "if our men want to battle for more rights, so be it, but we women better stay home and make meals" (187), Masi conveys her faith in the gendered hierarchy.

Upon Leela's husband's death, her upper-caste family abandons her to widowhood to secure their family's caste status and access to caste privileges. Furthermore, older widows from the same caste demonstrate internalized sexism by carrying out the terms of Leela's widowhood. They remove tinkling and noisy jewelry, shave Leela's hair, and dress her in chidri, "a widow's sari" that announces to the world that the wearer of chidri is a bringer of bad luck (62). Although Leela is the main target, her close women relatives, Ba and Kaki, also share the burden because "when there was a widowed daughter in the house, the elder women gave up wearing flowers, nose rings, and bright saris" (*Keeping Corner* 55). When Leela's older brother Kanubhai questions their family's decision regarding Leela's widowhood, Ba and Kaki explain, "You know we had to […] If we want to live in society, we have to follow its rules" (69). If they did not follow the rules, they would be thrown out of caste and shunned for the rest of their lives. Although Leela reluctantly submits to the terms of widowhood, she feels the burn of injustice and unfairness.

At several points in the story, Leela is forced to feel the disgrace and misfortune of being a widow. After her husband's death, Leela suffers a crisis in identity because "once the woman ceased to be a wife, especially a childless wife, she ceased to be a person; she was then neither a daughter nor a daughter-in-law" (Chakravarti 78). Her family and caste community are quick to supply deleterious identities and purposes and fill the gap. Although Leela is often called a "widow" in *Keeping Corner*, other more offensive words capable of psychological wounds are mentioned in the story. When Leela's Masi cursed her as "Raand"[8] (103), she felt stung, humiliated, and worthless. The man who attempted to assault Leela sexually also cursed her as "Raand" (249) because Leela managed to wound him with her knife-like khili[9] and escape to safety. Another less vitriolic word is "widhwa" (54, 63), the Gujarati colloquial word for "widow." The slew of offensive words and victim-blaming attitudes prod her to decide, "I don't want to be a widow" (141). The journey from "not a widow" to something else starts with imagining resistance. Leela mirrors bell hooks's mind as a site of resistance, where one could "vicariously experience, dare to know and feel, without threat of repression, retaliation, and silencing" (54). Accordingly, Leela creates a "site of resistance" through exposure to news updates from the anticolonial freedom struggle and Gandhi's and Narmad's[10] ideas gained via homeschooling with Saviben. The freedom fighters struggled for anticolonial freedom, and the social reformers advocated for gender equality by openly challenging customs and traditions that oppressed women and lower castes. Leela cultivated an alternative future from the social reformers' targeted efforts to uplift widows by opening schools and advocating widow remarriage. In a letter, her cousin Jaya had encouraged moving to the city of Ahmedabad for higher education, where "you will be Leela and nothing else" (146). Latching onto the possibility for change, Leela realizes that she would not be "Leela the widow" but "Leela the teacher" (146). Through Saviben, she encounters the life stories of pioneer women such as Doctor Kashibai Navrange, the first lady doctor in Mumbai. Leela thinks to herself: "Someday I could be like them [...] I could study in Ahmedabad and become a teacher or a doctor" (156). Leela's imagined resistance powers her desire to be something other than a widow for the rest of her life. In her quest to find an appropriate channel for expressing resistance, she settles on satyagraha.

A Dual Struggle

As a story set amid many layers of freedom struggles, *Keeping Corner* strives to uncover individual layers while also visualizing the osmosis of ideas between them. Events from the anticolonial struggle punctuate *Keeping Corner*'s plotline. Through radio and word of mouth, the villagers in *Keeping Corner* discuss events and developments in the anticolonial struggle. While some villagers side with the nationalist leaders, others side with the British Raj, preferring not to go against a global superpower. Leela's Bapuji (father), an affluent upper-caste farmer, is impressed by Gandhian satyagraha. He teaches his daughter: "*satya* means truth, and *agrah* means insistence. Gandhiji believes that if we use the force of truth, we can fight injustice" (*Keeping Corner* 84). He participates in Kheda satyagraha, a farmers' satyagraha protesting the injustice of heavy taxes despite droughts and crop failures cutting into farmers' livelihood. Referring to the Rowlatt Act, which authorized the British administration to apprehend any Indian without sufficient justification, Leela's older brother Kanubhai declares, "This affects every Indian. *We* all have to fight [...] Soon it will be time for *you* to march with everyone" (198) (emphasis added). He plays an important role as Leela's ally by openly challenging the exclusionary norms defining widowhood and including Leela in the anticolonial struggle's united front. However, *Keeping Corner* is not a story of a white or brown male savior but of one child widow's path to reshape her own fate or kismet.

Bapuji's faith in satyagraha inspires Leela's choice of satyagraha to fight the injustices she encounters as a child widow. After deciding on the method of satyagraha and the path of education for empowerment and service, Leela recognizes the essential first step of convincing her family elders, Ba, Bapuji, Kaki, and Kaka. There are two critical reasons behind Leela's decision to negotiate her freedom in collaboration with her family. First, satyagraha is renouncing radical violence and embracing a nonviolent protest for truth and justice. Despite knowing that resisting the British came at the cost of getting beaten up and thrown in jail, Bapuji insisted on participating in Kheda satyagraha, protesting the unfair taxes on starving farmers. His persistent refusal to pay taxes resulted in the sarkar confiscating the family's bullocks and milch cows. The loss of bullocks resulted in the loss of livelihood, as they relied on the bullocks to plow their fields. Yet Bapuji does not renounce the path of satyagraha. When numbers among the confiscated cattle perish under the government's negligence, Bapuji remains unperturbed and insists: "Nonviolence means you must show restraint" in the face of adversities (234). He teaches Leela to protest injustice persistently through the quest for truth, satyagraha. Accordingly, she embraces truth and reason to protest the injustice of widowhood and aspires to be "Leela, the teacher." Second, unlike Fat Soma, who openly renounced his caste privileges to become a wandering monk, Leela cannot afford to become an outcaste. Since she does not possess patriarchal authority, as Fat Soma did, and is vulnerable to sexual assault targeting widows, she needs her family's support and protection.

When Leela first mentions to Ba, "I want to become a teacher or a doctor" (236), Ba points out, "You're a widow," a sobering reminder that there is no room for dreams and alternate futures in widowhood (*Keeping Corner* 236). Leela counters Ba's argument with Gandhi's and Narmad's ideas on child marriage, widowhood, and advocacy for girls' education. She adds: "What good are all their ideas if widows and their families don't take the lead?," stressing the vital role families play in supporting their members (236). Convinced by Leela's argument, Ba tells Bapuji, "Jamlee can offer Leela nothing […] She needs to learn to take care of herself. She's a smart girl and she can make a new life for herself" (242). However, Bapuji remains unconvinced because supporting Leela's higher education requires challenging traditions and customs and potentially becoming an outcast.

Nevertheless, Leela does not give up. She recognizes a crucial contradiction in Bapuji's understanding of satyagraha, a gap to plant her resistance. Leela asks: "If Bapuji was for truth and fairness, then he should know that what was happening to me wasn't fair. Why didn't he fight for me?" (86-87). Gandhi's definition of satyagraha mirrored a similar contradiction when he opposed Mahad satyagraha[11]. Although Gandhi approved satyagraha to protest colonial oppression, he opposed the Mahad caste community's application of satyagraha to challenge casteist oppression (Roy, "The Doctor and the Saint," 107-8). Likewise, Bapuji supports Gandhi's satyagraha against British colonial oppression but not Gandhian ideas on uplifting women. He marks the difference by saying: "Fighting the sarkar [the British] is one thing and breaking tradition is another. They have nothing in common" (245-46). Leela deconstructs the difference and reasons, "Following the truth is the same, whether it is against the foreign government or our own society. It requires courage. It's easier to follow customs than to question them. Bapuji, we have to take a pledge to fight against all that is wrong and cruel, including customs and prejudices. Don't our scriptures, Vedas, say that truth is whole? So how can we fragment it? How can we fight against cruelty and unfairness in some cases but not in others?" (*Keeping Corner* 246). Citing the unfairness of suffering imposed only on widows but not on widowers, Leela asks: "I didn't do anything wrong, but I have to suffer [widowhood]. Don't I have a right to wage satyagrah against that?" (246). When she places the injustices of colonization and widowhood side by side, Bapuji is finally convinced about the rightness of Leela's satyagraha. Finally he gives his consent for Leela to study in Ahmedabad, saying: "You made me realize that this is not just about you, it is also about something bigger" (247). He joins Leela in expanding the method of satyagraha and the meanings of freedom to fight cruelty and unfairness in all contexts.

Discussion and Conclusion

It is easy to discredit Leela's resistance and see her as a silenced victim when reading about stereotypes regarding South Asian women through the Western gaze. However, Leela asserts her agentic subjecthood by actively adopting and adapting satyagraha to fight the injustice of her widowhood. First, she expands the anticolonial freedom struggle's satyagraha to liberate widowhood from the clutches of brahmanical patriarchy. Second, her support of the anticolonial freedom struggle is accompanied by a critique of anticolonial nationalist feminism. While Gandhian call for all Indian participation in the freedom struggle eased the women's movement in public spaces, it also confined women to the nationalist vision of womanhood that prioritized men's freedom and citizenship over women's. The nationalist leaders, many of whom were upper-caste men, encouraged their womenfolk to participate in the Gandhian anticolonial struggle informed by ahimsa and satyagraha. The newly empowered women participating in satyagraha and anticolonial struggle used their will and voices only to the extent of supporting the nationalists' goal without reaching for broad definitions of freedom. However, Leela's expression of resistance is cognizant of intersecting oppressive structures in supporting anticolonial struggle while also daring to resist the clutches of oppressive customs, such as child widowhood and female illiteracy.

Through Leela, Shani, and Fat Soma, *Keeping Corner* exposes readers to multiple equations of domination and resistance sketched across transnational and domestic power structures. Although resistance accompanies all forms of domination, it "is not always identifiable through organized movements" because "resistance inheres in the very gaps, fissures, and silences of hegemonic narratives" (Mohanty 83). Accordingly, Leela's satyagraha exposes hypocrisies in Gandhian satyagraha. Her persistence toward "Leela, the teacher" unveils shortcomings in feminist reforms articulated by both colonizers and colonized nationalists. In choosing education, she relies on her upper-caste privilege but also deconstructs the upper-caste monopoly over education through her mission to serve other girls and women as a teacher. The model of education that

Saviben imparts to Leela in *Keeping Corner* celebrates knowledge and pedagogies that prioritize learners' experiences and cultural knowledge toward empowering them for social justice action. In the last scene, as Leela takes in the bustle of Ahmedabad and the ongoing social and political changes resulting from the anticolonial struggle, she observes, "Traditions bound people as foreign rule had bound our country. Even when they hurt us, we could not leave them, because we were so used to them" (272). Drawing a parallel between traditions and foreign rule, she invites readers to ponder long-standing traditions and norms that continue to bind people in the present day.

Keeping Corner's approach to oppression and resistance in colonial-era upper-caste child widowhood facilitates the space to observe transnational movements in definitions of womanhood and feminist resistance. As Mohanty argued in *Feminism without Borders*, the damage and deficit stereotypes attributed to colonized women continue to haunt their modern-day descendants, the Third World women. Studies of the South Asian diaspora reveal that girls and women of South Asian descent labor under the weight of the "Western gaze" that exoticizes them (Rayaprol 144; Acosta 271). When learners are provided with spaces such as ethnic studies programs that support their academic, personal, and ethnic identities, they are empowered to reclaim an authentic sense of self beyond stereotypes and apply agency for social change (Acosta 274). Research on youth literacy and young adult literature shows that readers and reading spaces play equally vital roles in expanding worldviews and nurturing narrative empathy. Because young people are aware of different power structures shaping their worlds, educators recommend texts and pedagogies that empower them to use their voices to "become active, empowered, democratic, and justice-oriented citizens" (Selvestor and Summer 20). But this is possible only when learning is not snuffed out by standardized education. In "Pedagogies of Resistance," Leigh Patel advocated for fugitive acts of learning that emerge against the stratifying structures of the formal and standardized education system designed to hierarchize students (397). Literature and stories can facilitate the spaces to nurture critical thinking in readers.

In a study of South Asian American writing, Rajini Srikanth notes the gaps left by multicultural reading practices that support benign tolerance of difference as a laudable achievement without seeking more profound engagement with diversity (22). Instead, she argues for the need for South Asian American literature that can "supply the narratives and images that are compelling enough to make readers in the United States aware of the gaps in their consciousness, and intriguing enough to move them to fill these gaps by reading with care and living with vision" (33). As a South Asian story published in the United States, *Keeping Corner*'s narrative engagement with intersections of caste, gender, and colonization carries great potential to enhance readers' awareness and empathy. The authorial tryst with re-orientalism challenges readers to strive beyond exoticized tourist readings of South Asia.

Works Cited

Ashcroft, Bill, et al. *The Empire Writes Back: Theory and Practice in Post-Colonial Literatures*. 2nd ed., Routledge, 2002.

Acosta, Curtis. "Tipu: Connections, Love, and Liberation." *Rethinking Ethnic Studies*, edited by Tolteka Cuauhtin et al., Rethinking Schools, 2019, pp. 269-74.

Bhalla, Tamara. *Reading Together, Reading Apart: Identity, Belonging, and South Asian American Community*. U of Illinois P, 2016.

Bose, Sugata, and Ayesha Jalal. *Modern South Asia: History, Culture, Political Economy*. Routledge, 2004.

Chakravarti, Uma. *Gendering Caste: Through a Feminist Lens*. Sage, 2018.

Crenshaw, Kimberlé. "Mapping the Margins: Intersectionality, Identity Politics, and Violence against Women of Color." *Stanford Law Review*, vol. 43, no. 6, 1991, pp. 1241-1300.

Cook, Mike P., et al. "March and the Struggle for Historical Perspective Recognition." *The ALAN Review*, no. 2017.

Cuauhtin, Tolteka, et al., editors. *Rethinking Ethnic Studies*. Rethinking Schools, 2019.

Davis-Undiano, Robert. "Mildred D. Taylor and the Art of Making a Difference." *World Literature Today*, vol. 78, no. 2, 2004, pp. 11-13.

Dirks, Nicholas B. *Castes of Mind: Colonialism and the Making of Modern India*. Princeton UP, 2001.

Gómez, Sarah Hannah. "Decolonizing Nostalgia: When Historical Fiction Betrays Readers of Color." *The Horn Book Magazine*, 2016, https://www.hbook.com/?detailStory=decolonizing-nostalgia-when-historical-fiction-betrays-readers-of-color.

Gopal, Priyamvada. "Reading Subaltern History." *The Cambridge Companion to Postcolonial Literary Studies*, edited by Neil Lazarus, Cambridge UP, 2004.

hooks, bell. "Narratives of Struggle." *Critical Fictions: The Politics of Imaginative Writing*, edited by Philomena Mariani, Dia Centre for the Arts, 1991.

Krishna, Sankaran. "Methodical Worlds: Partition, Secularism, and Communalism in India." *Alternatives: Global, Local, Political*, vol. 27, no. 2, 2002, pp. 193-217.

Lau, Lisa, and Ana Cristina Mendes. *Re-Orientalism and South Asian Identity Politics: The Oriental Other Within*. Routledge, 2014.

Marx, John. "Postcolonial Literature and the Western Literary Canon." *The Cambridge Companion to Postcolonial Literary Studies*, edited by Neil Lazarus, Cambridge UP, 2004.

Mohanty, Chandra Talpade. *Feminism without Borders: Decolonizing Theory, Practicing Solidarity*. Duke UP, 2004.

Nankani, Sandhya. "Rising Tide: The Boom in Historical Fiction About India and the Indian Diaspora." *Multicultural Review*, vol. 18, no. 2, 2009, pp. 23-27.

Pandey, Iswari. *South Asian in the Mid-South: Migrations of Literacies*. U of Pittsburgh P, 2015.

Pandey, Gyanendra. "Subaltern Citizens and Their Histories." *Interventions*, vol. 10, no. 3, 2008, pp. 271-84.

Parmar, Y. A. *The Mahyavanshi: The Success Story of a Scheduled Caste*. Mittal Publications, 1987.

Patel, Leigh. "Pedagogies of Resistance and Survivance: Learning as Marronage." *Equity & Excellence in Education*, vol. 49, no. 4, 2016, pp. 397-401.

Patil, Vrushali. "From Patriarchy to Intersectionality: A Transnational Feminist Assessment of How Far We've Really Come." *Signs*, vol. 38, no. 4, 2013, pp. 847-67.

Rangachari, Devika. "Writing History for Children." *Muse India*, 2007.

Rayaprol, Aparna. "Being American, Learning to Be India: Gender and Generation in the Context of Transnational Migration." *Transnational Migration and the Politics of Identity*, edited by Meenakshi Thapan, Sage Publications, 2005, pp. 130-49.

Riechel, Aimee. "Our Oral History Narrative Project." *Rethinking Ethnic Studies*, edited by Tolteka Cuauhtin et al., Rethinking Schools, 2019, pp. 107-12.

Roy, Arundhati. "The Doctor and The Saint." *Annihilation of Caste*, edited by S. Anand, Verso, 2014.

Schaull, Richard. "Foreword." *Pedagogy of the Oppressed*, by Paulo Freire, translated by Myra Bergman Ramos, Bloomsbury Academic, 2018, pp. 9-15.

Selvester, Paula M., and Deborah G. Summers. *Socially Responsible Literacy: Teaching Adolescents for Purpose and Power*. Teachers College P, 2012.

Sheth, Kashmira. *Keeping Corner*. Disney-Hyperion Books, 2009.

Sinha, Mrinalini. "Gendered Nationalism: From Woman to Gender and Back Again?" *Routledge Handbook of Gender in South Asia*, edited by Leela Fernandes, 2nd ed., Routledge, 2022, pp. 3-17.

Spivak, Gayatri. "'Can the Subaltern Speak?' Revised Edition, from the "History" Chapter of Critique of Postcolonial Reason." *Can the Subaltern Speak?*

Reflections on the History of an Idea, edited by Rosalind Morris, Columbia UP, 2010, pp. 21-78.

Srikanth, Rajini. *The World Next Door: South Asian American Literature and the Idea of America.* Temple UP, 2004.

Sunder Rajan, Rajeswari. *Real and Imagined Women: Gender, Culture and Postcolonialism.* Routledge, 2003.

Sunder Rajan, Rajeswari. *The Scandal of the State: Women, Law, Citizenship in Postcolonial India.* Duke UP, 2003.

Thomas, Ebony E., and Amy Stornaiuolo. "Restorying the Self: Bending Toward Textual Justice." *Harvard Educational Review*, vol. 86, no. 3, 2016, pp. 313-38.

Tolbert-Mbatha, Waahida. "'My Family's Not from Africa — We Come from North Carolina': Teaching Slavery in Context." *Rethinking Ethnic Studies*, edited by Tolteka Cuauhtin et al., Rethinking Schools, 2019, pp. 91-95.

Young, Robert. *Postcolonialism: An Historical Introduction.* Wiley, 2016.

Zaidi, Annie. *Un Bound: 2,000 Years of Indian Women's Writing.* Aleph Book Company, 2015.

Notes

1. The trend since 2007, starting with Kashmira Sheth's *Keeping Corner*, has brought forth several titles exploring significant moments in South Asian history, notably featuring female protagonists (Nankani 2009). It continues in the writings of more recent authors, such as Supriya Kelkar and Veera Hiranandani.

2. Upper-caste women were required to follow *pativrata* customs that were "ideological 'purdah' of the Hindu woman as chastity and wifely fidelity came to be regarded as the means to salvation" (Chakravarti 70). The upper-caste membership also forced women to "regard their husbands as 'honoured' beings who must be respected at all times" (Chakravarti 83). Drawing on the critical writings of early feminists, such as Pandita Ramabai and Tarabai Shinde, Gail Omvedt called *pativrata* a "double standard" that demanded chastity of women while encouraging wives to overlook their husbands' excesses and sexual licensure.

3. Sati is the practice of immolating Hindu widows on the funeral pyres of their husbands (Bose and Jalal 58). It was practiced in certain parts of South Asia, particularly among upper-caste communities.

4. The nonviolent freedom struggle in 1947 was preceded by an armed insurrection in 1857 called the Sepoy Mutiny, named for the Sepoys (a branch of British Indian armed forces composed of native soldiers) who sparked the insurrection (Bose and Jalal). Despite the

spread of mutiny across large parts of present-day north India, it was mercilessly crushed by the British Trading Company's forces. At the end of the mutiny, the trading company's holdings were taken over by the crown as a direct colony of the British empire.

5. In addition to determining an individual's standing in the social hierarchy, the caste system also played a significant role in determining a person's profession. Traditionally, professions were fixed to one's caste identity and could not be changed. In *Keeping Corner*, Leela explains that the Rabari caste were traditionally "nomads who went from one place to another with their animals and tents" (139).

6. In *Gendering Caste*, Uma Chakravarti uses the term sexuality to convey girls' and women's fertility and childbearing abilities in the context of marriage, endogamy laws, and brahmanical patriarchy.

7. Saviben is Leela's teacher in *Keeping Corner*. Saviben's father had been against her college education, saying it was a man's world and that "a woman's place was at home" (156). Saviben had been disowned by her father for continuing school.

8. In *Keeping Corner*, Leela explains, "Raand meant widow, but in a hateful, disgusting way. It was a swear word" (63)

9. "A gold hair ornament. It was round with a sturdy gold rod for the back" (*Keeping Corner* 215). Kaki advises her to "keep in your poulka pocket — all the time" and to use it "if you ever find yourself in danger" (215).

10. A nineteenth-century Gujarati social reformer who rejected child marriage, advocated for women's education and widow remarriage, and ran the periodical *Dandyo* (Parmar).

11. When a lower-caste community applied the peaceful protest of satyagraha to challenge caste restrictions in their village (Dirks 266; Roy, "The Doctor and the Saint" 107-8), Gandhi disapproved of this movement, labeling it "Duragraha" as "devilish force," as opposed to "Satyagraha" informed by "soul force" (ibid. 109). Gandhi condemned the Mahad Satyagraha, urging "Untouchables to fight for their rights by 'sweet persuasion and not by Satyagraha'" (ibid. 109).

Three

"Let Me Tell You a Story"

Healing, Environmental Justice, and Resistance in Mark Oshiro's *Each of Us a Desert*

Sonia Alejandra Rodríguez

Xochitl, the sixteen-year-old protagonist of Mark Oshiro's *Each of Us a Desert* (2021), carries the importance of stories in her body. As a cuentista, Xochitl consumes her village's stories and regurgitates them to the earth before the stories go home to Solís, their deity. Not giving voice to the village's stories might mean catastrophe for everyone. Xochitl's role as a cuentista highlights the significance of storytelling as a process for healing and liberation. As I demonstrate throughout this chapter, storytelling that liberates requires sharing and speaking one's story into existence. In *Critical Race Theory: An Introduction*, Richard Delgado and Jean Stefancic explain that "Stories can give [those silenced] a voice and reveal that other people have similar experiences. Stories can name a type of discrimination (e.g., microaggression, unconscious discrimination, or structural racism); once named, it can be combated" (52). Delgado and Stefancic write specifically about stories in the courtroom and the influential role of a diversity of stories in a law context to achieve equal justice for all. In the quote above, they describe the important process of using stories to name the oppressions experienced. It's in the naming that challenging oppressive ways of knowing or being can begin. In my research on "conocimiento narratives," I explain that Gloria Anzaldúa calls a similar naming process "el arrebato," a nebulous place where one must acknowledge that a trauma has even occurred (2019). Delgado and Stefancic elaborate further, saying, "Powerfully written stories and narratives may begin a process of correction in our system of beliefs and categories by calling attention to neglected evidence and reminding readers of our common humanity" (52). In other words, stories can be used to challenge dominant ideologies and biases. Stories by those who have been silenced shine a light on "neglected evidence," and, in doing so, stories create possibilities for more liberating ways of knowing and being. I analyze *Each of Us a Desert* from the point of view that storytelling as a tool for liberation stems from community. Second, my critical approach to storytelling as a theory and a praxis is informed by critical race theory and ethnic studies. These fields of study further reiterate what communities of color have been saying about storytelling as having the potential to being about self and community liberation and to counter dominant oppressive narratives. In *Each of Us a Desert*, Xochitl's knowledge creation through storytelling allows for her and her communities' liberation. Their represented liberation permits me to showcase the importance of centering youth as intellectuals and storytellers.

In *The Courage to Imagine: The Child Hero in Children's Literature*, Roni Natov (2017) says that empathy "involves the ability to hold onto the self and listen to the other, not to become the other, not to merge with overidentification" (146). In this sense, empathy is striving for the balance between caring for oneself and caring for another. Becoming the other or overidentifying with the other, as Natov explains, is not empathy. The desire for balance and the struggle with overidentification, in regard to empathy, is at the heart of Mark Oshiro's *Each of Us a Desert*. Xochitl is her village's cuentista, a healer who consumes confessions and returns them to Solís by physically purging the stories into the earth. In doing so, Xochitl prevents her peoples' sins from becoming nightmares, or material manifestations, that could threaten their lives. While the role of the cuentista is recognized as one that merits respect and honor from the community, Xochitl doesn't want this role, which was bestowed upon her at the age of eight by her dying aunt. She feels burdened by this responsibility and sets off on a journey to Solado, a city where she can find a cuentista who will remove this gift. In this chapter, I read *Each of Us a Desert* as a novel that intersects the power of storytelling with healing, environmental justice, and resistance. I am interested in the ways that Xochitl's gift as a cuentista, with the ability to consume and regurgitate stories, challenges not only the purpose of storytelling as a tool of liberation but also the expectations of care and empathy that often fall on young women.

In this way, I closely examine storytelling as having multivalence roles in the novel in regard to healing, both the self and a larger community; in terms of considering how storytelling is an important aspect of environmental justice, in particular for people of color; and in terms of resistance against oppressive epistemologies that influence the self and inform cultural, familial, and communal expectations. My reading of the novel additionally is grounded in larger concerns in ethnic studies and youth literature as fields of study. The present attacks on critical race theory across the US, the desires to limit inclusion of ethnic studies in the K-12 classrooms, and the growth of challenges and banning of books that center young protagonists of color signal a larger fear of challenges to the US as a powerful empire and indicate the longevity of white supremacy. It's in these perilous times that centering youth as intellectuals and storytellers is even more important.

Storytelling and Healing

I situate Xochitl within a tradition of curaderas in order to read her cuentista gift as having multivalent healing purposes. In *Letras y Limpias: Decolonial Medicine and Holistic Healing in Mexican American Literature*, Amanda Ellis (2021) argues, "Curanderas mark the tensions within uneven and ongoing histories of violence, they recall past cross-cultural encounters, and they invite us to think about the ways in which Eurocentric ideologies continue to (dis)order our worlds, shape what we think of ourselves, and manifest themselves in the present day" (8). In this way, curanderas embody and become repositories for trauma while simultaneously offering decolonial methods of healing. In *Each of Us a Desert*, Xochilt is forcefully placed in the position to carry her neighbors' trauma to offer reprieve to the individual confessing and as a ritual of praise and obedience to Solís. The position of cuentista is not one of simply healer but more specifically healer through storytelling. A literal translation of cuentista from Spanish to English is that of "storyteller." In *Decolonizing Methodologies: Research and Indigenous Peoples* (2023), Linda Tuhiwai Smith describes storytelling as an indigenous project wherein "The story and the story teller both serve to connect the past with the future, one generation with the other, the land with the people and the people with the story," and in the passing of stories so too are a culture's values and beliefs (146). The role of the curandera as prescribed by Ellis and that of the storyteller as explained by Smith suggest these positions to be those of powerful and significant intermediaries — serving as a connection between the past and present, as a bridge from trauma to healing, and as a container of multiple truths and realities. I resist reading the curandera and the storyteller as passive forms of healing and resistance because, as exemplified by Xochitl's character, the acts of healing from trauma and decolonizing knowledge are practices that can take a toll on the body.

In Empalme, Xochitl's village in *Each of Us a Desert*, it's believed that if the townspeople don't confess their sins, they will manifest into actual physical creature–like monsters referred to as pesadillas or nightmares. Xochitl explains: "This is the story I was told of how las cuentistas were born; You [Solís] gave some of us the ability to devour the truth of others, and You warned us. We would all know if someone had harmed another, if they had kept their truth from You. The longer one of us went without a cuentista, the worse our pesadillas became" (23). While the reason and the process by which the characters must confess to gain atonement and salvation resemble colonial and Catholic rituals, I instead read these acts of confession through a decolonial lens that examines trauma through storytelling to exist and know differently and posits the dangers of not processing one's trauma. Cathy Caruth's definition of trauma is useful here: "trauma describes an overwhelming experience of sudden or catastrophic events in which the response to the event occurs in the often delayed, uncontrolled repetitive appearance of hallucinations and other intrusive phenomena" (12). In employing trauma theory, I reject the notion of confessing one's misdeeds as understood through a binary of good and bad behavior, which suggests there is a correct and wrong way of being. The characters of *Each of Us a Desert* reveal sins that relate to alcoholism, stealing, and lying. I read these behaviors as a response to trauma created by environmental injustice, including a devastating fire and an attempt to privatize Empalme's water supply. Oshiro's use of fantasy provides a brilliant opportunity to look at trauma that often goes unrecognized and turns the villagers' trauma not into "hallucinations and other intrusive phenomena" but into real and dangerous monsters.

The burden of ensuring that the collective trauma of Empalme does not overrun the village falls on the cuentista, or at least what Xochitl and her village believe. The responsibility of being a vessel for another's trauma, however, also has physical consequences for the cuentista. The ritual of taking a story requires the consumption of a story that momentarily lives inside Xochitl's body. At the beginning of the cuentista ritual, after extending her hands and letting one of the characters place theirs on top of hers, Xochitl feels depleted. She says: "As Rogelio's story filled my body, it jostled for space. It stretched between bones and organs, and I pushed the pain and discomfort down, down, farther away from my heart. I stood and wobbled, trying to separate my own sadness and loneliness from Rogelio's. They were so *similar*, and it haunted me every time. You [Solís] let me keep that part of the memory; the ritual left me confused, bewildered, uncertain where I ended and where the story began" (20). That Rogelio's story temporarily lives within Xochitl during the cuentista ritual is an example of the way storytelling connects past and present with each other and signals to the way an individual's pain can be situated within a collective trauma. In writing about curanderas' rituals, Ellis explains, "The ritualized process of the limpia is a set of choreographed embodied actions wherein practitioners engage in illness-specific rituals, prayer, and care work to transmit a sense of healing with the aim of restoring balance" (91). Xochitl embarks on this cleansing "choreographed embodied" act to restore balance to Rogelio and in turn maintains balance between Empalme and Solís. Such balance means Solís is content and the pesadillas don't physically manifest in Empalme. In this way, the cuentista's ritual demonstrates that healing the individual can in turn heal a collective. However, while this cuentista ritual is about balance, about using storytelling to maintain balance between healing and trauma, Xochitl is left with residual trauma. As I argued earlier, healing the collective is an important aspect of challenging and changing dominant oppressive ways of knowing.

As part of Xochitl's cuentista ritual, after taking a story, she must wander into the desert, touch the earth, and vomit the story into the earth as a symbol of returning the story to Solís. In returning the story, Xochitl doesn't have a complete memory of the story and is left disoriented after the process. In a way, she loses a bit of herself. While Xochitl recognizes the importance of this ritual for Empalme's future, she also recognizes that she doesn't want to be the one to do it. From the beginning of the novel, it's clear to the reader that Xochitl does not want the cuentista role, nor did she ask for it, but she plays the role because it's expected of her. That Oshiro has positioned Xochitl as a young person who recognizes and understands that the expectations of her society are not for her is an outstanding example of the ways understanding childhood and consent are progressing in our society. It also demonstrates the importance of recognizing young people as intellectuals. Xochitl feels isolated for the majority of the novel, as she has no one with whom to share her doubts about the expectations and burdens she carries. In speaking about her parents, Xochitl says, "It wasn't that I thought my parents didn't care about me. But I couldn't bring myself to tell them how I really felt. Would they think I was ungrateful? Selfish? I just wanted more. Was that so bad?" (26). Xochitl's sentiments are not unfamiliar to young people whose parents or relatives have survived traumatic events, like immigration, and more specifically like the climate crisis that Xochitl's family endured.

In questioning her positionality, Xochitl signals to the power dynamics in traditional family structures. Youth and children are seen as having less authority than their parents (or guardians), and that imbalance of power is both influenced by and further cements learned cultural and gender expectations to be followed. Sarah Ahmed says in *Willful Subjects*, "The aim of education is to bring the will of the child into line not only with parent will, but the moral law, upon which parental law is assumed to rest" (68). Children and young people are supposed to learn to obey their parents because obedience is what society expects of adults. Understood in this way, the power imbalance and hierarchy between children, young people, and adults is purposeful. Xochitl's question about what might happen if she does not follow the path laid out for her also points to an idea that there is a dichotomous way of being, a correct and a wrong way, a safe and an unsafe way, an accepted and an unaccepted way. Additionally, Xochitl questions the way her community treats her role as a cuentista. She says, "They claimed to understand me, but they understood only the need for the ritual. They didn't get how much I needed to be away from home; away from all the responsibilities and the sad, needy faces; away from feeling stuck in a life I never chose" (32). Xochitl is well aware that being a cuentista gives her value in her community, but in the aforementioned quote she clearly calls out that this value is not for her as a person but for her as a cuentista. In the position of cuentista, she's privy to the feelings and truths about her neighbors in a way they are not. Ellis, in writing about respect for curanderas, says, "even though curanderas are deeply respected for their ability to heal, like all women, they are still subject to being accused of being brujas, dubbed evil, and persecuted and maligned because of their gender, autonomy, knowledge, and power" (98). Xochitl, like Ellis, points to the ways the healers, who also read and identify as women, are nonetheless beholden to colonial gender oppression where their value, and in turn, respect, only goes as far as they are seen as useful in their society.

Xochitl has the awareness to know that the way she is treated by her family and her village is dependent on her power as a cuentista. Early in the novel, she begins to question this positionality and the limits of empathy — hers and that of the people around her. Xochitl says, "Take, consume, return. Tuve que honrar a Solís. Proteger mi aldea. Amar a mi familia. That was it. I protected others, but who protected me? Who listened to *me*? Who cared about the things that made me scared, worried, or angry?" (84). Xochitl's questions are an expression of her needs and an affront to the hierarchical power dynamics between youth and adults. She is holding up her responsibilities as a cuentista but her community is failing her, and she is left to ask, "who protect[s] me?" Xochitl's frustration, while fictional, resounds with a real question that might impact readers of all ages: When adults fail young people, how do adults learn from young people to do better? As the novel progresses, Xochitl's urgency to leave Empalme intensifies. Xochitl's personal journey for liberation quickly becomes entangled with the liberation of her community's after piecing together a story that predicts impending danger for Empalme. Julio, a local gang leader, arrives in Empalme with plans to privatize the little water that exists in the village. The privatization of the water means the control of the town. Xochitl learns about Julio's plans during one of her cuentista rituals with a neighbor. In a turning point in the novel, Xochitl decides to not give the story to Solís and instead decides to have the story, and the truth, live inside herself. To not lose this one story, Xochitl must then keep within herself every story she takes thereafter. Again, because Xochitl feels abandoned by her community, she must take matters into her own hands. In another instance when Xochitl takes someone's story, she says, "Marisol's guilt tore at me, but I ignored it. How was this my life? How was I expected to consume such horrible traumas over and over again? Now that I had kept so many stories inside me, refusing to give them to the desert, Empalme no longer looked the same to me" (94). I find Xochitl's question a powerful one: "How was I expected to consume such horrible traumas over and over again?" While she's clearly referring to the traumas of the people in her village, I can't help but connect this question to the reality of young people of color today. To change her outcome, Xochitl is left in a position where she must put herself first over her family and her community. *Each of Us a Desert* starts as a tale about a "chosen one," but Xochitl quickly subverts that trope by refusing to be a martyr for her community.

Storytelling and Environmental Justice

In Oshiro's novel, La Quema was a wildfire that devastated the land, forcing Xochitl and her community to move farther into the desert to create a new village, Empalme. Throughout the novel, readers learn that this climate catastrophe has had a deep traumatic impact on those who survived. Because of La Quema, access to water is scarce. It's evident throughout the novel that La Quema has had a lasting effect on the environment, forcing people to continue to migrate throughout the land in search of better jobs, water, and healing. In Empalme, the people who can't migrate are forced to endure Julio's violence. As Marek Oziewicz and Lara Saguisag explain in the introduction to a special issue of *The Lion and the Unicorn*, "Children's Literature and Climate Change," "Those without the means to move elsewhere [after a climate catastrophe] will eke out diminished lives in what Dorceta E. Taylor calls 'toxic communities': sites decimated by pollution, disasters, and racial and social injustice" (vi). Oziewicz and Saguisag make clear that the effect of a climate crisis doesn't end when the crisis has been contained. Instead, the effects, including the trauma and violence, endure and morph long after visible signs of a climate crisis have disappeared. In other words, as it relates to *Each of Us*, while the literal fire of La Quema no longer burns, that doesn't mean that the people aren't still suffering from the wounds the fire created.

Searching for water in Empalme was becoming increasingly difficult, forcing Xochitl to walk farther away from her aldea to find it. In an effort to privatize water, Julio resorted to physical violence to enforce water rations in Empalme. Xochitl explains, "After Julio and his men took over the well and started charging la comunidad to withdraw water, some of us devised our own means of surviving. It was extra work, but it also meant that sometimes our family could go days without seeing Julio" (37). It also meant they could go days without water. In "Against Ecocidal Environmentalism," Hannah Doermann explains, "Numerous scholars have demonstrated that capitalism is the primary cause of planetary destruction, and that our only hope for limiting the ecological damage of global warming is a radical restructuring of society" (141). I agree that capitalism has led to "planetary destruction" and add that capitalism is also the reason that solving and healing from climate catastrophes is challenging. Indeed, "a radical restructuring of society" is necessary. As Julie Sze reminds us in *Environmental Justice in a Moment of Danger* (2020), "Capitalism depends on control, specifically control of nature" (7). Such control of natural resources like water is evident in *Each of Us* through Julio's corrupt intentions to privatize water in Empalme. But Xochitl reminds readers that a restructuring of society is possible — if dominant narratives can be used to oppress people and exploit the planet, then stories can also be used to liberate us.

Julio's capitalistic greed to control the water and the people is one of the reasons why Xochitl leaves Empalme, and it's also the reason she decides to return at the end. While taking a story, Xochitl learns that Julio plans to not just take the water but also has bigger plans to cause more severe violence. Xochitl does not return this story to Solís because she can't let herself forget that her community is in grave danger. After learning the truth about Julio's plans, Xochitl explains to Solís that Julio and his men:

> had refused our rituals and our guidance, and they didn't care if we were worried that You [Solís] would return and scorch it all out of existence again. We were superstitious and silly to them, and that's why Julio had said we deserved to be conquered.

> "You are all like this," he slurred to Papá one morning during that first week he arrived; it was also the last day that we relied on our weekly portion from the well. "The last aldea I controlled, they were just as weak as you. Waiting for Solís to save them." He brushed his hand across the face of mi papá. "Their god didn't show when I slaughtered them all." (53)

Toward the end of the novel, the reader learns that there is a long history of conquering and controlling the land that has led to the present timeline of corruption and greed. As Sarah Wald et al. explain in the introduction to *Latinx Environmentalisms*, "discussions about the environment ought to engage colonialism, or they risk extending colonialism by ignoring this ongoing legacy" (5). Julio's language of conquering, controlling, and slaughtering a people echoes colonization and genocide. Xochitl's explanation makes clear that her community's stories and beliefs are being corrupted and exploited to justify violence and establish dominance. Additionally, Julio's rejections of Empalme's rituals and the guidance of the people are indicators to stay away from the water well Julio attempts to control. The multilayered exchange of stories in the quote above — between Julio and Papá, between Xochitl and Solís, and between the narrator and the reader — demonstrates the complex ways storytelling ties the past to the present to the future. Julio reveals past experiences of conquest and genocide, exercises similar violence presently, and predicts a similar future for Empalme. But Xochitl and her father know a different story, one that's taught them to search for their own water without relying on exploitative systems. Xochitl's affront to Julio's power is an extraordinary display of rebellion against people and systems that seek to oppress her and her people. Xochitl's acts of rebellion through storytelling will ultimately lead to a rejection of narratives that seek to harm the environment, the people, and their futures.

I read *Each of Us a Desert* as a representation of the ways storytelling and the environment are intertwined. For Xochitl, as a cuentista, the ritual of returning the stories she takes from her neighbors' confessions requires that she go into the desert and commune with the earth. Throughout the novel, Xochitl refers to the process of returning the stories as needing to return them to the earth. In *Each of Us*, the stories belong to and in the earth. In an early example in the novel of Xochitl's cuentista ritual, Xochitl explains, "I opened myself up to the earth. I climbed up to the other side of the gully, and the earth spoke to me. I let it pull me to the ground, the dirt biting into my knees and my palms […] and [the story] spilled onto the waiting earth, filling the cracks and seeping deep within" (20). Xochitl demonstrates that to be a cuentista, one must also be in tune with the environment. In this way, Xochitl listens not just to the stories of her neighbors but also to those of the earth. This is why she is called and pulled from within by the earth so often throughout the novel. In an interview in *Latinx Environmentalisms*, Helena Maria Viramontes says, "we carry our environments within ourselves" (166). Viramontes speaks of the ways that one's environment is a part of them despite any distance. For Xochitl, her environment churns in her belly with every story she consumes. After deciding not to return these stories to Solís, this becomes physically painful for her. The keeping of the stories allows Xochitl to piece together the truth about her world, including the truth about La Quema and the continued effects of such a monumental climate catastrophe. In collecting the stories, Xochitl is privy to the climate trauma her people endured. But it is through these collected stories, and through her migration journey to Solado, that she is able to challenge oppressive powers in her life. Xochitl explains, "I was not even aware that the rigid rules of my life were *stories*, passed on from generation to generation because that's all we knew. Tia Inez believed it, and la cuentista before her did, too. And so, we gave every cuentista of Empalme the same rules, the same restrictions, and we held them down, and we forced them into a life they couldn't possibly have chosen" (375). Xochitl describes the prescribed role of the cuentistas as stories that have been passed on for generations without giving chosen healers an option for other ways of knowing and being. However, I argue, Xochitl's revelations also make clear that "from one generation to generation" cuentistas have been collecting climate trauma stories. I insist on reading La Quema as a climate catastrophe that cannot be removed from the climate trauma the people in the world of *Each of Us* continue to experience, even generations later. I read the cuentistas' role, which emerged after La Quema, as an example of the importance of storytelling in perilous times of various environmental injustices. Already in the desert, Xochitl says: "I sank into the earth, letting it accept me as I accepted it. We both benefited from each other; it was what mi gente had taught me. We all knew that one reason Solís had sent La Quema was because of the violence that humanity had subjected the earth to. It was why I gave the stories back to the desert first before they were sent home. The earth deserved our contribution, too" (118). Here, Xochit details the stories consumed and then returned to the earth by the cuentistas as an example of a healing process meant for both humanity and for the environment. While Xochitl rejects the imposed and prescribed role of the cuentista, what she can't reject, what her people have taught her, is that storytelling is a powerful healing tool.

Another way that storytelling and the environment are connected in the novel is through Xochitl's search for water, which often leads to her finding pieces of paper with poems written on them. Xochitl explains,

> I had been hunting for water weeks earlier, and I thought that You were guiding me to a new source. I rarely went to the east, but as I walked in that direction, it was as if something had looped twine around my heart and kept tugging me. *Closer, closer*, it said, and I obeyed, always did what I was told. I was the dutiful daughter, wasn't I? The one who honored her parents, the one who kept herself available to all in case las pesadillas were close. (33)

The quote above demonstrates another instance of the way the earth pulls at Xochitl and the way her environment lives within. What tugs at Xochitl in this example are poems stuffed in leather pouches buried deep in the earth written by Emilia, Julio's daughter. Oshiro, through Xochitl, connects earth, water, and poetry to demonstrate a connection between storytelling and the environment. As the novel progresses, Xochitl digs, burying her hands in the dirt to find water and poems. In the above passage, Xochitl also connects the tug of the earth with the expectations she feels to be a "dutiful daughter." Regardless of her conflict, the poems buried in the earth give Xochitl solace and company. In "Seeking Refuge *Under the Mesquite*: Nature Imagery in Guadalupe García McCall's Verse Novel," Cristina Herrera argues, "Through the mesquite's example, the novel suggests that nature may offer vulnerable girls important lessons such as resilience, even acceptance of life's unpredictability and our powerlessness to control such events as illness and death" (202). As Herrera argues, nature is bountiful with life lessons accessible to "vulnerable girls." In *Each of Us a Desert*, nature and the poems offer Xochitl a connection that is different, and more powerful, than the connection she has with nature because of her search for water or because of her role as a cuentista. In each case when Xochitl finds a poem buried in the earth, nature indeed teaches her there are other ways of being. Xochitl elaborates on her connection when she finds the first poem:

> I was good at hunting water, at picking up the signs Papá had taught me, but the earth shouted at me, guided me farther east, until I was in the shade of a thick patch of mesquites. […] That first time I read la poema, I couldn't make sense of the words. They were too real, too close, and I dropped the scrap of paper back to the earth, stood up, and walked away from it. But it sang to me, called me back, and I returned, devoured it over and over. (33)

The beautiful image of buried poems in the earth is one that further established the relationship between storytelling and the environment. While Xochitl has an existing relationship with nature because of her role as a cuentista, las poemas begin as sources of positive interactions with nature. Searching and finding a poem reminds Xochitl of her own power and her own connection to her environment that isn't tied to her role as a cuentista. In the quote mentioned above, the earth called her to a poem with words that offered her healing. Throughout the novel, the earth pulls at Xochitl to a location of water or a poem. In this way, the earth nourishes Xochitl with the water she needs to live but also with words that help her endure, survive, and liberate herself:

> Este mundo de
> cenizas
> This world of ashes
> > no puede contenerme

cannot contain me
>   No hay paredes
There are no walls
>   para detenerme
to stop me
>   *Soy* libre.
I am free. (40)

The stories Xochitl collects throughout her migration journey to rid herself of her cuentista gift and the poems she finds buried along her path are examples of how storytelling and the environment are connected in *Each of Us a Desert*. Oshiro links words and earth, making it clear that a path toward environmental justice must include the dismantling of harmful, dominant narratives and the embrace of new, more empowering messages. As Julie Sze reminds us: "In a nation [the US] where rapacious corporate capitalism is plundering natural resources, and oil and gas interests fund climate change denial and direct what passes for environmental policy, a world with clear air and without war, rampant consumerism, and extractive capitalism seems nearly impossible to imagine. It is precisely now that imagination and action become essential" (1). It's Sze's call for imagination in the face of increasing climate catastrophes that leads me to climate fiction like *Each of Us a Desert*. The poems Xochitl finds allow her to imagine other ways of knowing and being. Her imagination for a different world and a different self push her on her journey that ultimately liberates her, her community, and her environment.

Storytelling and Resistance

In writing about Alexandra Villasante's *The Grief Keeper* and Adam Silvera's *More Happy Than Not*, Cristina Rhodes says of each protagonist that their "traumatic pasts inhibit their movement toward the promise of [a] queer future" (1). The same is true for Xochitl in *Each of Us a Desert*. The consumption of "traumatic pasts" makes it impossible for her to exist as a person, rather than a cuentista, and to exist in a "queer future" with Emilia. By queer future, I mean both in a romantic relationship with Emilia and in a queer future where a climate catastrophe doesn't dominate their lives. Xochitl's fight for a queer future requires that she unlearn what she knows about being a cuentista and about her world. A discussion of resistance also fits into the previous two sections of this chapter, as healing and protecting the environment require persistent resistance and resilience. I focus on resistance in this section specifically to highlight Xochitl's fight for a queer future by taking control of the cuentista narrative. When Xochitl finds the inner strength to stop living by other's expectations, she is able to do what she's been wanting to do — to make choices about her own life. Xochitl's new agency doesn't reject her cuentista traditions or her community, but instead gives her the power to decide both how to use her gift and what role to take in her community.

To explain how Xochitl can resist the traditional role of the cuentista, I first explore how she must resist roles and expectations placed upon her by familial relationships. Xochitl's resistance to her role as a cuentista is one that speaks to the ways young women are forced into caregiving roles and expected to fulfill those duties above all else. In the novel, Xochitl explains that Tia Inez taught her to be a cuentista, and that meant putting herself aside for the role. The role of the cuentista is a prescribed role that has significance within the family structure and the community. For the majority of the novel, the role of a cuentista is a gendered role often bestowed on women. Later in the novel, Xochitl will learn this isn't and hasn't always been the case. It's important to note that any rejection of a prescribed, gendered role doesn't always mean a rejection of the family or the culture in which that role originated and survived. In *Contemporary Chicana Literature: (Re)Writing the Maternal Script*, Cristina Herrera argues that the daughters in the Chicana literature she analyzes "do not reject their mothers, but they do reject and contest cultural, patriarchal, and heteronormative gender roles that would have them follow in their mothers' footsteps. Although at first the daughters attempt to distance themselves from what they view as their mothers' complicity in gender role socialization, the same daughters grow to rewrite motherhood and daughterhood as a unifying, empowered experience that need not stifle or constrain Chicanas in achieving subjectivity" (11). In Xochitl's case, she does not seek to resist Tia Inez but does want to reject the rules, stories, and expectations passed down to her that further reinforce "cultural, patriarchal, and heteronormative gender roles." Later in the novel, it's revealed that Julio is also a cuentista, but the expectations to behave like one do not cage him in the same way they do Xochitl. In fact, Julio rejects the expectations, only to use his powers for manipulation and corruption. Throughout the novel, Xochitl uses her cuentista powers to provide healing, even when she doesn't want to. Herrera further asserts, "tolerance of abuse is a feminine ideal that highlights women's presumed natural capacity for forgiveness" (128). In other words, women in patriarchal societies are expected to tolerate abuse and to forgive such abuse simply because they are women. I argue that other characters in *Each of Us* continue to ask Xochitl to take their stories because they expect her to "play [her] part" of a cuentista but also of that of a woman (310). In distancing herself and rewriting the prescribed roles, Xochitl creates opportunities for daughters and mothers, or whoever is passing on knowledge to the next generation, to exist outside oppressive narratives.

Xochitl's resistance to Solís happens gradually. In one instance, Xochitl is upset with Solís for the suffering Emilia has endured because of her father, Julio, and after trying to escape him. Xochitl exclaims, "Did You ever care about her? Or did You think she had to suffer in order to become worthy of Your attention? She gave me her story. And *I* listened" (149). Xochitl differentiates between what she expected Solís's empathy to be and her own, greater, empathy. Pointing out the difference suggests that Xochitl doesn't see herself in Solís's light anywhere. The moment of differentiation is also an opportunity to further investigate and question dominant narratives. In other words, if Xochitl was wrong about Solís's empathy, there are likely other things she can also be wrong about. In the novel, Xochitl recounts being an "obedient daughter" by following the ritual she was told she had to follow: take and return the story every single time to impart and maintain balance. But Xochitl "needed to be away from home; away from all the responsibilities and the sad, needy faces; away from feeling stuck in a life [she] never chose" (32). Xochitl does not reject her family but does reject her gendered role as a cuentista. To return to Herrera, "daughters distance themselves from what they view as their mothers' complicity in gender role socialization" (11). In Xochitl's case, the distance, both ideological and geographical, is not only from her mother but also from Tia Inez's memory and anyone else in her community who expects her to behave accordingly. It's in that distance, through Xochitl's resistance, that she learns that the scripts she's been expected to follow and the ones her community still believes are not true. She says, "My life had been so rigid in Empalme. But the rules that had been used to control my life, to make everything defined and perfect, were not even *true*?" (245). When Xochitl learns the truth about Solís, about La Quema, about the current state of their society, she says, "I *had* to go back home. And I had to break the cycle" (375). Later she says, "They have to know what I know" (377). Throughout her journey to Solado, Xochitl meets different people and groups that challenge what she knows about being a cuentista, a migrant, and a survivor of a climate catastrophe. In meeting these people, Xochtl is able to resist oppressive narratives and piece together a more empowering one for herself. Once Xochitl resists prescribed roles for herself, receiving a sense of liberation, she then makes the choice that this liberation cannot be for her alone but that she must share what she knows with her community.

Storytelling and resistance work in multiple ways in *Each of Us a Desert*. Xochitl resists the expectations placed upon her as her aldea's cuentista. Instead, Xochitl embraces a type of storytelling that sets her free from the "rules that had been used to control [her] life" (245). At the end of the novel, she tells Solís, "I believe that there is too much of me for You ever to take. I believe I am more important than the role You cast me into, and when all of this is over, I know I will never take another story from anyone" (426). Xochitl runs the risk of losing herself after purging all of the stories she's held onto to piece together the truth, but rejects this notion and affirms that she is more than the expectations used to cage her. In this way, Xochitl transforms the power of storytelling used to oppress her into a storytelling that is empowering and about resistance. At the end, as Xochitl purges herself, she's also created a path for a queer future where she can be free of her role, where she and Emilia can be together, and where there's a possibility of environmental justice through the truths she's learned. Resistance in *Each of Us a Desert* is not accompanied by complete resolution of the characters' oppressions but instead reminds readers that resistance is a journey.

Conclusion

Each of Us a Desert is an excellent example of the potential of speculative fiction and youth literature to create transformative change in the lives of young people and in our society at large. Sami Schalk explains, in *Bodyminds Reimagined: (Dis)ability, Race, and Gender in Black Women's Speculative Fiction*, that "For marginalized people, [speculative fiction] can mean imagining a future or alternative space away from oppression or in which relations between currently empowered and disempowered groups altered or improved. Speculative fiction can also be a space to imagine the worst, to think about what could be if current inequalities and injustices are allowed to continue" (2). Mark Oshiro's novel as speculative fiction offers precisely what Schalk describes. Xochitl's story, and that of her community, serves as an opportunity to "imagine the worst," to see how capitalism corrupts and damages the environment, to see how prescribed gender roles can trap people, to see death and tragedy follow climate catastrophes. Simultaneously, *Each of Us a Desert* offers ways to create a "space away from oppression." While readers follow Xochitl's own journey to imagine her own queer future, they can also learn from Xochitl to use storytelling for healing, resistance, to protect the environment, and to fight for their own queer futures.

Similarly, Hannah Doermann reminds of the potential of young adult fiction: "By creating futuristic societies that exacerbate the social issues of our time and allowing us to understand the potential future implications of our actions, dystopian Young Adult fiction provides an important avenue for exploring climate change problems" (137). Understanding the "potential future implications of our actions," in regard to environmental injustice, is a powerful way for young people to read climate fiction. For Xochitl, it was through finding her own voice that she was able to also address the climate trauma that was ingrained in her community. It's important to note that *Each of Us a Desert* doesn't end with a solution to Empalme's climate crisis, but it does end with Xochitl rejecting full responsibility for healing everyone's trauma. The ending is perhaps a call to adults to recognize the pressure we've placed on young people to address the environmental injustices created by our and older generations.

Climate catastrophes are becoming more of a daily reality. Books like Mark Oshiro's *Each of Us a Desert* become increasingly important in discussions of issues of climate change and queer futurity. As Oziewicz and Saguisag remind us: "given how deeply climate change is intertwined with the social, racial, and other forms of injustice that plague our world, children's literature and criticism must also become more deliberate in tying issues of inequity to the existential crisis of climate change we are facing. After all, climate change is a challenge that today's young people will confront throughout their lives" (viii). Using storytelling as a tool to tie "issues of inequity" to environmental justice is exactly what Xochitl does through the novel. Furthermore, Sze reminds us that "Critical consciousness and a focus on histories and storytelling are the environmental justice movement's major contribution to fighting during and through this moment of danger" (79). My analysis of *Each of Us a Desert* demonstrates the ways that storytelling and healing, the environment, and resistance all intersect to capture a holistic view of climate justice. Additionally, while Xochitl doesn't speak of climate change directly, she does talk about the environment and the violence the environment, the land, her home, and her people have experienced. In the end, it is at these moments when youth speak about the realities of their environments that the connection between environmental injustices and the people affected by climate change becomes the most obvious. We need more stories of queer young people facing the realities of climate catastrophes, and their consequential climate trauma, to both sound the alarm to the state of our planet but also to imagine a different future than the one that lies ahead of us today.

As I work on this chapter, *Each of Us a Desert*, a novel about an empath, has been banned in Texas classrooms (pending investigation). More policies, laws, and efforts are taking place to limit the rights of LGBTQIA people. Here, I return to Delgado and Stefancic to remind us that "The idea that one can use words to undo the meaning that others attach to these very same words is to commit the empathic fallacy — the belief that one can change a narrative by merely offering another, better one — that the reader's or listener's empathy will quickly and reliably take over" (35). In other words, dominant and oppressive narratives will not change overnight simply because we have more diverse stories available. I've argued throughout this chapter that storytelling is healing and liberating — and I believe that. Communities of color have demonstrated just that for generations and generations. Xochitl's character reminds readers that recognizing the limits of empathy can liberate one to continue to do the work that needs to be done to get toward the queer future we deserve.

Works Cited

Ahmed, Sara. *Willful Subjects*. Duke UP, 2014.
Caruth, Cathy. *Unclaimed Experience: Trauma, Narrative, and History*. 1996. John Hopkins UP, 2016.
Delgado, Richard, and Jean Stefancic. *Critical Race Theory: An Introduction*. 4th ed. New York UP, 2023.
Doermann, Hannah. "Against Ecocidal Environmentalism: Anti-Capitalist, Queer, and Decolonial Critiques of Mainstream Environmentalism in

Lilliam Rivera's *Dealing in Dreams*." *The Lion and the Unicorn*, vol. 45, no. 2, April 2021, pp. 137–53.

Ellis, Amanda. *Letras y Limpias: Decolonial Medicine and Holistic Healing in Mexican American Literature*. U of Arizona P, 2021.

Herrera, Cristina. "Seeking Refuge *Under the Mesquite*: Nature Imagery in Guadalupe García McCall's Verse Novel." *Children's Literature Association Quarterly*, vol. 44, no. 2, Summer 2019, pp. 194–209.

Herrera, Cristina. *Contemporary Chicana Literature: (Re)Writing the Maternal Script*. Cambia Press, 2014.

Natov, Roni. "Imagine Empathy: Kate DiCamillo's *The Tale of Depereaux* and *The Miraculous Journey of Edward Tulane*." *The Courage to Imagine: The Child Hero in Children's Literature*, by Roni Natov, Bloombury Academic, 2017, pp. 145–60.

Oshiro, Mark. *Each of Us a Desert*. Tor Teen, 2020.

Oziewicz, Marek, and Lara Saguisag. "Introduction: Children's Literature and Climate Change." *The Lion and the Unicorn*, vol. 45, no. 2, April 2021, pp. v–xiv.

Rhodes, Cristina. "Imagining the Future: The (Im)Possibilities of Queerness in Two Latinx Speculative Youth Adult Novels." *Label Me Latina/o*, vol. XI, Special Issue: YA Latinx Literature, pp. 1–10.

Rodriguez, Sonia Alejandra. "Conocimiento Narratives: Creative Acts and Healing in Latinx Children's and Young Adult Literature." *Children's Literature*, vol. 47, no. 1, 2019, pp. 9–29.

Schalk, Sami. *Bodyminds Reimagined: (Dis)ability, Race, and Gender in Black Women's Speculative Fiction*. Duke UP, 2018.

Smith, Linda Tuhiwai. *Decolonizing Methodologies: Research and Indigenous Peoples*. 3rd ed., Bloomsbury Academic, 2023.

Suhr-Sytsma, Mandy. *Self-Determined Stories: The Indigenous Reinvention of Young Adult Literature*. Michigan State UP, 2019.

Sze, Julie. *Environmental Justice in a Moment of Danger*. U of California P, 2020.

Vazquez, David J., Sarah D. Wald, and Paula M. L. Moya. "'We Carry Our Environments within Ourselves: An Interview with Helena Maria Viramontes." *Latinx Environmentalisms: Place, Justice, and the Decolonial*, edited by Sarah D. Wald, et al., Temple UP, 2019, pp. 164–76.

SECTION 2

Intersectionality and Counternarratives

FOUR

Representations of Asian American Girlhood in Contemporary Young Adult Literature

Jung E. Kim

The COVID-19 global pandemic brought to light the xenophobia and racism that have long been targeted at Asian Americans (AsAms). In March 2021, a House Judiciary panel held hearings on the rise of violence and discrimination against AsAms, and the evidence and testimony were overwhelming (Sotomayor). However, there were also members of Congress who spoke of AsAms as a model minority and brushed off the attacks as anomalous. The model minority myth (MMM) upholds that AsAms are successful because they work hard, don't make trouble, and have strong values (Chou and Feagin). It is built on a monolithic view of the Asian diaspora that erases differences of ethnicity, class, and im/migration status, and it also uses AsAms as a wedge to prove to other racial minorities that racism is not real. In tandem with the MMM is the notion that AsAms are "forever foreigner," the idea that all AsAms are "unassimilable aliens" (Takaki; Wu). AsAms are always seen as being from somewhere else and as "other," regardless of generational or im/migration status.

Despite decades of research and pushback from the AsAm community around the MMM (Poon et al.), it continues to be perpetuated both in youth literature (de Manuel and Davis; Endo) and in real life. In fact, the MMM has been so entrenched that people expressed surprise at the rising anti-Asian attacks; they assumed AsAms did not deal with racism, erasing the long history of exclusion, violence, and even forced incarceration of AsAms. This resistance to seeing AsAms as oppressed was noted decades ago by Mitsuye Yamada in her classic 1983 essay "Invisibility Is an Unnatural Disaster" (Yamada). She begins her essay relaying a student's angry response to a collection of AsAm writing: "It made me angry. *Their* anger made *me* angry, because I didn't even know the Asian Americans felt oppressed. I didn't expect their anger" (34).

When one looks at the types of limited representation AsAms have had until very recently — images of hypersexualized women, emasculated men, the "yellow peril" invading this country — it becomes clear how easy it has been to dehumanize and marginalize AsAms. This has been particularly true for AsAm women, who have reported the vast majority of attacks (Pillai et al.). This is connected to a long history of American domestic and foreign policies where Asian women have been seen as prostitutes, lotus flowers, and dragon ladies (Pyke and Johnson). The 1875 Page Act effectively barred Chinese women from entering the United States because of fear of their sexuality and their purported immorality. Since then, American military presence in multiple Asian countries has further contributed to this view of Asian women as prostitutes and short-term, disposable companions. From the submissive, tragic lotus flower who sacrifices herself in service of whiteness to the cunning, devious manipulations of the dragon lady (Espiritu; Shah), Asian women have been given limited roles in the American imagination. Similarly, we see these tropes and stereotypes perpetuated in media for the last century, from the dragon ladies played by Anna May Wong to Arthur Golden's purportedly authentic *Memoirs of a Geisha* (Rajgopal). Audiences are presented with stereotypical, two-dimensional characters where Hollywood becomes "the discourse of empire through its representation of Asian women as ahistorical and frozen in time" (Rajgopal 143).

With that said, while there is still room for improvement, there has been growing representation of AsAm girls/women in media. And while it is not clear what percentage of books features AsAm girls/women, there has been a virtual explosion of AsAm literature in children's/young adult (YA) publishing; 10.6% of books published in 2021 were about Asians[1] compared to 1.4% in 1994 (Cooperative Children's Book Center). This study examines what this representation looks like in contemporary realistic YA: How do these representations reflect the realities of the daily lives of average AsAm girls? How do they reflect or deflect AsAm stereotypes? And what messages might contemporary AsAm girls be receiving about what it means to be an AsAm girl or woman? Studying AsAm "children's literature plays a vital role in addressing, mediating, and contesting dominant representations of Asian American children in popular culture" (Thananopavarn 107). Jennifer Ho writes that female coming-of-age novels, in particular, acknowledge how the challenges of race and gender impact the development of female protagonists.

While there has been some work examining AsAm children's literature (e.g., Ho; Mathison; Thananopavarn) and a body of work on AsAm feminism (Fujiwara and Roshanravan; Moraga and Anzáldua; Sg; Shah), there have been very few studies examining representations of AsAm girlhood in children's and YA literature (Endo; Ninh; Thongthiraj). By drawing on the two critical bodies of literature — Asian critical race theory (Iftikar and Museus; Museus and Iftikar) and Asian feminist writings (Fujiwara and Roshanravan; Shah) — I hope to add to the extant literature by analyzing representations of AsAm girlhood in several award-winning YA books from the last decade. The use of both AsianCrit and Asian feminist writings allows for the critical exploration and analysis of the intersections of race and gender, along with other identity markers, as represented in these books.

Theoretical Framework

Asian Critical Race Theory (AsianCrit) is a branch of critical race theory (CRT), which came out of critical legal studies in the 1970s. The tenets of CRT are built around the centrality and intersectionality of race and racism, challenging the dominant ideology, commitment to social justice, importance of experiential knowledge, and use of interdisciplinary perspectives (Solorzano and Yosso). AsianCrit was developed in the 1990s (Chang) and builds on not only CRT but also two of the most dominant racial framings of AsAms, that of the model minority myth (Chou and Feagin; Poon et al.) and of being forever foreigner (Tuan). The MMM positions AsAms as aspirational minorities who have assimilated to (white) American culture and symbolize a post-racial society free of discrimination, and the forever foreigner trope alludes to the popular conception of all AsAms as being foreign regardless of actual citizenship or generational status.

AsianCrit was adapted and refined for use in education by Museus and Iftikar, who defined it as "a perspective that outlines a unique set of tenets that are designed to provide a useful analytic framework for examining and understanding the ways that racism affects AsAms in the United States" (23). The seven tenets of AsianCrit are 1) Asianization; 2) transnational contexts; 3) (re)constructive history; 4) strategic (anti)essentialism; 5) intersectionality; 6) story, theory, and praxis; and 7) commitment to social justice. This chapter draws more explicitly upon two particular strands of AsianCrit, those of transnational contexts and intersectionality. While all of the tenets could be applied to the texts and there is significant overlap between tenets, *transnational contexts* and *intersectionality* were the most immediately relevant and apparent in the selected texts. *Transnational contexts* emphasizes the importance of historical and contemporary national and international contexts for AsAms. *Intersectionality* is based on the notion that racism and other systems of oppression (e.g., sexism, heterosexism, ableism, etc.) intersect to mutually shape the conditions within which AsAms exist. Because of the nature and themes in the texts chosen for analysis, these two tenets were chosen as the most appropriate for analysis.

Data

This chapter is part of a larger study of AsAm female representation in YA literature and focuses on a subset of books that meet certain criteria:

- Contemporary (i.e., not historical fiction) realistic fiction
- Protagonist who is female, high school–aged, and AsAm
- Published after 2010
- Winner of the young adult/youth literature category of the Asian/Pacific American Award for Literature (APALA)

The APALA is awarded by the Asian/Pacific American Librarians Association, an affiliate of the American Library Association, and "the goal is to honor and recognize individual works of Asian/Pacific American experiences (either historical or contemporary) and/or Asian/Pacific American cultures by Asian/Pacific Islander American [APIA] authors and illustrators." Their current criteria for nominations can be found on their website ("Literature Award Guidelines & Nominations").

Notably, their criteria have changed over time. While previously the award was given to "works related to Asian/Pacific American experience or culture," the award was updated in 2016 so that only authors and illustrators who were APIA could win. This decision was made after members began to notice the increasing number of books about APIAs that were written by non-APIAs. They decided that "not only should works celebrate APIA experiences, but these stories should be told by members of the APIA community" (Dear). Thus, *Orchards* (2011-2012) would not have qualified to win, as it was written by a white woman. It is also unclear whether the 2013-2014 winner *Jet Black and the Ninja Wind* would still have qualified under these guidelines, as the authors are a white American woman and her Japanese husband (i.e., neither of the authors is APIA/Canadian). The honor book for that year, *Gadget Girl*, was also written by a white American woman and would not have qualified. All three white women live in Japan with their biracial or bicultural families and wrote biracial Asian *American* characters despite their own lack of experience as such.

The books that meet these criteria and are discussed in this chapter are the following:

- *It's Not Like It's a Secret* by Misa Sugiura (2017-2018) — INLIS

    * Sixteen-year-old Japanese American Sana Kiyohara moves with her family from Wisconsin to California with her father and stay-at-home mother. There, she must navigate her sexuality and the fact she is in love with her best friend while also uncovering her father's possible infidelity.
    * Reading age: thirteen to seventeen years (Amazon)

- *P.S. I Still Love You* by Jenny Han (2015-2016) — *P.S.*

    * The second book in a trilogy, this book explores biracial Korean American Lara Jean's growing romantic relationship with Peter, navigating the complexity of his ongoing friendship with his ex-girlfriend, and discovering a possible new love interest.
    * Reading age: twelve years and up (Amazon)

- *Jet Black and the Ninja Wind* by Leza Lowitz and Shogo Oketani (2013-2014) — *Jet Black*

    * After her mother dies, biracial Japanese American Jet Ryu (aka Black) goes to Japan to connect with her mother's family. There she continues developing the ninja skills developed by her mother and learns she must take on an international corporation to save her family's homeland.
    * Reading age: twelve to eighteen years (Amazon)

- *Tina's Mouth: An Existential Comic Diary* by Keshni Kashyap and Mari Araki (2012-2013) — *Tina's Mouth*

    * Indian American teenager Tina is fifteen, obsessed with Jean-Paul Sartre, recently best friend–less, and in love with skater boy Neil. Throughout the graphic novel, Tina and her siblings explore the meaning of love, life, and identity.
    * Reading age: thirteen and up (suggested)

- *Orchards* by Holly Thompson (2011-2012)

    * After a classmate's suicide, biracial Japanese American Kanako is sent to Japan for the summer to reflect on the aftermath of the tragedy. There on her extended family's farm, she confronts the truths about what happened and tries to heal.
    * Reading age: twelve to seventeen years (Amazon)

All books were read in mind with the larger themes of AsianCrit initially and then reread and analyzed for the specific tenets of *transnational contexts* and *intersectionality*. As one may see from the summaries, there are multiple themes of crossing borders and intersecting identity markers like sexuality and race present in the books, which made the two tenets most appropriate for analysis.

Findings

Transnational Contexts in AsAm YA: Immigration and Transnational Flows

Asians have been on the continent of North America since the sixteenth century (E. Lee). Regardless of im/migration or generational status, though, AsAms have been perpetually othered and seen as having deep ties "back" to Asia. This can be seen from incarceration of Japanese Americans during WWII to the killing of Vincent Chin, who was mistaken for being Japanese. Over the last few decades, several AsAm scientists have been wrongfully accused of spying for China when there was no basis for such accusations (Lai). The Chinese origin of COVID-19 has led to a spike in racist attacks on Asians regardless of country of origin, ethnic background, or citizenship. In other words, regardless of actual loyalties, citizenship, or affiliation, AsAms are "forever foreigner" (Tuan) and unwillingly accepted as "American."

In reality, 57% of AsAms, including 71% of AsAm adults, were born in another country (Pew Research Center, *The Rise in Asian Americans*). As the result of multiple race-exclusionary laws, im/migration from Asia to the United States was essentially barred for a significant part of the early twentieth century until the passage of the 1965 Immigration Act (E. Lee). This change in immigration laws and American military incursions into Asia — for example, the Vietnam War and the Korean War — brought significant waves of im/migrants to the United States in the 1970s. American military involvement in Asia also brought war brides, refugees, and orphans during this time. More recently, globalization and the creation of transnational flows of migrants between countries add another layer to the complexities of an AsAm identity.

Thus, the constant push-pull of connections to Asia for members of the diaspora creates a transnational context for understanding both historic and contemporary AsAm identity. All five books discussed in this chapter feature protagonists with at least one immigrant parent. This is one of the reasons the AsianCrit tenet of transnational contexts was selected as a lens for analysis. Two of the books, *Jet Black* and *Orchards*, feature an immigrant Japanese mother; two books, *It's Not Like It's a Secret* and *Tina's Mouth*, feature parents who are both immigrants, Japanese and Indian, respectively; and one book, *P.S.*, features a Korean mother whose origin is ambiguous (It is unclear where she was born or how long she lived in America). All of the parents immigrated as adults. None of the protagonists themselves are immigrants, although 31% of AsAm youth aged fifteen to nineteen are foreign-born (Asian American Federation). This raises questions about how representative these titles are of the AsAm experience and underscores the importance of greater diverse representation of AsAms.

Jet Black *and* Orchards: *Going Back "Home"*

At the outset, *Jet Black* and *Orchards* don't seem to have a lot in common. *Jet Black* is about a girl (Jet) who has been trained as a ninja all her life, travels to Japan to meet her grandfather after her mother dies, and then takes on an international conspiracy. *Orchards*, on the other hand, is about a girl (Kanako) who has finished eighth grade in the midst of a classmate's suicide and is sent to Japan for the summer to "get away." However, both feature Japanese mothers who fell in love with white American men and left their families and homes in Japan. While Jet's mother never returns to Japan, Kanako's mother visits regularly. Even as Kanako's mother tries to maintain her relationship with her family back in Japan, it is a strained and somewhat difficult relationship, as her family feels a sense of abandonment. They struggle with accepting the white American husband and, by extension, his children, while there is no indication of such tensions with her father's white Jewish family. In this juxtaposition, the Japanese family is the problematic one, and the white American family is the accepting one.

While differing in circumstance, Jet and Kanako both end up traveling to Japan, and the majority of both books take place in Japan. Despite having only one Japanese parent, being raised in America, and not being part of Japanese American communities, both girls have been raised to be relatively fluent in the Japanese language, which smooths their transitions to living in Japan. This is somewhat anomalous, as Japanese Americans "are among the least likely to place a high level of importance on keeping the Japanese language alive in the U.S" (Pew Research Center, *The Rise in Asian Americans*).[2] The ease by which Jet and Kanako adapt to being fully Japanese may not necessarily be reflective of the experience of many AsAms, particularly US-born AsAms, in returning to their ancestral homelands. While many AsAms believe maintaining some heritage language is important, only 14% would be comfortable having a conversation in that language (Pew Research Center, *The Rise in Asian Americans*). Language, specifically lack of heritage language proficiency, can be a significant issue for members of the Asian diaspora if they move between countries. Thus, the reality reflected in these two books does not represent the lived reality of many Japanese Americans.

Despite their initial misgivings, Jet and Kanako both end up feeling deeply connected to Japan during their time there. At the beginning of *Jet Black* when Jet's mother is dying and tells Jet she must "go back" to Japan, Jet responds, "How can I go *back*, Mom? I've never been there before" (23). Kanako is also resentful of being sent away for the summer. Yet they both fall in love with the Japanese landscape and find a sense of connection and healing. So strong is this affinity to their motherland that Jet remains in Japan at the end of the story, and Kanako speaks about returning the next summer. Both books allude to a deeper connection to culture and self and sense of returning home in traveling to the birthplace of their mothers. It is only by going to Japan that the girls learn more about their mothers' lives, choices, and sacrifices, and feel a deeper understanding of them.

The relative ease and fluidity with which Jet and Kanako seem to navigate their Japanese identities erase the very real differences that exist between being Japanese versus Japanese American, and also erase the difficulties many AsAms experience moving between two nations/cultures. This may be partially attributable to the fact that both books seem more focused on an exclusively Japanese identity, rather than on understanding or negotiating a Japanese American one. By locating the books primarily in Japan, the protagonists (and authors) can focus exclusively on being Japanese and not on the more complicated nuances of an AsAm identity. The fact that both books were written by non-AsAm authors who do not have the lived experiences of being AsAm and whose primary experiences were with living in Japan may underscore this disconnect.

P.S. I Still Love You: *Korea as Korean American Culture*

P.S. is the second book in a trilogy about a biracial Korean American girl with limited representations of Korean culture. With the exception of a few references to Korean food or beauty products and celebrating some Korean customs with the extended family, there are relatively few connections to Korean American culture. Lara Jean's mother was Korean (another deceased Asian mother), but her father is white, and they live in a predominantly white community. Perhaps that is why it seems incongruous that in the last book (*Always and Forever, Lara Jean*), Lara Jean and her two sisters go to Korea as a way to feel connected to their mother. It is not clear that their mother was born in Korea or even ever visited. While there are references to their maternal grandmother going to Korea on occasion, she seems relatively Americanized in the book, with no references to an accent or any other indication she is an immigrant. There is an implication that Lara Jean and her sisters feel they can only connect with their mother's Korean culture by going "back" to Korea itself, rather than by building more connections to their Korean American family or a Korean American community. Not unlike *Jet Black* and *Orchards*, the message here seems to be that being Asian/AsAm is tied specifically to Asia and less to an Asian *American* identity.

Of the three books in the Lara Jean trilogy, *P.S.* probably includes the most references to Korean culture. The book opens with a somewhat disconnected scene where the girls participate in sebae (although it is not named that in the book) — a New Year's ritual of bowing to show respect to elders — with the Korean side of their family. Midway through the book, there is a discussion where Lara Jean's father expresses regret that he did not keep them enrolled in Korean school after their mother died. Lara Jean responds that she wants to take Korean in college. This is surprising, as there are no indications that the girls have had any experience with the Korean language beyond a few food words.

There are no incidental words or phrases, and they don't engage in it with their grandmother or extended family. This is in contrast to the Pew Research Center study (*The Rise in Asian Americans*) that finds Korean Americans are one of the Asian ethnic groups most interested in maintaining their language and that 79% of Korean Americans use some Korean ("Korean Language Use by Korean Americans on the Decline"). Finally, toward the end of the book Lara Jean references a Korean concept of connectedness relayed by her grandmother, that of "jung" (sometimes written as "jeong"), in discussing her relationship with her boyfriend and his relationship with his ex-girlfriend. These three scenes are relatively disconnected and disjointed and relay a fairly fragmented depiction of a Korean American identity.

Despite these instances of Korean culture and the fact that Lara Jean and her sisters have relationships with their maternal grandmother and Korean extended family, they still bemoan in book three that "if we forget Korea, we forget Mommy." Their sense of being Korean is mostly tied to the idea of Korea, and they seem to struggle with forging a Korean American identity outside it. Whether this is a byproduct of living in a mostly white community, being biracial, or lack of heritage language fluency, the books imply a level of assimilation and white-adjacency that is troubling and does little to model how AsAm girls can "negotiate the levels of power that exist in the myriad social institutions within which they must function" (Couzelis 44). The implied message here seems to be that a lack of connection to their ancestral homeland erases their Korean American identity. With few references to their Korean American culture or identity, mostly marked by food and popular culture references, Lara Jean and her sisters could be read mostly as white characters.

It is interesting to note that one blogger (C. Lee) wondered if the author of the Lara Jean books, Jenny Han, who is not multiracial, created an interracial family where the Asian mother died so that she could avoid the typical immigrant parent conflict trope. By effectively removing the Asian parent, Lara Jean and her sisters can have "normal" (read as white, middle-class) adolescent lives that do not involve negotiating cultural conflicts and expectations with an Asian or immigrant parent. However, as indicated earlier, by tying the Asian or Korean identity to the dead mother, the girls' Korean American identities are also effectively rendered invisible for the majority of the books. This is an interesting contrast to an author like Tae Keller, whose Korean ties were only through one grandparent yet maintains strong Korean American references in her books.

As more and more AsAm girls are second-, third-, or even fourth-generation Americans, they need representations of AsAm identities that are not based solely on connections to Asia. It is striking that AsAms are often plagued by the "forever foreigner" ideal and seen as being unassimilable, yet Han's books paradoxically seem to imply that a Korean American identity can only be made through connections with the ancestral homeland while also conveying an underlying melting pot mythology. Lara Jean and her sisters rarely encounter any racial remarks or implications that they are different or anything but "just American" (i.e., white). Yet the Stop AAPI Hate reports indicate that the majority of AsAms have encountered hateful comments or even assaults during the COVID-19 pandemic (Cruz et al.). Ultimately, Han offers few resources or scenarios in her books for AsAm girls to make sense of their AsAm identity through her characters. This is in stark contrast to books like Joanna Ho's *The Silence that Binds Us*, which deals strongly with contemporary American racial issues, or Sayantani DasGupta's *Debating Darcy*, an Indian American update of Jane Austen's *Pride and Prejudice*. These books feature AsAm female protagonists who are thoughtful, persistent, and connected to their culture.

Tina's Mouth *and* It's Not Like It's a Secret: *Immigrant Ties and Forging an Asian American Identity*

Both *Tina's Mouth* and *INLIS* feature protagonists with two immigrant parents. Tina's parents are from India and immigrated to the US so her father could attend medical school. It is less clear exactly when or why Sana's parents in *INLIS* immigrate to the US, but Sana's father is a businessman. Both of the mothers in the story are stay-at-home parents. While Tina's parents are connected to the Indian community and socialize with other Indian families, Sana's parents are more insular. While Sana's father does go out on occasion with people from work, her parents do not seem deeply connected to a Japanese community — neither in Wisconsin where the book starts nor in California after they move.

Regardless of community connections, both families inculcate a strong sense of cultural identity in the young women. Early in *Tina's Mouth*, Tina tells a story of having a crush on the Hindu god Krishna and is racially aware enough to call out microaggressions she encounters. Sana's father tells her Japanese folktales growing up, and both parents share Japanese language and values with her. Both sets of parents seem to speak primarily in English to their daughters. While there are some cultural conflicts in *INLIS*, the major conflicts in both books revolve primarily around school-based romances. Contrary to the immigrant parent/culture clash trope that can often exist in AsAm literature (ninh), Tina's parents are refreshingly progressive and accepting of all three of their children. They do not chide Tina's sister for abandoning her Ivy League architecture degree to pursue her artistic interests, they support her brother's breaking off his engagement, and they give Tina the freedom to do what she wants socially and at school. While Sana's parents seem more traditional, it turns out that their marriage is much less conventional, and they are accepting of Sana's sexuality in the end. Both books, then, expand representations of not only AsAm adolescents — in depicting AsAm queer youth and their stories — but also AsAm parents. The stereotypical, overprotective "tiger" parents are replaced with more nuanced, complex characters.

In *Tina's Mouth* and *INLIS*, Tina and Sana have clearly forged a strong AsAm identity, one that braids both Asian and American values and understandings. Even as they navigate multiple cultural norms and their relationships with their immigrant parents, we see how ties back to India and Japan become negotiated within an American context for both parents and children. Not only do we see how the parents in *Tina's Mouth* and *INLIS* make sense of their AsAm children, we also see how they reflect on their own choices in immigrating to America and building a life for themselves here. We see how the values and norms the parents grew up with in Asia are adapted and modified to the context of America over time, and how what they pass on to their children is also then adapted and modified again. Thus, over two generations, we see how an AsAm identity is forged and negotiated through conflict and resolution. Books like *Tina's Mouth* and *INLIS* offer robust narratives of AsAm identity and girlhood for readers to engage with as they consider and negotiate their own identities.

Intersectionality

While women of color have long been familiar with the ways in which their race and gender (among other aspects of their identity like class and citizenship) multiply marginalize them, Kimberlé Crenshaw named and further theorized this phenomenon as intersectionality. Intersectionality explores the idea that individuals' identities fall along multiple axes of subordination or marginalization, and the singular prioritization of one of these identities obscures understanding and progress. Intersectionality is one of the key understandings of women of color politics and AsAm feminist understandings.

Women of color and Third World feminism emerged as a reaction to the ahistorical understandings of second wave feminism, which assumed an understanding of gender oppression from the perspective of white, middle-class women. For women of color, there is also a deep historical context for how they are racialized and gendered based on factors like American colonialism and empire abroad. This section draws on these understandings to better understand how race, ethnicity, gender, and other identities are represented in YA AsAm literature. Multiple books have multiracial protagonists, queer characters, and interracial love interests. While this analysis is foregrounding race and gender, it is not enough to examine the stories only from those lenses.

Multiracial Identity

Three of the five books, *Orchards*, *Jet Black*, and *P.S.*, feature biracial AsAm/white young women written by authors who are not multiracial. This proportion overrepresents the reality that 14% of AsAms are multiracial (Pew Research Center, *Key facts about Asian Americans, a diverse and growing population*). What is further noteworthy is that all three books do little to engage with the tensions many multiracial youths may struggle with. As previously discussed, *Orchards* and *Jet Black* take place primarily in Japan among their Japanese families. While Kanako in *Orchards* alludes to tensions with her mother's family and not being accepted on earlier trips to Japan — which may be attributed more to her father "taking away" her mother to the US than to her multiracial status — there are few other mentions of her whiteness. Her whiteness is described as most apparent in a specific physical feature, her "Russian Jewish bottom."

Similarly, there are a few references to Jet's multiracial identity, and it does not come into much consideration on the New Mexico reservation she grew up on or in Japan in her travels. Her greatest source of angst seems to stem from her childhood poverty, rather than from her race, biracial or otherwise. Surprisingly, despite growing up on the reservation, Jet never mentions Indigenous classmates and centers her white peers, even while her mother's longtime boyfriend is Navajo. There are references in the book to his culture, but it is unclear a) how accurate these descriptions are and b) whether the authors' attempts to draw parallels between Jet's Indigenous Japanese ethnic background and American Indigenous groups are accurate or appropriate.

In one early scene in the book, Jet dons a kimono, which transforms her from "tough res girl to geisha" (31). Neither of the authors of *Jet Black* is Native American or seems to have grown up on a reservation. Even though Jet is not Native American, her description of herself as a "tough res girl" summons stereotypical notions of what Indigenous people on reservations are like — connoting them with crime and rough living. Her self-described transformation into a geisha infers a costume element to being Japanese, that one "becomes" Japanese simply by donning a garment. In fact, both books contain scenes where the girls don kimonos and describe themselves as looking "entirely" or "so" Japanese. While authors like Chaudri and Reynolds have questioned YA texts that make being multiracial a "problem," they also question texts that minimize protagonists' multiple racial identities. Like their AsAm identities, both Jet and Kanako's multiracial identities are portrayed as mostly irrelevant.

This equating of traditional clothing with cultural representation is also seen in *P.S.* when Lara Jean and her sisters wear hanboks at their family New Year's party. However, as the only multiracial family members and the only ones wearing hanboks, it seems to emphasize their difference rather than similarity to their Korean family. In contrast to *Jet Black* and *Orchards,* where full Japanese-ness is assumed and whiteness incidental, Lara Jean's white-adjacency seems foregrounded and her Korean-ness made incidental. Most of the scenes are bereft of discussions of race or ethnicity except for a few key scenes previously mentioned. Lara Jean and her sisters are essentially portrayed as either Korean or white, never multiracial.

Furthermore, while there are a few scenes where race is an issue — like when her friend at the senior center, Stormy, demands she not like another resident just because "you're both Asian" (the other resident is Japanese American)

— they are superficial. In this scene, Stormy is jealous of Lara Jean's attention to another resident who happens to be Asian. Rather than call out this behavior, Lara Jean notes that she's "gotten used to the vaguely racist things old people say" with no reference to Lara Jean ever having addressed these comments. Han misses an opportunity to demonstrate to readers how contemporary AsAms can grapple with racist incidents when they happen. Instead, we get another example of a passive AsAm. Later on, when a video of Lara Jean in a compromising position goes viral, someone (presumably Asian) questions whether Lara Jean is "really Asian." Other than these rare instances that are dropped in as if to remind the reader that she is Asian, there is little engagement with the complexities of race, what these moments mean to Lara Jean, or how she feels about her identity because of them.

Love and Sexuality

Love and sexuality are big themes in many of the books. Four of the five books — all but *Orchards* — have romantic interests in them, and three of them feature them as the main conflict. Because Kanako in *Orchards* is mostly with her family, there are few opportunities for her to find love. Her mental state, dealing with the aftermath of a classmate's suicide, is also one that might be less conducive to romance. While Jet does fall in love with "the enemy" in *Jet Black*, the focal point of the book is about overcoming an international conspiracy. However, Jet's story does parallel her mother's story; they both fall in love with men who were sent to destroy them. This is a fairly troubling storyline given the long history of mainstream media depictions of the sacrificial Asian woman falling in love with her colonizer (Rajgopal) — from Madame Butterfly to Miss Saigon. While her mother does not die young like the Asian women in these other stories, her life is one of struggle and sacrifice until her death. Jet's romantic ending is less clear, but it is not necessarily a happy one. While Kanako's parents' story is not as troubled, her mother must leave her dreams of taking over the family business in Japan to settle in upstate New York where her father practices law. Her mother does eventually own a nursery, but her initial agreement to marry Kanako's father means leaving Japan, her family, and her dreams for the farm. Again, it is the Asian woman who must make the sacrifices in the relationship.

Jet's view of herself as an AsAm woman is also presented in problematic ways that feed into stereotypes. Early in the book Jet puts on her mother's wedding kimono after her death. She describes the dress as transforming her into a "geisha" (31). This calls to mind hypersexualized, subservient images of Asian women. The "geisha" description is surprising, as it does not represent an "average" contemporary Japanese or Japanese American girl but a historical figure that has been exoticized and fetishized in American culture. It is striking that she would call to mind a professional entertainer, one who is often associated with prostitution (albeit mistakenly) in the West, when putting on a kimono her mother wore at her wedding. The fact that a teenaged AsAm girl might see herself in such a stereotypical way may speak partly to the prolific problematic representations of AsAm women in the media and partly to the lack of direct personal experiences non-AsAm authors have. Rather than imagining powerful Asian or AsAm women, Jet's first thought when seeing herself as a Japanese American woman is of a fetishized Asian stereotype.

The main plot of *P.S.* is romance — Lara Jean's relationship with Peter and her reacquaintance with another childhood crush, John Ambrose McClaren. Struggling with Peter's ongoing friendship with his ex, Lara Jean becomes distracted by John's return to her life. Both love interests, as with the majority of the other characters, are white, cisgendered, and heterosexual. This is an issue for which some have critiqued Jenny Han's books — the perpetual fixation on white men as romantic leads (Nguyen). Furthermore, in referring to de Jesús's (2001) work, Endo writes: "heterosexual love triangles focusing on Asian-White adolescent pairings, particularly between AsAm girls and White American boys, are so pervasive that this representation has become normalized in mainstream young adult literature" (244). We see over and over again a woman of Asian descent falling for a white man, reinforcing notions of white supremacy and desire.

Even more disturbing is the reference in the third book to *Sixteen Candles,* a film Lara Jean loves. *Sixteen Candles* features Long Duk Dong, one of the most egregious AsAm stereotypes in film. There is no mention of the racist nature of this caricature in the book, and in the Netflix adaptation of the book, it is Peter who comments on its racist depiction while Lara Jean and her sister defend the film because "Jake Ryan is cute." This is very disappointing, as there is a long history of Asian men being emasculated in media and a trope that Asian women only date white men. Instead of demonstrating possibilities for AsAm engagement or resistance to such dominant narratives, it further reinforces and perpetuates harmful messages they may already encounter regularly. Finally, while one of Lara Jean's best friends is gay (white), he is not out in the book and not interested in anyone at their school. He is, in effect, made harmless in his sexuality. It provides a semblance of diversity by including a queer character but in a way that is sanitized and palatable to mainstream audiences.

While *P.S.* dodges many of the tensions surrounding adolescent sexuality for young women of color, *Tina's Mouth* confronts head-on some of the kinds of racialized and gendered microaggressions AsAm girls and women confront. Tina's white male love interest, Neil, assumes Tina knows about nirvana and spirituality because she is Indian. In fact, he says he seeks out her company so he can hang out with his "kooky Buddhist biking buddy" (for the record, Tina is Hindu). Furthermore, in an attempt to be romantic, he wades into a muddy pond and gives her a flower. Neil declares it a lotus because it is an "Indian flower" for his "Indian princess" — further muddling things with his conflation of the Native American Indian (whom the Indian princess is associated with) with the

South Asian Indian. Later, when Tina confronts Neil for hooking up with her (white) friend at the same party, he tells Tina not to be "so old school," implying she is culturally backward. Tina gives up on Neal and, unlike Lara Jean, ends up dating a non-white boy, Reza, an Iranian American classmate.

Tina's Mouth also deals with the various ways romance can develop outside traditional expectations. When Tina's older sister is set up by a family friend, she instead ends up falling for his younger brother — someone five years her junior. Tina's older brother, on the other hand, decides to settle down and gets quickly engaged to an Indian girl with his parents' help. When he has an existential crisis about the marriage, though, his parents ask him whether he is in love. This may challenge readers' assumptions that Tina's parents, who are in an arranged marriage, would not care about love. Toward the end of the book, Tina's brother realizes he is gay, and, while it is not explicitly stated as such, his engagement party becomes a "disengagement party" that looks very much like a coming-out party. In this way, *Tina's Mouth* offers a counternarrative to traditional expectations of love and sexuality and to popular representations of Asian immigrant parents; Tina's parents are loving and accepting of all their children's choices in life.

Finally, *INLIS* also pushes against stereotypical assumptions on a variety of fronts. Sana's love interest is someone of the same gender, a Mexican-American female classmate. In this, the book breaks from the white and heterosexual tropes previously mentioned. Moving from a white-dominant community in Wisconsin to a diverse one in California, Sana realizes the many microaggressions she had to deal with in Wisconsin and confronts biases in herself and her family as she befriends and learns from a diverse group of friends in her new town. There are few instances in contemporary AsAm YA literature that show how race and racism between different minoritized groups play out and even fewer that show an AsAm protagonist wrestle with their own internalized racism. In this way, *INLIS* provides opportunities for AsAm youth to see the evolution and ongoing development of AsAm perspectives on race and sexuality.

While Sana struggles with admitting her sexuality to her parents and friends for most of the book, it is not a traumatic experience. Some scholars (Hayn and Hazlett; Matos) have critiqued the tendency in youth literature to focus on the coming-out story as traumatic. Sana's family's loving acceptance of her sexuality — particularly as immigrant Asian parents — is a welcome departure from that trend. Sana's bisexuality is also important representation, as queer scholars and activists have critiqued "bi erasure" (Erickson-Schorth and Mitchell; Pallotta-Chiarolli) within media and our binary-driven society. Finally, Sana finds out that her own parents' relationship is far from traditional within Japanese or American expectations. And while Sana still struggles to fully understand their choices, she respects that they are doing what they think is best for everyone and themselves. Her mother's choices do not fall under a typical feminist paradigm, but her mother's assertion that she is making the choice to allow for the greatest happiness underscores her agency and not her victimhood.

Conclusion

The growth of AsAm YA literature is encouraging, but there is still much room for discussion and improvement. Despite the increased visibility of AsAm authors and books, we see there are still gaps in the contemporary realistic field regarding who is represented and whose stories are told, particularly among award winners. None of the stories involved protagonists who were multigenerational Americans, adopted, immigrants or refugees, Southeast Asian or Pacific Islanders, or those with disabilities; the list goes on. We need not only more stories but more diverse stories. A single window or mirror (Bishop) that only selectively reflects back or portrays some AsAm experiences is not enough. Just as AsianCrit argues that AsAms are not a monolith, AsAm YA literature must also work to better represent this understanding.

Using critical frameworks like AsianCrit and AsAm feminism allows for deeper inquiry and understandings into how AsAm identity is constructed within YA texts and how these texts can reinforce or counter dominant narratives about AsAms. Whether analyzing stereotypical representations of AsAm parents or hypersexualized images of AsAm girls, there is an opportunity to examine the messages about AsAms and their experiences readers of all backgrounds take away. What does it mean when an AsAm girl looks in the mirror and sees a geisha or when she is only interested in white boys? What does it mean for multiracial characters to be represented by non-multiracial people? No one doubts the power of YA literature to open minds and expand thinking, but we must also examine what kinds of messages texts (and other media) are perpetuating.

Within the current context of increased assaults on all AsAms, and AsAm girls and women in particular, it is even more important to understand how we can help support texts that are nuanced, thoughtful, and empowering for readers, and push back against worn-out stereotypes and racial tropes. These texts can be important resources for all readers, but particularly adolescent readers as they navigate their journeys into adulthood. The power of literature is to see not only the mirrors and windows but all the potential sliding glass doors of possibilities.

Works Cited

Asian American Federation. "The State of Asian American Children: 2014," https://www.aafederation.org/doc/AAF_StateofAsianAmerican Children.pdf, accessed 1 Feb. 2022.

Bishop, Rudine Sims. "Windows, Mirrors, and Sliding Glass Doors." *Perspectives*, vol. 6, no. 3, 1990, pp. ix-xi.

Chang, Robert S. "Toward an Asian American Legal Scholarship: Critical Race Theory, Post-Structuralism, and Narrative Space." *California Law Review*, vol. 81, no. 5, 1993, p. 1241.

Chaudhri, Amina. *Multiracial Identity in Children's Literature*. Routledge, 2017.

Chou, Rosalind S., and Joe R. Feagin. *Myth of the Model Minority: Asian Americans Facing Racism*. 2nd ed., Routledge, 2015.

Cooperative Children's Book Center. *Books by and/or About Black, Indigenous and People of Color 2018-*, 16 Apr. 2020, http://ccbc.education.wisc.edu/literature-resources/ccbc-diversity-statistics/books-by-and-or-about-poc-2018/#USonly. Accessed 5 Mar. 2022.

Couzelis, Mary J. Henderson. (2018). "Moving from the Margins: Confronting the Hypersexualization of Asian American Females in Graphic Fiction." *Growing Up Asian American in Young Adult Fiction*, 41-62.

Crenshaw, Kimberlé. "Mapping the Margins: Intersectionality, Identity Politics, and Violence against Women of Color." *Stanford Law Review* 43 (1990): 1241.

Cruz, Megan D., et al., and Stop AAPI Hate Report Youth Campaign. "Stop AAPI Hate Campaign," 17 Sept. 2020, http://stopaapihate.org/wp-content/uploads/2021/04/Stop-AAPI-Hate-Report-Youth-Campaign-200917.pdf. Accessed 5 Jan. 2021.

De Manuel, Dolores, and Rocío G. Davis. "Editors' Introduction: Critical Perspectives on Asian American Children's Literature." *The Lion and the Unicorn*, vol. 30, no. 2, 2006, pp. v-xv.

Dear, Jerry. "APALA Literature Awards by Jerry Dear (KR 18, Summer 2017)." *Kartika Review*, 30 June 2017, http://www.kartikareview.org/18/apia-dear.html. Accessed 24 May 2022.

Endo, Rachel. "Complicating Culture and Difference: Situating Asian American Youth Identities in Lisa Yee's Millicent Min, Girl Genius and Stanford Wong Flunks Big-Time." *Children's Literature in Education*, vol. 40, no. 3, 2009, pp. 235-49.

Erickson-Schroth, Laura, and Jennifer Mitchell. "Queering Queer Theory, or Why Bisexuality Matters." *Journal of Bisexuality*, vol. 9, no. 3-4, 2009, pp. 297-315.

Espiritu, Yen Le. "Race, Class, and Gender in Asian America." *Making More Waves: New Writing by Asian American Women*, 1997, pp. 135-141.

Fujiwara, Lynn, and Shireen Roshanravan. *Asian American Feminisms and Women of Color Politics*. U of Washington Press, 2018.

Han, Jenny. *P.S. I Still Love You*. Simon and Schuster Books for Young Readers, 2019.

Hayn, Judith A., and Lisa A. Hazlett. "Hear Us Out! LGBTQ Young Adult Literature Wishes Are Answered!" *The ALAN Review* vol 38, no. 2, 2011, pp. 68-72.

Ho, Jennifer. *Consumption and Identity in Asian American Coming-of-Age Novels*. Routledge, 2013.

Iftikar, Jon S., and Samuel D. Museus. "On the Utility of Asian Critical (Asiancrit) Theory in the Field of Education." *International Journal of Qualitative Studies in Education*, vol. 31, no. 10, 2018, pp. 935-49.

Kashyap, Keshni, and Mari Araki. *Tina's Mouth: An Existential Comic Diary*. HarperCollins, 2012.

"Korean Language Use by Korean Americans on the Decline." *Korea Times*, 16 Dec. 2014, www.koreatimesus.com/korean-language-usage-by-korean-americans-on-the-decline/. Accessed 10 Jan. 2024.

Lai, Alicia. "It's Wrong to Target Asian-American Scientists for Espionage Prosecution." *Scientific American*, 22 Mar. 2021, www.scientificamerican.com/article/prosecuting-asian-american-scientists-for-espionage-is-a-shortsighted-strategy/. Accessed 7 Mar. 2022.

Lee, Chris J. "'To All The Boys I've Loved Before' Has Creepy Racial Things Going On." *Plan A Magazine*, 19 Mar. 2021, www.planamag.com/to-all-the-boys-ive-loved-before-has-creepy-racial-things-going-on/. Accessed 7 Feb. 2022.

Lee, Erika. *The Making of Asian America: A History*. Simon and Schuster, 2015.

"Literature Award Guidelines & Nominations." *APALA — Asian Pacific American Librarians Association*, www.apalaweb.org/awards/literature-awards/literature-award-guidelines/.

Lowitz, Leza, and Shogo Oketani. *Jet Black and the Ninja Wind*. Tuttle Publishing, 2013.

Mathison, Ymitri, editor. *Growing Up Asian American in Young Adult Fiction*. UP of Mississippi, 2017.

Matos, Angel Daniel. "Complicating the Coming Out Story: Unpacking Queer and (Anti) Normative Thinking in Simon vs. the Homo Sapiens Agenda." *Engaging with Multicultural YA Literature in the Secondary Classroom.* Routledge, 2019, pp. 103-12.

Moraga, Cherríe, and Gloria Anzaldúa. *This Bridge Called My Back: Writings by Radical Women of Color.* State U of NY P, 2015.

Museus, S. D., and Iftikar, J. An Asian Critical Theory (AsianCrit) Framework. *Asian American Students in Higher Education*, vol. 31, no. 10, 2013, pp. 18-29.

ninh, erin k. *Ingratitude: The Debt-bound Daughter in Asian American Literature.* New York UP, 2005.

Nguyen, Hanh. "'To All the Boys I've Loved Before' Author Jenny Han Addresses Criticism for Not Including an Asian Male Love Interest." *IndieWire*, 23 Aug. 2018, www.indiewire.com/2018/08/to-all-the-boys-ive-loved-before-netflix-jenny-han-no-asian-male-love-interest-1201995975/. Accessed 7 Feb. 2022.

Pallotta-Chiarolli, Maria. "Erasure, Exclusion by Inclusion, and the Absence of Intersectionality: Introducing Bisexuality in Education." *Journal of Bisexuality*, vol. 14, no. 1, 2014, pp. 7-17.

Pew Research Center. *The Rise in Asian Americans*, 30 Apr. 2021, www.pewresearch.org/social-trends/2012/06/19/the-rise-of-asian-americans/.

Pew Research Center. *Key Facts about Asian Americans, a Diverse and Growing Population*, 29 Apr. 2021, https://www.pewresearch.org/short-reads/2021/04/29/key-facts-about-asian-americans/ Accessed 10 Jan. 2024.

Pew Research Center. *Japanese in the U.S. Fact Sheet.* 19 May 2023, www.pewresearch.org/social-trends/fact-sheet/asian-americans-japanese-in-the-u-s/?tabId=tab-e06a67fe-f52f-404b-82d1-23d86755033c. Accessed 10 Jan. 2024.

Pillai, Drishti, et al. *The Rising Tide of Violence and Discrimination Against Asian American and Pacific Islander Women and Girls.* Stop AAPI Hate, 28 May 2022, https://stopaapihate.org/wp-content/uploads/2021/05/Stop-AAPI-Hate_NAPAWF_Whitepaper.pdf. Accessed 5 Feb. 2022.

Poon, O., et al. "A Critical Review of the Model Minority Myth in Selected Literature on Asian Americans and Pacific Islanders in Higher Education." *Review of Educational Research*, vol. 86, no. 2, 2016, pp. 469-502.

Pyke, Karen D., and Denise L. Johnson. "Asian American Women and Racialized Femininities." *Gender & Society*, vol. 17, no. 1, 2003, pp. 33-53.

Rajgopal, Shoba Sharad. "'The Daughter of Fu Manchu': The Pedagogy of Deconstructing the Representation of Asian Women in Film and Fiction." *Meridians*, vol. 10, no. 2, 2010, pp. 141-62.

Reynolds, Nancy Thalia. *Mixed Heritage in Young Adult Literature*. Vol. 32, Scarecrow Press, 2009.

Sg, Geok-Unlim. *The Forbidden Stitch: An Asian American Women's Anthology*. CALYX Books, 1989.

Shah, Sonia. *Dragon Ladies: Asian American Feminists Breathe Fire*. South End Press, 1997.

Solórzano, Daniel G., and Tara J. Yosso. "Critical Race Methodology: Counter-Storytelling as an Analytical Framework for Education Research." *Qualitative Inquiry*, vol. 8, no. 1, 2002, pp. 23-44.

Sotomayor, Marianna. "In Wake of Atlanta Slayings, Lawmakers Clash During Emotional Hearing about Attacks on Asian Americans." *The Washington Post*, 18 Mar. 2021, www.washingtonpost.com/politics/hearing-asian-american-attacks/2021/03/18/90071f8c-8801-11eb-8a8b-5cf82c3dffe4_story.html. Accessed 5 Jan. 2022.

Sugiura, Misa. *It's Not Like It's a Secret*. HarperCollins, 2017.

Takaki, Ronald. *Strangers from a Distant Shore: A History of Asian Americans*. Rev. ed., Little, Brown, and Company, 1998.

Thananopavarn, Susan. "Negotiating Asian American Childhood in the Twenty-First Century: Grace Lin's Year of the Dog, Year of the Rat, and Dumpling Days." *The Lion and the Unicorn*, vol. 38, no. 1, 2014, pp. 106-22.

Thompson, Holly. *Orchards*. Ember, 2012.

Thongthiraj, Rahpee. "Negotiated Identities and Female Personal Space in Thai American Adolescent Literature." *The Lion and the Unicorn*, vol. 30, no. 2, 2006, pp. 234-49.

Tuan, M. *Forever Foreigners or Honorary Whites?: The Asian Ethnic Experience Today*. Rutgers University Press, 1998.

Wu, Ellen D. *The Color of Success: Asian Americans and the Origins of the Model Minority*. Princeton University Press, 2013.

Yamada, Mitsuye. "Invisibility Is an Unnatural Disaster: Reflections of an Asian American Woman." *This Bridge Called My Back: Writings by Radical Women of Color*, by Cherrie Moraga, edited by Gloria Anzaldua, Kitchen Table/Women of Color Press, 1983, 35-40.

Notes

1. It should be noted that the CCBC does not currently differentiate between books featuring Asian versus Asian *American* characters.

2. This may be the case because Japanese Americans have a longer history in the United States and are less likely to be immigrants (73% of Japanese Americans are native-born Americans; Pew Research Center, *Japanese in the U.S. Fact Sheet*). There was also a large decline in Japanese language schools in the early twentieth century as anti-Japanese sentiment increased and then the forced closure of all such schools during WWII.

—FIVE—

In the Spirit

WOMANIST NOTIONS OF BLACKNESS, INDIGENEITY, GENDER, AND DIS/ABILITY IN CHILDREN'S LITERATURE
Reanae McNeal

Sankofa One: Introduction

Se wo were fin a wo Sankofa a yenkyi (It is not a taboo to return and fetch it when you forget).

— W. Bruce Willis, *The Adinkra Dictionary*

The griot Carol Boston Weatherford, an award-winning African American children's book author, leads us into the doorway of Sankofa in her book *Moses: When Harriet Tubman Led Her People to Freedom*. Weatherford tells a fictional (her)story of Tubman's spiritual journey, grounded in her Christian beliefs and based on true facts. She centralizes Tubman's socially engaged spirituality from a womanist approach. That is, the interweaving of her spirituality with social justice activist endeavors. In doing so, Weatherford gives us an opportunity to go back and fetch the story of a shero, a woman who dared to defy the odds. A *dis/abled African American woman freedom seeker, an ascendant of Indigenous Africans,* who broke away from the shackles of slavery and freed other enslaved people. As Weatherford notes, "This fictional story is based on the spiritual journey of Harriet Tubman — as a slave in Maryland; a free woman in Philadelphia, Pennsylvania; and a famous conductor on the Underground Railroad" (n.p.). Weatherford's storytelling reveals Tubman's spiritual journey as a central component of her lived experience and activist endeavors.

I also include *an ascendant of Indigenous Africans* as part of Tubman's identity in recognition that Black Americans are also the ascendants of an Indigenous people; therefore, they should also be understood as displaced Indigenous people. Instead of using descendant, which has become a normative term, I use *ascendant* to recognize the rich heritage of Indigenous Africans, Indigenous and Black people in general, and the wealth within their wisdom systems. Notably, as activist-writer Cherríe Moraga also points out: "Black women are Indigenous women, once forcibly removed from their ancestral homeland" (xxv). In this way, Black Indigeneity is an essential component of Tubman's identity and other enslaved Black women in Turtle Island/North America.

For instance, Tubman's Asante grandmother was brought to the United States from Africa on a slave ship (Clinton 5). Recounting the power of "a Black American cultural tradition called generational transmission" in enslavement, Maya Cunningham conveys what Tubman may have learned about sound and songs from West African wisdom systems (Cunningham n.p.): "Tubman would have learned songs from her parents and grandparents, wholly informed by West African aesthetics and functionalities, but in a North American context. Tubman's Asante grandmother, Modesty, might have remembered the ivory talking trumpets and *Atumpan* drums of the Asante royal court" (n.p.). To ignore the histories of how enslaved and displaced Indigenous Africans continued to carry on wisdom systems from their homelands and pass it to their ascendants is to disregard an essential component of Tubman's identity and the nuanced networks of generational transmission of cultural (re)membering(s), particularly of enslaved people and their ascendants. Like Kyle Mays (Black/Saginaw Anishinaabe), I believe, "It is through maintenance and production of culture that we can find the core elements of Black Indigeneity within African America" (n.p).

While Tubman is an ascendant of Indigenous Africans, some Black Americans are also ascendants of both Indigenous Africans and Indigenous peoples of the Americas. As bell hooks points out, "white supremacist constructions of history have erased from public collective memory the recognition of solidarity and communion among Native Americans, Africans, and African Americans" (hooks 181-82). Thus, this collective erasure and intentional suppression in dominant narratives too often leaves these interwoven heritages, overlapping histories, and intermingling of Native Americans, Africans, and African Americans unacknowledged. White supremacist constructions of history often erase the multilayered identities and interrelated kinship between these communities, which also leaves these stories lacking in children's literature.

Notably, these erasures of Africans', Native Americans', and African Americans' interactions and kinships have also caused Afro-Indigenous/Black-Indigenous ascendants from these relationships and communities to often be overlooked in dominant and marginalized narratives in children's literature, which includes Afro Native people and African Americans with Native heritage.[1] For example, the Center for Native American Youth states, "Thousands of people in the United States identify as Black-Indigenous or Afro-Indigenous. This community often faces issues like colorism and the erasure of their identities. Their experiences raise questions about conceptions of Indigeneity — revealing the complex and often vexed relationships between cultures in the Americas" (n.p.). As part of our decolonial endeavors in children's literature in relation to ethnic studies, we must resist dominant narratives that leave many Black, Indigenous, and People of Color (BIPOC) children feeling invisible and not valuable. hooks notes, "It is a gesture of resistance to the dominant culture's way of thinking about history, identity, and community for us to decolonize our minds, reclaim the word that is our history as it was told to us by our ancestors and *not* as it has been interpreted by the colonizer" (184). Decolonial work must also include transgressing and resisting colonial, white supremacist historical accounts and dominant identity/community formations that leave out interwoven and overlapping identities and histories between groups, especially as we consider the *diverse Black-Indigenous people* from overlapping communities and ethnicities throughout the diaspora, including Tubman the ascendant of an Asante grandmother.

Importantly, connections between Blackness and Indigeneity are vital to acknowledge in our decolonial endeavors in children's literature in relation to ethnic studies to honor the overlapping, interrelated identities, and experiences of communities. Such connections also make visible the homelands, displacement, removal, and lived experiences of diverse Black and Indigenous people as well as pursuits of freedom and sovereignty. As E. Sybil Durand and Marilisa Jiménez-García assert, "With every wave of migration or displacement, we should expect interconnected histories and communities. These displacements, whether temporary, permanent, or forced, cause discursive shifts in how identities are understood and highlight their current and historical social constructions" (3). Decolonial work behooves us to honor the multifaceted identities and social locations of marginalized communities and the sheroes that come from them. In this way, we can more adequately speak to the rich heritage(s) that have sustained them and the interconnected histories of displacement, removal, and violence.

I contend that Weatherford's fictional (her)story of Tubman's spiritual journey expands children's literature in three ways: (1) reveals the power of spiritual activism through a womanist approach while exposing students to spiritual principles, literacies, and technologies to advance social justice endeavors; (2) offers students opportunities to discuss systemic, racial, gender, and ableist oppression; Blackness and Indigeneity; faith and religion; spirituality; and liberatory practices; and (3) invites students to break from dominant theological notions of God, creation, and the cosmos and interact with worldviews that recognize interrelatedness. Thus, I also underscore the importance of filling in *unnatural gaps of erasure* in children's literature on Blackness and Indigeneity in intersectional ways, particularly on girls and women in Turtle Island/North America.

In this fashion, I do not take what has become the conventional approach to scholarly discourse; instead, I ground this chapter in the concept of Sankofa, which is derived from the Akan people of Ghana, as my framework. This concept calls for looking back and taking from our past that which can propel us into a better future. At the same time, I situate this work in womanism, which is also rooted in Black Indigeneity. I also transgress monolithic identity and community formations as well as historical constructions that undermine the fullness of marginalized people's identities and lived experiences through my interaction with Weatherford's story. As Durand and Jiménez-García underscore, "Authors unsettle our understanding of history by constructing personal and complex historical narratives that challenge homogeneous characterizations of cultural groups and their histories" (10). In this way, my interaction with Weatherford's text complicates the intersectionality of Blackness, Indigeneity, gender, and dis/ability as well as our historical understanding of enslaved women such as Tubman who practiced what can be described as womanist spiritual activism.

Although Tubman did not refer to herself as a womanist, her life certainly embraces the principles. Weatherford also takes on a womanist methodology to document and record this ancestral story. She uses the story to inspire and engage children in liberatory practices. As Layli Maparyan notes, "The spiritual archaeology of womanism is basically about looking backwards through the personal spiritual journey of 'outrageous, audacious, courageous [and] willful' women who 'love Spirit' to observe how diverse spiritual influences have shaped the womanist idea" (112). By looking backward in the spirit of the Sankofa tradition, Weatherford gives us an opportunity to honor Tubman, a woman who encapsulates courage, perseverance, and audacity. For example, in her author's notes, Weatherford describes this sheroe leader as grounded in her faith and spiritual roots. "Courageous, compassionate, and deeply religious, Tubman saw visions and spoke to God. She believed the Lord called her to free slaves on the Underground Railroad. Her strong faith not only helped her to escape from slavery, but to lead others to freedom" (n.p.). The framework of womanism allows us to interpret and understand Tubman's embodied theological worldview that underscores her spirituality.

The story of Tubman's spiritual journey offers child readers the opportunity to engage with her socially engaged spirituality from a womanist approach. I explain about this womanist approach in more detail further into the chapter. Child readers learn about a sheroe and her resistance to a white supremacist, anti-Black, anti-Indigenous, misogynist, and ableist society. Weatherford's story, which exemplifies Tubman's socially engaged spiritual activism from a womanist approach, invites children to reflect on the ways that they can apply spirituality toward advancing social justice issues. This becomes important to children's literature when we consider the role spiritual principles and spirituality have played in BIPOC's lives and communities. Giving readers a thought-provoking account of Tubman's spiritual journey, Weatherford invites children into *other worldviews, epistemologies, theologies, and spirituality.*

Sankofa Two: Speaking through Creation

We need stories in children's literature of sheroes committed to decolonial and social justice endeavors that infuse spirituality through a womanist approach. Maparyan explains: "[Womanism is] a social change perspective rooted in Black women's and other women of color's everyday experiences and methods of problem solving in everyday spaces, extended to the problem of ending all forms of oppression for all people, restoring the balance between people and the environment/nature, and reconciling human life with the spiritual dimension" (xx). The womanist approach is grounded in an interrelated worldview derived from everyday problem solving and focuses on ending all oppression. This approach also focuses on restoration, balance, and reconciliation in relationships with people, the environment, and the spiritual dimension.

Thus, the womanist approach also focuses on community, survival, and wellness as well as moving in kinship with the natural environment. To be clear: "Womanism is a 'spirit,' a 'walk,' or a 'way of being in the world.' The womanist worldview and its associated social movement is rooted in the lived experience of survival, community building, intimacy with the natural environment, health, healing, and personal growth among everyday people from all walks of life" (Maparyan 33). In this respect, womanism is a practice that lends itself to the lived experiences of ordinary people and an intimacy *with the natural environment*.

An example of womanism is when Weatherford conveys throughout her story how God often speaks to Tubman through creation and the natural environment. In the passage below, God speaks through the song of a whip-poor-will, emphasizing how God values all living beings and their sacredness. Weatherford reveals an interconnected womanist worldview that the Spirit of God speaks and moves through diverse forms of creation. She emphasizes a God that embraces diversity and sees all creation as sacred while underscoring Tubman's reception to such an approach. Weatherford writes,

> God speaks in a whip-poor-will's song.
> I SET THE NORTH STAR IN THE HEAVENS
> AND I MEAN FOR YOU TO BE FREE.
> Harriet sees the star twinkling (n.p.)

Weatherford also reveals creation as one infused with God's voice, signs, and wonders. In other words, God speaks through all of creation for the purposes of Tubman's liberation: the whip-poor-will's song and a twinkling star. The twinkling star serves as a sign to Tubman on how to get to the North — to freedom. Tubman uses these signs to make her way toward freedom.

In this fashion, Weatherford's compelling story of Tubman's spiritual journey situates God as an accomplice to Black-Indigenous liberation via her escape to the North and her abolitionist activism. Additionally, Weatherford reveals a relational God that values kinship, speaks, and infuses themselves throughout all of creation; a cosmic God that honors and occupies the embodied sacredness of a dis/abled African American woman freedom seeker, an ascendant of Indigenous Africans. In Weatherford's story, Tubman is valued by her God and not considered less than. For example, Christina Cleveland critiques the dominant theological narratives of the created white male God by dominant society that has often been used as a deity to maintain white supremacy. Like Cleveland, Weatherford rejects Black women being "at the bottom of the white male God's pecking order," which she exemplifies throughout Tubman's story in her theological interaction with a God of liberation and an accomplice to freedom (Cleveland 17). Weatherford demonstrates and focuses on a God that honors Tubman's ingenuity and brilliance while transgressing derogatory and devaluing definitions of her humanity and what had become normative demeaning relating with enslaved women like Tubman. The liberatory God that Tubman relates to in her spiritual journey shows that she "not only matter(s) but [is considered] sacred" (Cleveland 17).

Children are invited to reflect on a God who works with and through a cosmic universe that aligns itself with Tubman's liberation from bondage while demonstrating Tubman's faith and spiritual experience in the context of an interconnected womanist worldview grounded in Black-Indigeneity. Melanie Harris points out, "While it is imperative to be mindful of how ecological colonial assumptions, such as the equation of Africanness to nature must be examined, African cosmology generally presents a holistic perspective. That is, it regards the realms of nature, humanity, divinity, and spirit as interconnected" (n.p.). Children can engage in womanist/Black-Indigenous interconnected cosmological worldviews where God/Spirit is acknowledged as existing and working through all of creation. Likewise, Gloria Anzaldúa also underscores a womanist and Indigenous interconnected cosmological worldview when she asserts that "Spirit exists in everything; therefore God, the divine, is in everything" (100). In this fashion, Weatherford's story can open up conversations with children about womanist/Black-Indigenous/Indigenous cosmological worldviews that acknowledge everything and everyone as *connected* and *sacred*.

These types of conversations on womanist/Black-Indigenous/Indigenous cosmological worldviews can lead into other discussions of identity formations. As Anzaldúa notes about this spiritual connection: "You share a category of identity wider than any social position or racial label. This conocimiento motivates you to work actively to see that no harm comes to people, animals, ocean — to take up spiritual activism and the work of healing" (558). Engaging children in these types of conversations invites them to rethink identity formations and cosmology. Thus, this transgresses a Western knowledge system that categorizes according to a hierarchal system that places lesser and higher values on things. Engagement with interconnected cosmologies invites children to consider what it means to place sacred value on humans, animals, plants, and earth.

Weatherford's demonstration of Tubman's spiritual cosmological interactions offers children an opportunity to delve more deeply into the multifaceted and epistemological world of a dis/abled African American woman freedom seeker, an ascendant of Indigenous Africans. In this respect, like other Black educators and writers, Weatherford uses storytelling to transgress and disrupt epistemological violence incurred by the mainstream curriculum while expanding the multifaceted layers of marginalized women's lives in children's literature. As Jarvis R. Givens explains, "the art of black teaching included the work of rewriting the epistemological order" (143). This reordering requires advancing other ways of being in the world and recentering embodied marginalized knowledges from the margins to the center. Weatherford's story of Tubman affirms the right of enslaved people to have absolute freedom. In essence, Weatherford's story of Tubman gives students a strong invitation to freedom dream. That is, to imagine a socially just world. At the same time, Weatherford invites students to recognize their spirituality as another viable knowledge system to advance social justice.

Sankofa Three: Dreams of Liberation

Womanism's most prominent characteristic is spirituality. In this fashion, womanists apply spiritual activism to social justice issues. Maparyan defines spiritual activism as significant to womanist praxis when she points out: "Spiritual Activism is the key to womanist praxis. Defined as social or ecological transformational activity rooted in a spiritual belief system or a set of spiritual practices — or, more simply, as *putting spirituality to work for positive social and ecological change — spiritual activism is the bedrock of spiritualized politics*" (119). This socially engaged spirituality interweaves spirituality with political activism for social and ecological change. Maparyan further states that spiritual activism "can involve the active application of metaphysical knowledge toward material ends" (119), for instance, using such things as spiritual principles and spiritual technologies for the advancement of social change. Likewise, Anzaldúa has described spiritual activism as the "work of concimiento-consciousness work — [it] connects the inner life of the mind and spirit to the outer worlds of action in the struggle for social change. I call this particular aspect of concimiento spiritual activism" (178). This consciousness work requires putting our spirituality into action for transformation in the world.

Weatherford's story of Tubman's spiritual journey reveals a womanist worldview, methodologies, and spiritual activism. This story also speaks to other ways of knowing that are often overlooked when dealing with BIPOC women's activism. These other ways of knowing that are often integral to BIPOC women's worldviews and activism include belief systems in God/Creator/Lord/Spirit/Spirit(s) and the employment of spiritual literacies as important wisdom systems for survival and resistance. For too long, spiritual activism and systemic oppression have been overlooked by mainstream curriculums, ignoring the multiple ways that this type of activism incorporates subjugated knowledges and other ways of knowing through spiritual technologies and literacies.

For example, in Weatherford's story, dreams become essential and viable forms of knowledge on Tubman's journey for her own freedom and to liberate others. Weatherford writes,

Then, God speaks about a dream Tubman had:

> HARRIET, YOU DREAMED
> THAT SAINTS SAVED YOU,
> BUT MORTALS WILL GIVE YOU REFUGE
> The woman in the wagon who always spoke kindly to me —
> YES, HARRIET —
> I must go to her.
> The woman points Harriet to safe havens —
> hiding places for runaways — (n.p.)

God reveals the interpretation of the dream that the Saints represented mortals who would save Tubman. However, Weatherford illustrates how Tubman receives information through dreams that God discusses with her and interprets. Without saying who those mortals are, Tubman draws on the spiritual technology of discernment that God was talking about a woman who had been nice to her before. God confirms "yes." As a result, the woman is able to assist Tubman onto freedom.

Weatherford invites children into spiritual ways of knowing — spiritual literacies grounded in social justice. She reveals Tubman's embodied ways of knowing as viable sources of wisdom and knowledge: *visions, dreams, and discernment*. In womanism, "the invisible world exists, it is real," and "it is lawful and knowable" (130). The invisible world is something to learn and know from. Rarely, if at all, are children taught this in mainstream curriculum. Weatherford gives children an opportunity to discuss other ways of knowing through interacting with the spiritual journey of Tubman.

At the same time, Weatherford's story of Tubman also revolts against the dominant normative curricula that erase and/or disregard (dis)abled African American women freedom seekers, ascendants of Indigenous Africans. Weatherford reveals a womanist worldview and spiritual activism through the embodiment of a BIPOC woman, which is rarely taught in the mainstream American curriculum. Givens points out the ways that Black educators "rebel against established schools of thought in the American Curriculum" (Givens 134). Thus, Weatherford centralizes Tubman's embodied experience as a known sheroe across communities and invites students across social locations to delve into a womanist worldview and spiritual activism that embrace Black Indigeneity and socially engaged spirituality.

For instance, Weatherford also highlights one of Tubman's recurring dreams in her real life within the picture-book story, which included assistance from women, and underscored the power of women in her womanist worldview and spiritual activism. Weatherford writes: "[Harriet] recalls dreams where she flew like a bird, sank, and was lifted by ladies in white who pulled her north. FLY, HARRIET. YOUR FAITH HAS WINGS" (n.p.). These types of dreams underscored the power of women to be encouragers of faith and *saviors* who supported liberation. Deirdre Cooper Owens writes: "Focusing on a recurring dream of freedom while she was enslaved, Tubman spoke of her fatigue, vulnerability and how her liberation was held in the hands of other women. In her dream, when her strength wanes, a band of 'ladies' stretched out their arms to protect Tubman from her fall. These women cradled her as she rested, while simultaneously laboring to ensure her freedom. In her dream state, she envisioned women as saviors, as the rescuers of her enslaved body" (n.p.). In such dreams, women played powerful roles in liberation and lifting Tubman up when wearied. Building on Owens's commentary, Tubman's dreams contradicted and rejected the position of women as inferior and disposable based on their gender. Instead, she recognized their sacred value. As Owens notes, "Perhaps this recurring vision motivated Tubman to imagine herself as not only a savior of weary laborers but also to serve as a flesh and blood symbol of communal democracy" (n.p.). These types of images of women moving in their power and as saviors debunk patriarchal images, messages, and stories that underscore the superiority of boys and men in children's literature while perpetuating the leadership, activism, and communal persistence of women for social change.

Simultaneously, the spiritual technologies used and honored by Tubman reveal ways of knowing while legitimizing them. Stories that convey the richness of a socially engaged spirituality from a womanist approach "can also offer opportunities both to expand literary understandings and to encourage critical examination of issues that plague our democracy, such as inequities tied to race, gender, income, and disability" (Bishop 120). At the same time, Weatherford's work continues to implement liberatory pedagogies enacted by Black educators and writers. As Givens explains, "Black educators imparted to students that their citizenship and entitlement to complete freedom was bought and paid for by those who came before them. ... These lessons gave students the language and the historical context to refuse the myths shaping the world around them" (157). Weatherford's teachings through the picture book insist on critical engagement with the story and call for a deeper understanding of those who paved the way toward freedom through her story line while encouraging children that they can do the same.

Weatherford shows Tubman's agency and power to discern and interweave her socially engaged spirituality as an integral part of her embodied experience. While the overarching mainstream society discounted enslaved women's wisdom systems, Tubman and others survived, resisted, and depended on them. Cleveland underscores the embodied wisdom of enslaved women like Tubman when she points out: "Rather than allowing the white patriarchal establishment to dictate what is true, they relied on their own embodied wisdom. . . . [The] experiential knowing of a God who saw, affirmed, and liberated them" (58). This conveys lessons to children to honor their embodied wisdom and spiritual knowing.

Unsurprisingly, BIPOC women such as Weatherford have been at the forefront of making known socially engaged spirituality from a womanist approach in children's literature, as illustrated by Weatherford's centralization of Tubman's spiritual journey. As Irene Lara explains, "Within a western framework, writing about spirit and spirituality, as well as writing from a spiritual epistemology that is embodied and ensouled in a woman of color consciousness, is cause for silencing and marginalization" (30). Despite a Western framework's limiting worldview in conceptualizing the vastness of BIPOC women's spirituality through their embodied experiences and its impact on social change, spirituality remains a central component of womanism. As Maparyan writes, "womanism is not just [a] social movement, but a spiritual movement" (49). The spiritual journey and spiritual activism of womanists play a central role in their activism in the world, making this rich heritage of socially engaged spirituality an important component to learn when reflecting on social justice issues and BIPOC women.

When children's literature is integrated with stories of socially engaged spirituality enacted by BIPOC women in the womanist tradition, children are able to learn diverse ways of knowing, other forms of activism, and liberation pedagogies that often go unrecognized by dominant culture. Weatherford and other writers disrupt this normalization by dominant culture that the ideal reader of children's literature is "only" white children; instead, Weatherford imagines diverse children in need of stories that remain marginalized. Rudine Sims Bishop asserts, "When diversity is absent from the literature we share with children, those who are left out infer that they are undervalued in our society, and those whose lives are constantly reflected gain a false sense of their own importance, a sense that they are the privileged 'norm'" (120). This lack of diversity has been deadly to marginalized children while also perpetuating the fictitious idea that Eurocentric ways of knowing, dominant definitions of activism, and hegemonic pedagogies are superior. Thus, this sends a message to children that the primary and superior knowledge producers on the planet are white while maintaining the status quo.

Sankofa Four: A Dis/abled African American Woman Freedom Seeker, an Ascendant of Indigenous Africans Shall Lead Them

This powerful story of historical fiction calls for child readers to learn valuable lessons from Tubman's spiritual journey that played a key role in her being one of the most prolific women leaders in history — and dare I say one of the most prolific leaders in history. Thus, Weatherford's historical contextualizing of

Tubman's spiritual journey naturally constitutes a pedagogy that digresses from and disrupts the mainstream curriculum in schools. Entering into the characteristics of what Givens refers to as "fugitive pedagogy," this type of pedagogy by Black educators "demanded thinking and imagining beyond Western canons of knowledge, thus leading Black Americans to develop an undercanon that shadowed and critiqued the master narrative" (158). Weatherford's story is part of that undercanon that goes beyond the Eurocentric Western canons of knowledge. Simultaneously, Weatherford invites children to other wisdom systems that constitute the survival and resistance employed in enslavement by a dis/abled African American woman freedom seeker, an ascendant of Indigenous Africans, and another leadership model enacted by a BIPOC woman.

Weatherford conveys in her story that God calls Tubman Moses. Moses is a biblical character who was a leader who liberated his people, the Israelites, from the Egyptians under the guidance of God. The fact that Weatherford titled the book *Moses* demonstrates her dependency on the reader's knowledge of the story of Moses in the Bible. In knowing the story of Moses, the readers can create strong parallels and comparisons between Tubman, a woman, and Moses, a man, as strong liberation leaders who freed their people from the bondages of slavery. This underlining theme of Moses and liberation underscores the powerful call of Tubman to a major leadership position of her people to free them from bondage. For instance, God says, "HARRIET BE THE MOSES OF YOUR PEOPLE" (n.p.) This passage underscores a call to leadership and advocacy to deliver others from the grip of oppression. Tubman's story models that it is not enough to be concerned about yourself and your own family, but that one must also be concerned about others who are oppressed. Thus, being the Moses of her people entailed being the liberator of her people.

However, Tubman's answer speaks to her positionality and the societal messages of the devaluing of women's gender in her answer to what God is saying about this leadership, advocacy, and deliverer position. Tubman responds to God by saying, "But I am a lowly woman" (n.p.). This line of Weatherford's historical fiction story of her spiritual journey invites children to think about the way that racialized gender oppression can make girls and women question their competency and purpose in life when it goes beyond the scripted roles of gender that have become normalized. After all, Tubman went from being labeled as property to being free in the constraints of a society that still saw her social position as a (dis)abled African American woman freedom seeker, an ascendant of Indigenous Africans, as being inferior and therefore defining her as expendable. Critiques of racialized gender oppression become valuable to helping children interpret and go deeper into Weatherford's story.

Notably, the images on the page shows an enslaved woman, most likely Tubman, working in the field with what appear to be enslaved men. Thus, denoting the ways enslaved women such as Tubman were expected to and did work as hard as the men did. Such an image sends a message to child readers that women were not inferior to men and had just as much strength to carry out tasks, even under the hostile and horrific conditions of slavery. This type of imagery with the story can possibly translate into being strong and capable leaders. The enslaved woman, Tubman, is centralized in the picture, making her presence the most prominent. Furthermore, there is no comparison picture of the male Moses, which emphasizes Tubman's centralization as a *strong* woman leader of liberation.

God's response to Tubman speaks to her gifts that are her special attributes. God says,

> HARRIET, I HAVE BLESSED YOU
> WITH A STRONG BODY, A CLEVER MIND,
> YOU HEAL THE SICK AND SEE THE FUTURE.
> USE YOUR GIFTS TO BREAK THE CHAINS. (n.p.)

The gifts pointed out encompass her body, mind, healing, and prophetic gifts. In other words, God points to her strength, intelligence, ability to heal, and her ability to see the future, never mentioning her gender as a deficit for leading — reminding Tubman instead of her valuable physical, mental, and spiritual gifts. Children receive an invitation from Weatherford's story to think about natural and prophetic gifts as an intimate part of their makeup and their ability to lead regardless of one's social location. Tubman's God recognizes that gifts come in diverse embodiments that deserve to be honored despite the fact that Tubman lives in a social order that employs markers of difference for the sake of defining those considered less valuable and inferior in dominant society and discourse.

With this said, in complicating ancestral lineages, we must include sheroes in children's literature who have had parts of their identities erased, including the rich legacies of sheroes with dis/abilities. Unfortunately, "most biographies of Tubman do not examine her as a disabled woman" (Owens n.p.). Yet Weatherford directly speaks about the incident that precipitated Tubman's dis/ability and the impact for the rest of her entire life in her Author's Note when she writes, "the Master struck Tubman in the head with a two-pound weight, nearly killing her. For the rest of her life, she bore a scar and suffered severe headaches, blackouts, and fits of speechlessness" (n.p.). This important information invites children to reflect on Tubman as a dis/abled woman and make connections to dis/ability and enslavement when engaged with ethnic studies. Children are grounded in deeper understandings and critiques of the literature they read. As Sami Schalk notes, "The relationship of blackness to systemic disabling violence in the past impacts the relationship of blackness and dis-ability today" (42). Weatherford's story of Tubman can encourage discussions that assist children in making these vital connections to the long-term impact of systemic violence in children's literature through an ethnic studies lens.

However, Weatherford does not directly in the story speak about Tubman's dis/ability, but I believe she is alluding to one of her blackouts (a deep sleep) when sharing about her being chased by enslavers when she says : "In the underbrush. Harriet sinks into a deep sleep, God cradles her. When she wakes, the men on horseback have passed. And day breaks. Thank You Lord, *for watching over me*" (n.p.). In the images that correlate with Weatherford's story, Tubman is lying on the ground in tall grass sleeping with her head turned to the side and her eyes closed. One of her arms is flung haphazardly over her body while her other arm is stretched out on the grass. Animals of all kinds — foxes, rabbits, racoons, and possums — surround her body as she is in a deep sleep. Looming behind her are tall trees with the night sky and twinkling stars shining between them with an owl perched on the branches of one of the trees as Tubman lies in *a deep sleep*. Yet Tubman's enslavers are unable to catch her even in this temporary vulnerable state as God watches over her.

Weatherford demonstrates the way Tubman navigated multiple identities on her spiritual journey. With this said, Owens asserts, "We owe her the respect to add the adjective 'disabled' to Tubman's list of descriptions when we discuss her identities. More importantly, understanding Harriet Tubman as a 'disabled' figure can also help us to see the powerful intersections between disability and strength" (n.p.). This inclusion of all her multiple identities, including dis/ability, assists in passing on stories and wisdom systems of sheroes that reveal a more holistic and intersectional view of their lived realities while breaking away from deficit analyses that ignore the relationship between dis/ability and strength. While Weatherford does not refer to Tubman as dis/abled in the story at any time, I have in my interaction with the story.

Acknowledging Tubman as dis/abled can assists children in reflecting on the importance of understanding how dis/ability intersects with other identities. As Schalk points out: "Close and careful consideration of the real-world relationship of disability to gendered, racialized, sexual, and economic violence, such as slavery, is essential to interpreting representations of disability because this relationship impacts the creation and reception of representations of disability by groups impacted by such violence" (41). Weatherford's centralization of a dis/abled African American woman freedom seeker, an ascendant of Indigenous Africans, can assist children in more readily understanding the relationship of dis/ability to interlocking oppression and intersectional identities as well as learning about other forms of activism.

Notably, Weatherford reveals a multifaceted layer of Tubman's lived experience at the intersections of her identities, which can lead to viable discussions by children on dis/ability in intersectional ways that honor the embodied experiences of dis/abled BIPOC when in relationship with ethnic studies critiques. Schalk notes, "Understanding disability as a complex experience means remaining attentive to positive, negative, and ambivalent aspects of disability (physically, mentally, and socially) as well as the relationship between all three" (24). Stories such as Weatherford's can initiate conversations on the complexity of dis/ability that are critical for children in gaining a deeper understanding of multifaceted lived realities.

Children also can be invited to discuss BIPOC women, dis/ability, and leadership. As Moya Bailey and Izetta Autumn Mobley point out: "despite the higher prevalence of disability within Black and other communities of color, the disability rights movement and disability studies remain white in leadership and in stated objectives and outcomes" (n.p.). This prevalence of dis/ability among BIPOC communities and the inequities in leadership, objectives, and outcomes in disability rights movements and disability studies emphasize the need for Weatherford's story in children's literature. Highlighting a dis/abled sheroe who models leadership, courage, and resistance to interlocking oppression is necessary to bring to light the stories of BIPOC communities' experience with dis/ability. Bailey and Mobley also assert the importance of addressing the intersections of dis/abled "historical Black figures" while also accentuating women freedom fighters: "Whether it is the painful epileptic seizures of Harriet Tubman that helped her stay ahead of bounty hunters or the Mississippi appendectomy that spurred Fannie Lou Hamer's activism, the intersections of disability and race in the bodily praxis of historical Black figures needs to be more deeply addressed" (n.p.). Tubman's inferior positionality in a social order that ignores and devalues the sacredness of dis/abled African American women freedom seekers, ascendants of Indigenous Africans, does not disqualify Tubman for the God that infuses her faith and spirituality.

In fact, Tubman's God gives her a bold call to be a liberation leader activist. By speaking through the cosmos and supporting Tubman on her journey, Tubman's God does not see dis/ability as a deficit but works with her in all of her embodied states. Schalk reminds us that "we must not only remember slavery as the oppression of black people, both enslaved and free, but also remember it as a systemic racial violence that often produced black disabled bodyminds via ableist discourses of blackness" (45). Giving a historical account of the history of Black dis/ability within the context of oppressive systems engaged with the critiques of ethnic studies scholars gives children deeper understandings of the relationship between identities, positionality, and systemic oppression. In this fashion, Weatherford further demonstrates that the God Tubman communicates with believes in equity for dis/abled BIPOC women in leadership roles in activist liberation endeavors. Tubman's God's role as an accomplice in her liberation as an enslaved woman is interwoven throughout Weatherford's story.

Weatherford's weaving of this historical fiction of Tubman's spiritual journey speaks to the possibilities of not only womanist spiritual activism, but also a type of liberation that invites community, autonomy, equity, and belonging through the embodied spiritual journey of a dis/abled African American woman freedom seeker, an ascendant of Indigenous Africans. Notably, Owens writes, "Yet, as an enslaved woman who lived in a patriarchal and anti-Black America, Harriet Tubman's freedom dream and fugitive activism demonstrated something else. She offered up a version of freedom where a disabled Black [Indigenous] woman sat at the center of it, where Black [Indigenous] women were liberators, and where liberation was communal and democratic" (n.p.). In this way, Tubman refuses to be decentered in her liberatory quest as she created communal and democratic space for others. Bailey and Mobley point out how Black people model collectivity and interdependence: "Black Studies research suggests that Black people are employing a different model, one of collectivity and potential interdependence that eschews the individualist model of a disability rights framework" (n.p.). Weatherford's story in conversation with ethnic studies can assist marginalized children to see and understand more deeply sheroes represented in children's literature with multiple identities.

Importantly, more nuanced understandings of Blackness, Indigeneity, dis/ability, gender, and enslavement remain essential catalysts to helping children unpack historical and present-day oppression. As Violet J. Harris notes, "There are many people who suffer from various disabilities and who are African American, Latino, or Native American. But, the overall impression one would get from books is that "in-clusion" is only accessible to disabled persons who are White or European American" (qtd. Turner 124). As a result, many BIPOC children rarely see their experiences or their intersectional identities in relation to dis/ability reflected in children's literature, which speaks to the importance of ethnic studies being in continual conversations with children's literature for future generations.

Sankofa Five: Roots, Herbs, and Reading Signs in the Cosmos

Preserving stories for our most precious and sacred gifts, which are our children, is vital to (re)membering histories, validating lived experiences, and (re)imagining another world. As activist-scholar Ebony Elizabeth Thomas explains, "This process of restorying, of reshaping narratives to better reflect a diversity of perspectives and experiences, is an act of asserting the importance of one's existence in a world that tries to silence subaltern voices" (314). Weatherford invites us to a restorying of Tubman's life that puts children in direct interaction with Tubman's socially engaged spirituality from a womanist approach. Durand and Jiménez-García points out that "historical fiction [has] the potential to reveal to young readers that cultural communities have deeply entangled histories due to colonialism and their enduring struggles for civil rights" (10). The potential of historical fiction to bring more nuanced understandings of histories makes an analysis of Weatherford's work important to children's literature in relation to ethnic studies.

For instance, Weatherford reveals how Tubman is taught to work in collaboration with the land, read the signs of creation, and work with plants to heal. In other words, she works with creation and learns to read and listen to its language through the lessons learned from her father. The story Weatherford shares of Tubman's spiritual journey also encompasses "[a]n ecowomanist perspective [that] acknowledges African, Native American, and Indigenous cosmological perspectives as valid spiritual and religious worldviews with earth honoring ethical systems. For many of these cosmologies the earth is understood as sacred and divine" (Harris n.p.). For instance, Tubman becomes wearied on her journey fleeing to the North and grieves about missing her folks.

However, God reminds Tubman of how she has learned to work with and understand creation from her father:

> HARRIET YOUR FATHER
> TAUGHT YOU TO READ THE STARS,
> PREDICT THE WEATHER,
> GATHER WILD BERRIES,
> AND MAKE CURES FROM ROOTS.
> USE HIS LESSONS TO BE FREE.

This passage underscores her ability to understand the stars and weather, how to recognize and gather food to eat and mix roots to heal. Tubman's ecowomanist worldview allows her to see the sacredness and allyship of the cosmos, land, and plants by understanding the language and abilities of creation through an interrelated worldview. Thus, these cosmological lessons, grounded in Black-Indigenous cosmologies, handed down to Tubman from her father on how to work in relationship with the stars, weather, food, and roots underscore a cultural inheritance that assisted Tubman in her liberation goals.

In this fashion, engaging Weatherford's story with ethnic studies as a means to complicate the multifaceted layers of Tubman's identity becomes an important component of understanding her Black Indigeneity, identities, and overlapping ancestral histories that assisted her in the pursuit of liberation. As Mays also explains, "Black Indigeneity therefore is how Black Americans produce culture and maintain the cultural elements that their ancestors brought with them in spite of enslavement" (n.p.). This type of overlooking of overlapping histories and identities by dominant culture and marginalized communities can perpetuate so-called "convenient categories" of essentialized representations of identities in children's literature and white supremacist narratives that erase the connections between people and their interconnected histories and rich heritage(s) passed down.

The rich inheritance of lessons passed down by Tubman's father speaks to the ingenuity of cultural technologies distributed across generations. This is why ignoring Tubman's collective wisdom systems gathered from her ancestors to navigate such a hostile terrain in Turtle Island/North America is to disregard her individual history, the histories of her people, and the complex generational networks of (re)membering. Additionally, this type of disregard ignores the value in Black-Indigenous people's nuanced transference of their wisdom systems across generations and continents as well as across the homelands of Indigenous nations/people.

Tubman's relational ecowomanist worldview invites children to reflect on the sacredness of land, environment, plants, and cosmos while resisting oppression. As Harris explains, "Echoing the spirit of the ancestral and ecological knowledge embodied by Harriet Tubman, ecowomanism as an approach simultaneously points to the realities of Black and African women's experiences navigating oppression while also problematizing the theological epistemologies that frame traditional environmental thought that are arguably shaped by euro-centric, western theories including colonialism that lay dormant until one examines them closely" (n.p.). Tubman's faith and theology that inspired her spirituality negate domination and destruction of the environment and reveal other ways of ecologically relating and interacting for the purposes of healing and liberation. Grounded in ancestral and ecological knowledge, Tubman uses this knowledge to assist others while underscoring an earth-honoring womanist ethics grounded in Black Indigeneity. In this respect, "A subversive stance of resistance lies at the heart of Ecowomanism" (Harris n.p.). Moreover, Weatherford's story of Tubman can also be summarized as a form of resistance to dominant curriculums that leave BIPOC children erased and/or on the margins. Like Harris, I believe that "multicultural literature is much more than telling the story about an individual in a particular place or time; it is a story of a group's experiences that reflect their history, their current existence, and their future" (qtd. Turner 125).

Sankofa Six: Moving into the Future of Children's Literature

Divestment from dominant culture's way of thinking in our analysis of and writing of children's literature is imperative to the ties between children's literature and ethnic studies. Children's literature and ethnic studies in relationship allow the critique and disruption of settler colonialism and interlocking oppression while perpetuating stories that empower children to enact activism, tell their unique stories, and engage in multiple realities. Children are able to interact with overlapping and interconnected histories, identities, and communities while garnering survival and resistance skills. It is vital to acknowledge and honor "interconnected histories and communities" (Durand and Jiménez-García 3) and contribute to the disruption of "previous approaches to identity representations based on strategic essentialist discourses" (Durand and Jiménez-García 1). Essentialist discourses ignore the multifaceted histories and identities that have shaped the experiences of communities. As a result, these discourses have left a legacy of unnatural gaps in children's literature of erasure and invisibility of communities at the expense of BIPOC children's lives (Durand and Jiménez-García 1).

Even when enacting a decolonial analysis, we must simultaneously continue to fill in the unnatural gaps in children's literature of BIPOC communities and experiences that are marginalized and/or erased, such as the diverse experience(s) of Afro-Indigenous/Black-Indigenous people in Turtle Island/North America. Continuing to complicate Blackness and Indigeneity in children's literature in intersectional ways while delving into the rich, vibrant layers in communities is essential to the progress in children's literature. For example, the inclusion of diverse stories of Afro-Indigenous/Black Indigenous girls/women is essential in filling in those unnatural gaps in children's literature. The interwoven heritages and interactions of Indigenous Africans, African Americans, and Indigenous People of the Americas become vital to document in children's literature. Notably, as we advance and imagine a more just future, the diversity of Blackness and Indigeneity must be embraced in intersectional ways that give room for multiple identities and diverse lived experiences

Although some children's and youth literature has underscored these stories and brought visibility to them, such as *Black Indians* by William Loren Katz and *UNSPEAKABLE: The Tulsa Race Massacre* by Carole Weatherford, as well as stories revealing the interactions and communion between African American and Native people such as *Crossing Bok Chitto: A Choctaw Tale of Friendship and Freedom* by Tim Tingle (Choctaw), the centralization of the diverse stories of girls and women who are Afro-Indigenous/Black-Indigenous remains lacking. However, recently YoNasda Lonewolf (Oglala Lakota/African American) and Safiyyah Muhammad have published through an independent publisher a book called *Adventures of Star Song* about a Lakota and African girl who is eight years old. These books are seeds to the continual flourishing of these varied stories.

In conclusion, to reiterate: Connections between Blackness and Indigeneity are vital to acknowledge in our decolonial endeavors in children's literature in relation to ethnic studies to honor the overlapping, interrelated identities, and experiences of communities. Such connections also make visible the homelands, displacement, removal, and lived experiences of diverse Black and Indigenous people, as demonstrated with Tubman, a dis/abled African American woman freedom seeker, an ascendant of Indigenous Africans.

I end my chapter with an *invitation to activist-scholars, storytellers* invested in the bridge between children's literature and ethnic studies: We must continue complicating the stories that we convey further about our lived experiences for future generations. Like other womanists, I know "cultural diversity [remains] under assault," and "many groups cultural or subcultural, which have been marginalized by existing politico-economic systems and structures are subject to ongoing forces of annihilation" (Maparyan 13). In this fashion, we must be diligent in telling our often overlapping and interwoven histories, lived realities, and rich intermingling embedded in our stories.

Works Cited

Bishop, Rudine Sims. "Language Arts Lessons: A Ride with Nana and CJ: Engagement, Appreciation, and Social Action." *NCTE*, vol. 94, no. 2, 2016, pp. 120-23.

Center for Native American Youth. "What It Means to Be Both Black and Indigenous." *Aspen Institute*. 18 Feb. 2021, https://www.aspeninstitute.org/blog-posts/what-it-means-to-be-both-black-and-indigenous/. Accessed 20 June 2022.

Clinton, Catherine. *Harriet Tubman: The Road to Freedom*. Little, Brown and Company, 2004.

Cleveland, Christina. *God Is a Black Woman*. Harper One, 2022.

Coleman, Monica A. *Making a Way Out of No Way: Womanist Theologians on Salvation*. Fortress Press, 2008.

Cunningham, Maya. "The Sound World of Harriet Tubman." *Ms.*, 17 Feb. 2022, https://msmagazine.com/2022/02/17/harriet-tubman-music-sound-slavery-underground-railroad/. Accessed 20 Mar. 2022.

Durand, E. Sybill, and Marilisa Jiménez-García. "Unsettling Representations of Identities: A Critical Review of Diverse Youth Literature." *Research on Diversity in Youth Literature*, vol. 1, no. 7, 2018, pp. 1-24.

Davis, Fania E. *The Little Book of Race and Restorative Justice*. Good Books, 2019.

Givens, Jarvis R. *The Fugitive Pedagogy Book: Carter G. Woodson and the Art of Black Teaching*. Harvard UP, 2021.

Harris, Melanie. "Ecowomanist Wisdom: Encountering Earth and Spirit (@ theTable: Planetary Solidarity)." *Feminist Studies in Religion*. 22 Mar. 2018, https://www.fsrinc.org/planetary-solidarity-ecowomanist-wisdom/. Accessed 28 Mar. 2022.

Hooks, bell. *Black Looks: Race and Representation*. South End Press, 1992.

Keating, AnaLouise, editor. *Interviews/Entrevistas*. Routledge, 2000.

Lara, Irene. "Bruja Positionalities: Towards a Chicana/Latina Spiritual Activism." *Mujeres Activistas en Letras y Cambio Social*, vol. 4, no. 2, Spring 2005, pp. 10-45.

Maparyan, Layli. *Womanist Idea*. Routledge, 2012.

Mays, Kyle. "A Provocation of The Modes of Black Indigeneity: Culture, Language, Possibilities." *Ethnic Studies Review*, vol. 44, no. 2, 2021, pp. 41–50.

Moraga, Cherríe. "Catching Fire." *This Bridge Called My Back: Radical Writings by Women of Color,* 4th ed., edited by Cherríe Moraga and Gloria Anzaldúa, State U of NY P, 2015, pp. xv-xxv.

Moya, Bailey, and Izetta Autumn Mobley. "Work in the Intersections: A Black Feminist Disability Framework." *Gender & Society*, vol. 33, no. 1, 2019, pp. 19-40.

Owens, Deirdre Cooper, "Harriet Tubman's Disability and Why it Matters." *Ms.,* 10 Feb. 2022, Harriet Tubman's Disability and Why It Matters — Ms. Magazine (msmagazine.com). Accessed 23 Mar. 2022.

Schalk, Sami. *Bodyminds Reimagined: (Dis)ability, Race, and Gender in Black Women's Speculative Fiction.* Duke University Press, 2018.

Thomas, Ebony Elizabeth, and Amy Stornaiuolo. "Restorying the Self: Bending Toward Textual Justice." *Harvard Educational Review*, vol. 86, no. 3, 2016, pp. 313-38

Turner, Jennifer D. "Tales and Testimonies: Viewpoints on Diverse Literature from Duncan Tonatiuh and Violet J. Harris." *Language Arts*, vol. 94, no. 2, pp. 124-29.

Phillips, Layli. *The Womanist Reader*. Routledge, 2006.

Weatherford, Carol. *Moses: When Harriet Tubman Led Her People to Freedom.* Little, Brown and Company, 2006.

Willis, W. Bruce. *The Adinkra Dictionary. A Visual Primer On The Language of Adinkra.* Pyramid Complex, 1998.

Notes

1. I have used the term Afro-Indigenous/Black-Indigenous people interchangeably to be as inclusive as possible because of the history of erasure and diversity of Afro-Indigenous/Black-Indigenous people while also honoring the names used by individuals and communities. Please note that even these names are limited and general and do not encompass the multiple specific names used by diverse Afro-Indigenous/Black-Indigenous people, especially the names of specific nations/communities, which are often preferred.

SIX

The Power of Story, Images, and Policy in Native Studies

AN INTERVIEW WITH TRACI SORELL AND ALIA JONES

Marilisa Jimenez Garcia and Sonia Alejandra Rodríguez

Editors' note: Traci Sorell is an award-winning Native children's author, member of the Cherokee Nation, and lawyer. Sorell is the author of titles such as We Are Grateful, At the Mountain's Base, *and* She Persisted: Wilma Mankiller. *Sorell is a two-time Sibert Medal and Orbis Pictus honoree. She has also received awards from the American Indian Library Association. Sorell is also a graduate of the University of California, Berkeley, including taking courses in its historic ethnic studies program.*

Alia Jones is a master of arts in library and information studies (MLIS) student at the UW Madison Information School, focusing on Black and Indigenous children's literature, family and communities. Jones is also an experienced librarian and award committee member, having worked in the Cincinnati Public Library system and served on children's book award committees including the Caldecott Award Committee in 2020. Jones is a graduate of Cornell University in East Asian and American Indian studies.

This interview grew out of a desire to include the experiences of creators, influencers, and practitioners in youth literature and its connections to ethnic studies movements, particularly around Native studies and youth literature. We also saw an opportunity to consider picture books and younger readers, rather than young adult literature and teens, which perhaps are not as prevalent in conversations about ethnic studies. Sorell and Jones reflect on the relationship between ethnic studies and youth literature, the history of ethnic studies in the academy, their educational experiences and roles of youth literature in communities, and how to improve research on youth literature diversity and policy. Sorell and Jones also center the importance of centering youth of color, as a growing majority in the US, and their intersectional realities and stories.

***

Sonia Alejandra Rodríguez: Thank you so much for meeting with us. We're excited to have this very important conversation with you about the intersection of ethnic studies and youth literature. How did you get involved in the profession of children's literature?

Alia Jones: My journey to children's lit and libraries was kind of winding. It started as a teacher. I started in education, working with youth in South Korea. Working directly with those children got me interested in stories and storytelling. When I came back to the United States, I needed a job and I knew that I loved books, so I jumped directly into bookselling. I was a children's bookseller for about two years. That is really the core of where I got interested in children's literature. Learning about the current state of children's lives, while working directly with books, in the public retail space was really where I just gained most of my knowledge.

After that I jumped into libraries, because I wanted a little bit more depth and I wanted to work more with communities, so I transitioned to public libraries. Through those fields and working with the public directly is how I found a love for children's lives in libraries, especially diverse books, it was through working with people.

Traci Sorell: When I was an undergrad at University of California, Berkeley, I was a Native American studies major and an ethnic studies minor. One of the ethnic studies courses taught by a professor from Native studies was called "People of Mixed Race Descent." We had to examine how people in this race might not look like this or that in children's literature, but in doing so, what we realized, you know, is one, there were books that were coming on the scene, certainly Children's Book Press had things that were being published at that time, but there wasn't a lot about just children that we could find in single terms of, let's say Native students. Like just a Native topic book.

But when you looked at children and mixed race status [there was more variety]. We read *Black Is Brown Is Tan* (2004). But there just weren't a lot of depictions. It got me looking at bookstores, looking at museums. Any kind of historical society things I might go through. After years, I always look and see what they are representing for children in their children's section, and so I would look at things and I started a collection of children's books that didn't exist when I was a kid.

Once I had my son, then I became a little more analytical about what my collection was and what that looked like to share that collection with him.

And I realized very quickly that the majority of the stories that I had been collecting were traditional stories, sometimes retellings by non-Native people that didn't really adhere to the tribal stories. There were a few contemporary stories, but not many, so then I went to the library. So I was like, "oh I can't just be sharing all this stuff from the past, like where's contemporary things?" My concern only continued as he got started in school, but that's really what propelled me, was looking at my own books and then going to the library. At the time, I was living in Kansas City, I had a very robust city public library system in Johnson County. And then I lived in Alaska. I had three library systems that I could look at, and I checked out books from all of them. And it was lacking and this was 2013. That's really what galvanized me to see, "If this is a problem, is there something that I can do to address the problem?" [Also] you know, given that I have a background in Native studies, in ethnic studies, and *that* class which I took [at Berkeley] was in 1991 or 1992, and all these years later, we're not seeing the progress. It was concerning to me — and I'm not saying that there weren't books published in [that time] and that they haven't been wonderful — it's just not nearly enough for the population reality that existed in 2013 and even more so now that exists.

SAR: What role models did you have in the field?

TS: Again, you know I had contacted a friend from undergrad that I met from graduate school and Arizona who's actually [a] white Jewish author, but he's a professor. And he's published for young people and adults, and so I said, "If I want to publish a book for young people, how would I go about that?" He told me to join SCBWI (Society of Children's Book Writers and Illustrators) and check out their conferences. And to finish whatever I was writing, etc. He was a role model, in essence, because he was like: "Finish whatever it is you're writing since the majority of people never do that. Share with others, and get it out in the world and get some feedback on it." I followed his advice and then I found a great group in Kansas — the SCBWI chapter there who are wonderful mentors for me and really helped me with my craft and figuring out how this works — answering questions. They put on great conferences, so I would listen to agents and editors talk. I went to the late, great Karen Blumenthal in Texas. I went to a nonfiction conference she spoke at. She laid it out on the [issue] of money. She taught [about] the money side of the business. She talked about contracts. You know, and that was a whole side of the business. You have to learn the craft side, but you better know the business side, and if you don't know, then you are going to get taken advantage of. I had come from universities and nonprofits and they have to disclose a lot about the way they operate. That is not so with trade publishing. And I think that is something we still struggle with today. That is, how do we have equity in a situation where you haven't had access to and you don't know much about, and people are not forthcoming? You have to have those authors or those illustrators who are willing to share that information with you. Because I hear that even people in, you know, MFA programs aren't really getting that stuff taught to them. That's disturbing, right? Because it creates a huge barrier. I would say, those folks really have been my role models. They were people who had come from various walks of life. They were not necessarily people who had been English majors or creative writing majors and they had been able to get published. I was like, "Okay, surely, I can figure this out and just do the work necessary and read and write," and so that's what I did.

AJ: Again, my path was kind of winding in a lot of ways, so the role models I gained were, first of all, the authors and illustrators. Because I kind of entered into this field through making connections with contemporary people in the field, just reaching out through social media and getting to know some of these awesome illustrators at conferences, while simultaneously really getting to know librarians across the country. In a lot of ways I am grateful for the connections I've made through ALA (American Library Association) because they have allowed me to find this rich community connecting with you both, connecting with people [like] Sujei Lugo (Boston Public Library) and Sam Bloom (Cincinnati Public Library) and many people who are willing to take me in and show me [and who] introduced me to this whole world I had no idea existed. I just knew I would go into a bookstore and there's a *shiny* medal on these books. And I didn't know what that meant and there's a lot of learning that way. I definitely learned through practitioners, I guess you would say in the field of librarianship. I'd also give a lot of credit to people who inspired me, like Dr. Rudine Sims Bishop. She still inspires me, and just through her work and also her care and deep love for children, especially children of color and the experiences they have while reading. I think those are my major inspirations, and they continue to be my peers — the people I work with. My colleagues.

SAR: Could you describe some of your childhood experiences as a reader? How did you learn about the world through books?

AJ: I have always been surrounded by books. I still am. My father was a *big* reader and was always reading a book. And my parents. I'm grateful that early on, they took the time to give me books, but also to take me places to pick my own books, so to have that agency of finding stories that I related to. I have talked to friends about this topic quite a lot, you know, especially what books we connected to when we were little. And for me it always goes back to John Steptoe's with *Mufaro's Beautiful Daughters* (1987). That is one that I still have. One that I connect to deeply. The styling is beautiful, but it showed me the idea of African royalty and beauty and storytelling. Also, I was really into the *Addy* books, the American Girl series, as a lot of us were in the early 90s. I really connected to those stories and those depictions of Blackness — through a slavery narrative. I have always had a close connection to books and I will say I grew up in the mid-90s really when I started to bloom as a reader. I was lucky in that that was kind of the period where we were starting to get a little more multicultural lit right? And so there wasn't a lot, but I have some good examples of where I could see myself and connect to those types of images.

TS: My mom and my grandma and her mother were always swapping books and reading, and so it was just something that I grew up with being very normalized. Now, those could be Erma Bombeck, you know, funny comedy, life of women type books. They could be romance novels. They could be all kinds of different things — mystery, crime, thrillers, whatever they were reading. They would swap those back and forth so that was what I thought people did for fun. This is just part of their lifestyle. My dad was not a reader and that's largely because he was allowed to graduate high school functionally illiterate. So he was not able to read stories to us. My mom helped him learn to be a reader. But my mom told us a lot of stories before bedtime and then she'd also read books to us. She'd read a chapter a night. And I loved that part of school — it was my favorite part of the day when, after lunch, the teacher would read you a book — or a chapter — you know, after lunch time. Because the power of story is: It unifies you as a group, but it also sparks your imagination, right? I love that.

Unfortunately, what I didn't have any exposure to, though, were any books that represent my community and or any really Native community actualized in its humanity. There were no discussions of, you know, Native families, Native communities, Native sovereignty ... anything that would have reflected anything I was experiencing growing up. The depictions that were there were completely nothing I identified with. I mean, if you would have asked me, I wouldn't have said those people were Native, right? I mean because it was kind of this Western thing — something over there — that doesn't compute. Because that's how hollow and one-dimensional those stereotypical depictions were. What I really learned as a reader were certainly those kind of coming of age stories or just the first time something happens to you [stories]. I enjoyed the adventures of *Ramona* by [Beverly] Cleary. Judy Blume's books. I was like, "Who are these people that live in tall buildings and these kids that have no yards?" I couldn't understand getting in an elevator to go to your house. It just blew my mind that they would have no animals. I mean when Peter gets the fish in *Tales of a Fourth Grade Nothing* (1972) it's this big deal. I'm thinking [we've got] chickens and we've got horses. We lived in the country — even when we lived in town, we still had pets. So there were definitely ways that I learned that kids were living very differently than the one I was living. But overall they were always portals or you know other dimensions that I felt I entered. It was nothing that looked like my life. Even though they weren't sci-fi that way and that's not what I was reading, it always felt like you are in this otherworldly place.

SAR: What motivates you to continue working in this field?

AJ: The kids. Like literally everything that I do, from when I started lecturing, when I started talking to librarians and trying to get them to think about what they do. The kids always center my work. Because we wouldn't be here, if not for thinking about their needs and caring about how they see themselves — caring about and listening for what *they* want. I think when it gets frustrating . . . when I need to take a break from social media, I think what grounds me is really thinking about these youth populations who will be reading this work, hopefully, who will be getting more of this good content if we continue going the way we need to. So yeah, kids always ground me. And the kids that I worked with in the library and the kids that I will never meet you know that, hopefully, will benefit from some of the things I've been able to talk to these educators and librarians about.

TS: I would absolutely echo that. Because, like I say, what started with my son as a kind of my entry point and being concerned with what other Cherokee children and their families, and then, by extension, other Native families. [Asking] teachers and librarians, what are they putting on the shelves, what are they reading? And really being aghast at the fact that as my son entered school, the K-12 curriculum hadn't changed since I was younger. So, I'm going, "Okay, so fiction and nonfiction are both really problematic, and I want young people, whether they're walking into their public library, whether they're walking into a bookstore . . . whether it's their classroom, you know, whatever it is, I want them to have a rich variety of books." With accuracy in them, right? With cultural accuracy in full bodied humans. And the only way I know to do that is to stay focused on the fact that they don't have what they need yet. They've got more than they've had previously, but it's still a paucity of books available compared to where we need to be. That is true across BIPOC communities in general. When you have the majority of your population that are under 18 in this country that now reflect the population around the world, meaning they're not majority white here, just as we have not been majority white around the globe forever. Okay, this is the time to say we are so far behind we have got to start reflecting who our readers are. Right? Because you're not preparing them for the future. Now, again, I don't want to be overly negative about this, but you have to on some level acknowledge that it's intentional ignorance. I mean you could even say it's diabolical, that we have not recognized these population shifts, which have been happening for a while. Because people generally under the age of 30, if we look at the census, are non-white. It's not just our youth that we're writing for right now, or for the books that are coming in a few years, this has been happening for a while and we (collectively in terms of curriculum on the educational side or on the trade publishing side) moved to where we need to be going and change. I realize it happens slowly, but at the same time some days it doesn't feel like it's happening.

To Alia's point, I stay focused on the kids and how I can help other people enter this industry and provide that content. But I also want to see a widening of who is publishing books. More tribal presses, more independent presses owned by Native people, etc. Because the trade folks ... You can open up any *Publishers Weekly*, *The Children's Bookshelf* emails on a Tuesday or Thursday that come free to anybody who wants it, and you still see a lot of whiteness announced every week. We cannot depend on them to do what needs to be done. Which is unfortunate, I don't know if you have to go to mandates, or what. But when I start thinking about that and I get really discouraged, I go okay, the kids, I gotta stay focused on the kids. And encourage them to tell their stories and encourage them to bring their art and to share with the world. Because it's not about just what we're getting published right now, it's that, "Are we making a place for them to be able to do that?"

AJ: I wanted to piggyback on what you said, Traci. I feel like one good thing about what we both do is that we both know the experience of working directly with kids. Also, we understand money is a big part of this industry. You, as a person who is actively creating these books and me as a former bookseller literally seeing what comes in every week, seeing what sells, being told what books to push, but also on the flip side, having worked with these people in these spaces and seeing when a kid comes in and sees that book on the shelf and gets excited.

When a parent or grandparent comes in and they are of color, and specifically they see me as a person of color and they say, "Oh, it's cool. We might be able to get some good stuff today." I am able to give them what they were looking for. That matters. Yes, it's about money, we know that it's all about capitalism. But at the end of the day, it's about those connections in getting these books into the hands of people who need them.

TS: And piggybacking off that whole thing about capitalism, it's like, "Okay so, then the majority of your people are BIPOC, right? And so you need to have books that represent them right because they're the ones who are buying and reading the books." And yet there's stereotypes that only white kids and white families are somehow interested in reading. Even though that's completely been disproven. And not recently. There are still marketing and sales decisions that feel like they're being made off of that premise and in terms of whether the books are acquired or again how they're pushed out into the world and marketed and sold. You know, like Alia's point, what gets placed [book] face out at the bookstore, and publishers decide those things. They pay fees to have [books] face out versus not. I mean all that stuff. It's intentional, it's intentional.

AJ: It's like there's a very conscious disconnect between what's actually happening in the world and what publishers are willing to do.

TS: I mean it feels like it mirrors the political system, right? Where you have politicians who are very out of touch with what is the day-to-day reality of the populace. Much the same in the trade field and it's so strange to me. Not strange in that I didn't see it in the "people in the ivory tower" kind of thing [as opposed to who are the actual people in the world]. But I guess being in nonprofits just prior to this and doing those services and seeing the needs, I'm like, "Y'all need to get on the sidewalk and start observing what is happening and get with the program now." It's the lives that our kids are living and what they lack. Because you can walk into any bookstore, library, classroom and see what they're lacking.

Marilisa Jimenez Garcia: I love the naming of institutions. I think that that's something we would like to see more of in children's literature, right? Instead of, "[This notion] that this is just happening in the industry. People are doing things and making choices." So I think this is a collection where we would like to hold those institutions accountable and visibilize those institutions more and center the voices of those that end up seeing those consequences. My questions are about growing the field, and thinking through those frameworks, and the roles of academics, practitioners, and publishers . . . also some of these folks never talk to each other, right? How can the academic-practitioner-publisher relationship be more fruitful? How can that be a more fruitful conversation? How can those people work together a little bit more?

TS: What's interesting to me is that if you look at how things work in other industries, you'll have the government come together with nonprofits with private companies and they will have a task force. They'll have people that are exchanging these ideas and writing papers. They'll have policy forums. I'm used to that. Here, I don't see that in the industry ... like upper level professionals sitting and talking with scholars and talking with creators about how to move things forward. It's so strange to me because, again, we're not publishing for adults. We're publishing for people that, by and large, other people are acquiring the books and making them available to them. It's a different audience than those who are just buying for their own consumption, you know. Children by and large are going to depend on those around them to give them access to the books, whether it's buying them at the bookstore, buying them to stock in the library or in their classroom or whatever it is. So why aren't those conversations happening? Why aren't their task forces about, how do we take this research and integrate it into our sales and marketing plan? Not that I want the industry to start pushing what people research and things. I'm not trying to go down that road, because I want people to have the freedom to do what they want to do, but there's a lot of good work that can be done with those intersections and the synergies there, and so it baffles me that what a practitioner, say, such as myself who is in schools, in libraries, is listening to readers, is talking with teachers and librarians — there's information there that could help academia. It could help publishing, sales, and marketing editorial folks. I want to go, "Why isn't this happening?" I think the models have already been established in other places, but it just hasn't been applied here and it seems like the perfect place for it to happen because of who our audiences are and the fact that they are not buying this literature on their own.

AJ: I think, for me, what I have seen modeled has definitely been more of a conversation between academia and libraries just based on my experience talking with you all right now, but also thinking about how involved academics such as Dr. Ebony Elizabeth Thomas or Sarah Park Dahlen [are]. I have kind of a different idea of how, at least in kid lit, in literature, in children's studies, there seems to be an effort to have this cross conversation, which is good. We obviously need more of that, but I can see it happening.

The part that is the roadblock to me is publishing. And it's almost like publishing knows that it doesn't have to open its doors, and so it won't. And I've had direct conversations with publishers and editors at conferences. I've been like, "We need more transparency. What's going on?" And I can't get a straight answer and it's almost like they know they don't have to be held accountable as these institutions. And therefore things continue to be the way that they are. Remember, Traci, we did that "Racism in Kid Lit" thing in New York City that was put on by a publisher a couple years ago. And they brought all these people out to discuss racism and "What's happening in the industry?" All this stuff is great, but what came of it? I couldn't tell you. It's a lot of going through the motions. Until I see publishing really being transparent and open about how they are a problem — their problems, such as keeping people of color, hiring people of color, you know, promoting and making people feel like they're welcome in these spaces. Because it all affects the content that we end up getting for our kids. Lee & Low has the Diversity Baseline Survey, which is great, but we need more. And until we really have that I don't think that we're going to really be able to get these conversations. I know they're hearing them because we see those slight uptick [of books published stats] and the quantity and the quality of books. But we are not getting any feedback, I feel. And that also is connected to institutions like the CCBC (Cooperative Children's Book Center) who does amazing work, and has done for a long time. They publish all the stats, and then their position is kind of, "Well, there you go." And publishing is like, "Okay." What are these conversations that actually need to happen to actually get things happening? You can't just be like, "here you go" and then walk away. We need more direct conversation.

TS: It's almost like we need an annual "State of Kid Lit address" where someone calls together the press and says, "Here is our data. Here are our numbers. Look at how many problematic books are still in these categories and yet." Where is that "State of the Kid Lit" national address so that this is a focal point. A point of high [policy] awareness.

MJG: It's almost an inability to recognize how political a medium children's literature really is. I'm going to shift now more specifically to Native or Indigenous studies in children's lit. How can the field grow in terms of Native scholarship and criticisms, specifically? How can Native lit be more intersectional? How can we have more diversity within diversity?

AJ: We need exactly what you just said: more diversity. As far as whose voices are being heard, I mean just to be completely clear, a lot of people go to *American Indians in Children's Literature*, which is a very good resource, but if we're really going to start talking about the diversity in this field, we need more people to be writing about and analyzing children's literature beyond one person. Because you can't get a multitude of perspectives and understanding if there's one person controlling the narrative of what criticism and analysis of Native children's lit.

I always think: how do we build [youth literature scholarship] in Native studies programs, especially tribal colleges? How are we encouraging Native students to start their own blogs and get into putting their voice out there? How do we get Native academics to come over to the children's lit side too and start giving us some of your opinions on what is being published and what has been published? My opinion: there needs to be more voices. Because I think what we see is that when we have one voice, people, especially people who are non-Native and non-BIPOC, tend to flock to that one voice to get an understanding of what they think indigenity is, and especially indigeneity in kid lit. And we need more diversity. Period.

TS: You know, we have 574 federally recognized Native Nations, which means those are Native Nations that have formal relationships with the United States. Then you have tribes that have signed treaties that the US Senate never ratified. So a lot of tribes in California are not recognized because the Senate didn't recognize those treaties. Why? Because then the [government] would have had to have been beholden to them and honor very rich lands that those tribes had as ancestral homelands and still live on today. Then there are other groups that are state recognized. It's a very layered and complex history. And the majority of scholars and many Native people have no real in-depth understanding about that, but we need folks who do. To be writing in this field, we need folks who have that background in Native studies that have studied history and political science. Also, in our Native studies courses, in our literature courses, students will read books that are written by Native authors for adults, but we also don't have them read children's literature, which is important because that is where identity outside of family and community is being formed. I mean I didn't learn about tribes outside of mine, other than the Shawnee and Delaware which I grew up around, until I was in college. And then I learned about the systematic laws put in place right that impacted all of these different Native nations, some of the things that happened to mine happened to others, which I didn't even realize. So we need people with that kind of appreciation. It's fine to have people with a background in education or in libraries, but, because of our weird dual-citizenship status, first of our Native nations, and second of the United States, we have a completely different political and legal status in this country. We are subject to criminal and civil laws on a tribal level, on a federal level, sometimes on a state level, depending on the state you live. Again, people do not know this.

Many Native people cannot write about this because they don't know it, so that helps in terms of whether you are also accurately evaluating children's literature on these topics. I read a lot of stuff that's written by Native people, and it needs to have [a complex analysis of the laws and citizenship] in there. But, I know they don't know since they are coming through our educational system, it wasn't something they studied in college. We have a need for more people coming from a really good background in history of tribes and understanding differences between them. Again, one person or two people in that team can't understand or be experts on everyone. And it shouldn't be expected to be on [one person], but there's just such a lack of analysis that goes into it. The other thing is knowledge of craft which is a huge part of writing criticism. In terms of Native scholars, those who are writing about our books, there is really no discussion of craft.

AJ: I wanted to add [that because of how] stuffy academia and libraries are, "mommy blogs" are a big thing. [In other words] people are creating their own content about how they feel about books. I'm reminded of the work that *Children of the Glades* [Indigenous youth blog in Florida] is doing. You have these Native teens who are enjoying, reviewing, and thinking critically about books and the craft and art of storytelling. Going back to the importance of mommy blogs, they do move the needle. As a blogger, I've seen how these publishers prey sometimes on pitting bloggers against each other, for, you know, getting the exclusivity of being able to review books. So there's kind of this weird relationship between publishers meeting reviewers and bloggers. But is there really a beneficial relationship both ways? I don't know, but seeing how these readers are really moving [audiences] to pick up these books, I would hope to see publishers do more work in reaching out to Native readers of all types: parents, caregivers, students, and Native studies teams, and more teen bloggers who are up to date [on the market] to get their opinion [in terms of] what they are reading and putting that information out there and also compensating them.

TS: It's also a matter of us [as writers and scholars] kind of reaching out and trying to help facilitate this. But I don't even know all the options there are out there. I feel like Instagram is a much better way to learn about Native books or Bookstagram. That's where I found a number of Native moms and other Native readers who are writing, but there has to be a way to help them grow their platform.

MJG: We have been talking a lot about how to grow Native studies and whose voices seem missing from the conversation . . . what kinds of stories do you think are missing for Native peoples? And I am thinking about intersectional lives and not essentializing what "Native" means. Both of you have an expertise in the picture-book medium. Why is the picture book important for Native representation, and who's missing from Native stories?

AJ: I think picture books are universally appreciated and loved for their art. I think it's a natural reaction for people of all ages to connect to a well thought out and beautifully created book of pictures that has a story that threads everything together. For me, I've just been drawn to picture books, not only all my life, but especially as I've been in the bookseller and librarian field. I just have seen the power of people walking into a library and seeing that cover art and being immediately drawn to those visual narratives. I think we're all just drawn to art in general across cultures. If it moves us, we are more inclined to pick it up and dive into the story. We've seen how educators have used picture books across age ranges in the classroom, in different ways, and it's a testament to the depth of the types of picture books that we're getting and we've had in the past that are tackling some really important, and sometimes difficult, topics and in very deep ways. [You can even see how] back matter is its own separate beautiful part of picture books that don't get enough love. As far as what's missing, it's like what you said, intersectionality. We need more of that in Native kid lit. A big part of what I hope to study in grad school is the intersection of Black[ness] and Indigeneity. Afro-indigenous stories and lives and thoughts and how kid lit can be enriched by thinking in a more intersectional way. Black and Native people are rich in many ways, so we just don't have really much at all, and not enough of that in Native kid lit. With all types of kid lit, we need more Native kid lit that talks about and explores sexuality and gender and our two-spirit communities. There's just no way that being more intersectional is going to ever be a bad thing for Native kid lit. It is the direction we have to go to make up for these historical inaccuracies and this historical harm that a lot of these representations have done through caricature and stereotypes. We have to go this [intersectional] way.

TS: In terms of picture books, often it's the picture book that kids see first. It's their first introduction to books and reading. Some will get board books but picture books really are the entry point for the majority of kids whether that's a story time at the library when they're very little or Head Start or pre-K program or in their house. And we know how powerful images are. So for me it is critical and I don't care if it's fiction or nonfiction. Those images need to be accurate, because for so long, the representations have been inaccurate and you've planted that seed early. I have a particular love for picture books because I want to reach children early and want them to have accurate information. If you're going to be entertained by a story, if you're going to learn something, whatever your experiences with that book, I do not want to further what has come before that has been problematic. We also reach those that are older that have been miseducated and we can bring them into the fold more quickly to realize what has been lacking — where the gaps are — with a picture book. It's a very succinct lyrical language where you are getting images that often go beyond the words, so it is two stories in one. And that is often more powerful than asking someone to go through a book of prose. What is also missing is also just more creators — bringing in more voices and their experiences.

AJ: In [our] work, we need to do more careful curation of past works because what I've seen as a practitioner in libraries is a lack of care for what is being put on the shelves, what is being picked for story times, and displays and programs given to children. A lot of people who do not understand Native kid lit, Native stories literally do not care to make sure they pick up a book that's accurate, that is contemporary, that is by a native author. In the first place, they use all of these past books, many of them, which are harmful, which are anthologies, which are retellings by white people ... they don't care enough — that's the key — they don't care enough to vet that content in their collection. So we need more people who care enough to vet out these books that are in a lot of ways harmful, to get rid of them from your collection. Prioritize collection development that cares and centers stories from the heart and written by Indigenous people over just picking up a book from 1994 that was written by white person. Librarians can't just be willing to do the work; they have to *care* enough to do the work.

TS: I would definitely say going forward that the Youth Media Awards of the American Library Association are getting some things right. They are taking books from everyone. Independent presses, Native-owned, small presses ... they get books from everyone so their content is so much richer than the majority of award lists. In terms of diversity, I don't really see young people using diversity. They know what their intersections of [identity] are. "Diversity" is really for the Gen-Xers and maybe the millennials who are older now. This generation, this is just their reality, and they are looking at this and saying, "Where is the equity? Where is the inclusion?" But they don't have whiteness as the majority. The systems around them still center whiteness, heterosexuality, male dominance, but they themselves are much more conscious of each other and themselves in ways that we were not.

AJ: I want to add to what you're just saying with diversity. On the flip side, the whole movement [in 2020] to move away from the term "own voices" kind of put a bad taste in my mouth, a little bit. I understand why people felt the need to move away from it. But I also know that a lot, especially a lot of young people, really gravitated toward that term, especially BIPOC people, to find content that they needed. It's almost like we've kind of shifted more toward the middle again with the term diversity. There is a collective abandonment of the term "own voices." We tend to shift toward the middle instead of thinking about terminology that helps us find the content that we need, especially our youth. But also going back to the kids, if this work we do is really for kids, then are we hearing the stories that they want? Are we listening to them tell us what it is they want to read? What is it they don't see we're publishing? Are we centering their needs and their desires? On the flip side, are we doing what we can to encourage them to write their own stories published, even without traditional publishing? Are we doing enough?

MJG: Which goes back to the heart of ethnic studies because it is all about centering students and youth as intellectuals.

References

Adoff, Arnold, and Emily Arnold. *Black Is Brown Is Tan.* Harper Collins, 1973.

Blume, Judy. *Tales of a Fourth Grade Nothing.* Dutton, 1972.

Children of the Glades. *Indigo's Bookshelf: Voices of Native Youth.* https://indigosbookshelf.blogspot.com/. Accessed March 29, 2023.

Cleary, Beverly. The Ramona Books. HarperCollins, 1955–1999.

Reese, Debbie. *American Indians in Children's Literature.* https://americanindiansinchildrensliterature.blogspot.com/.

Porter, Connie Rose. *Meet Addy: American Girl Series.* Scholastic, 1994.

Steptoe, John. *Mufaro's Beautiful Daughters: An African Tale.* Scholastic, 1987.

University of Berkley, Native Studies program: https://guide.berkeley.edu/undergraduate/degree-programs/native-american-studies/. Accessed March 29, 2023.

SECTION 3

Community Frameworks

SEVEN

African American Children's Literature

THE FIRST 100 YEARS (REPRINT)
Violet J. Harris

Editor's note: I (Marilisa) first met Dr. Violet Harris as part of the National Council for Teachers of English Cultivating New Voices Among Scholars of Color Fellowship. The two-year fellowship allows current students, recent graduate students, and junior faculty to work with a seasoned mentor in literature, literacy, and reading studies. I remember seeing Violet Harris's name on the list of possible mentors, and I immediately placed a neat "X" next to her name, still thinking she might not have the time. I was overjoyed when I got the envelope and letter listing her name next to mine as a mentor-mentee pair in the program. The first time I met her was in Washington, DC, in 2014 at our first CNV institute. I remember standing in front of my poster board with my research notes and charts taped up behind me and trying to get my words out just right for Dr. Harris. She listened to me quietly but then completely blew me away with all of her keen insights on my work. Dr. Harris's work in gathering other scholars such Rudine Sims Bishop, Debbie Reese, and Sonia Nieto in her volume *Multicultural Children's Literature in the K-8 Classroom* inspired this volume in part.

Harris is one of the first scholars in youth literature to apply a historiographical analysis to Black children's literature — she was one of the first to tell us how, why, when, and what it meant for the larger field. Her career is also marked by her ability to publish in multiple disciplines, noting the importance of rigorous study of Black children's literature in Black studies. The following reprint is her essay in the *Journal of Negro Education,* published in 1991, where Harris lays out the case for understanding the intertwining of Black history, Black literacies, education, and children's literature. Harris's methods employ what we call community frameworks by narrating the history of children's literature from the perspective of the Black community and placing that intellectual legacy front and center.

Introduction

African Americans have been depicted in general literature since the seventeenth century. Essentially, the depictions are stereotyped, pejorative, and unauthentic (Brown; Baker; Broderick; Sims). Literature created by African Americans for children first appeared in the late nineteenth century. This literature has never been a central component of schooling. Not unlike that of African American literature written for adults, African American children's literature has a tumultuous past, including limited awareness among readers; circumscribed publication and distribution; omission from libraries, school, and bookstores; and uninformed criticism. Several factors contribute to this state of affairs, but one important factor is the existence of literary canons.

Canons, or sanctioned lists of works perpetuated by critics, educators, and cultural guardians, constitute the literature many students read. For example, in primary school, students read "classics" such as Beatrix Potter's *The Tale of Peter Rabbit*, Watty Piper's *The Little Engine That Could*, and Robert McCloskey's *Make Way for Duckling*s. Elementary school students tend to read classics such as Laura Ingalls Wilder's *Little House on the Prairie*, Katherine Paterson's *Bridge to Terebithia*, and E. B. White's *Charlotte's Web*. By the time most students have graduated from high school they will have read books from a canon that includes Nathaniel Hawthorne's *The Scarlet Letter*, William Golding's *Lord of the Flies*, and other works deemed necessary for cultural literacy. Unfortunately, literary canons tend to include a preponderance of books that reflect the experiences, values, perspectives, knowledge, and interpretations of Whites, particularly Anglo-Saxons. Few texts written by African Americans or other people of color are designated classics, even though many exhibit extraordinary literary merit, expand or reinterpret literary forms, or provide a forum for voices silenced or ignored in mainstream literature. The vast majority of students do not read African American classics such as *Roll of Thunder, Hear My Cry* by Mildred D. Taylor or *M. C. Higgins, the Great* by Virginia Hamilton because literary canons perpetuated in schools have become a part of a selective tradition. The same cultural processes that have led to the development of selective traditions have tended to ignore the contributions of African Americans to children's literature.

The purposes of this chapter are to examine, broadly, the historical development of literature written for African American children from the late nineteenth century to the present, to discuss possible trends in African American children's literature, and to assess the value of that literature to literacy education. Explanation of and justification for the development of African American children's literature is evident when one examines the selective tradition in children's literature and the depiction of African Americans within that tradition.

The Selective Tradition in Children's Literature

Because literature is a valued cultural commodity, traditions evolve around its definitions, functions, and value (Williams). The same holds true for children's literature, which is indeed a valuable and valued cultural commodity. Children's literature serves the important role of mediator between children, cultural knowledge, and socialization by adults. Moreover, because children's literature has long maintained this traditional role in society, it possesses both symbolic and real power. However, when a tradition is selective or, worse, when it sets up inaccurate and damaging stereotypes, the meanings and knowledge shaped by it become significant because they shape individuals' perceptions of the world and their roles in it.

The selective tradition in children's literature regarding African Americans has been replete with stereotypes. Critic Sterling Brown analyzed the images of African Americans in American literature and determined that the literary depictions of African Americans entertained Whites and, when combined with prevailing theological arguments and "scientific" data from the social sciences, provided literary justification for institutionalized racism. As Brown concluded, "[T]he Negro has met with as great injustice in American literature as he has in American life. The majority of books about Negroes merely stereotype Negro character" (180). Brown identified seven prevalent stereotypes of African Americans in literature and in the works of the literary canon: "the contented slave," "the wretched freeman," "the comic Negro," "the brute Negro," "the tragic mulatto," "the local-color Negro," and "the exotic primitive."

Each of these stereotypes existed in children's literature as well. For instance, Martha Finley's *Elsie Dinsmore*, a tale of a pious planter's daughter, abounds with contented slaves, one of whom is Elsie's faithful "Mammy," Aunt Chloe. Aunt Chloe epitomizes endurance, strong religious convictions, and loyalty to the slave system. The following excerpt captures the relationship between Aunt Chloe and Elsie and the attributes of the contented slave:

> [Aunt Chloe:] My precious pet, my darlin' chile, your ole mammy loves you better dan life; an' did my darlin forget de almighty Friend dat says, "I have loved thee with an everlasting love, an' I will never leave thee, nor forsake thee"? (64-65)

Indeed, most early literary texts that depict slavery present it in this manner or as an idyllic institution; few portray the horrors of slavery. Another example of a stereotype in children's literature is the comic Negro. African American males are usually the victims of that stereotype, whereupon they are depicted as dim-witted children who constantly grin, eat, misunderstand simple directions, and scratch their heads. For example, in Sara Cone Bryant's *Epaminondas and His Auntie*, the male slave Epaminondas is depicted as inherently stupid:

> O' Epaminondas, Epaminondas, you ain't got the sense you was born with; you never will have the sense you was born with! Now I ain't gwine tell you any more ways to bring truck home. (14)

Such texts were not aberrations or exceptions; they were typical of their time. Many remain in circulation today as reprints or are available in libraries. Other copies are passed down within families as treasured artifacts. For example, a graduate student of mine recently refused to sell me her copy of Blanche Seale Hunt's *Little Brown Koko*, a book similar to *Epaminondas and His Auntie*, because the former was one of her favorite books as a child and one that she recently shared with her own children.

Perhaps the one book that cemented stereotyped images of African Americans in popular culture is Helen Bannerman's *The Story of Little Black Sambo*. For many, primarily Whites, the title engenders fond memories. While some will admit their embarrassment for liking the story, a few still defend their childhood reactions and admit they do not understand the negative reactions of African Americans to the story. By contrast, some African Americans conjure up images of discrimination, name-calling, and grotesque caricatures of their race's physical features when references to the book are made. Many also remember their own acute embarrassment when the story was read or recall their intense anger when they themselves might have been referred to as "Sambo." An examination of the text, particularly the illustrations, demonstrates the validity of African Americans' responses. In some of the editions, the illustrations show Black people as simian-like or with protruding eyes; large, red lips; extremely dark skin; and, in the case of males, long, gangly arms.

Again, one cannot label a book such as *Little Black Sambo* atypical; rather, it is a typical depiction. Stereotypes of African Americans are pervasive in all aspects of American culture. For example, businesses adopted the "mammy" and "uncle" stereotypes to sell pancakes, hot cereal, and other commodities. Further, movies such as *The Birth of a Nation* aided in the entrenchment of stereotypes, and the literary images were reinforced in school texts from elementary schooling through university training. For example, Elson notes that African Americans are portrayed in social studies and science texts as intellectually and physically inferior to all other racial groups. The very pervasiveness of the stereotypes in all aspects of life suggests that African American children have difficulty encountering literature or other cultural artifacts that portray them truthfully. Additionally, the sociocultural milieu of the early periods did not bode well for the creation and distribution of authentic literature. Those who desired to offer alternative images had to battle against the institutions and processes involved in the development of popular culture.

The Beginnings of a New Tradition: 1890–1900

Recent research suggests that literature for African American children did not appear until the 1890s (Fraser; Muse). Nonetheless, it is probable that some African American religious, social, fraternal, or economic organizations created literature for children prior to this period. Quite possibly, those works languish in attics, rare bookstores, or archives. Many extant copies no longer exist; they survive only as references noted in equally obscure texts. For example, in *The Horizon,* an early twentieth-century periodical published by W. E. B. DuBois, an advertisement appeared for a periodical for African American children titled *The Young Set.* However, a search of periodical catalogs and archival holdings reveals no evidence that the magazine was ever published.

Thus far, early writers and contemporary researchers cite the work of Mrs. A. E. Johnson in the 1890s as the beginnings of African American children's literature (Penn; Fraser; Muse).[1] Johnson's first novel, *Clarence and Corinne; or, God's Way,* usually is cited as the first work by an African American writing in this genre. Johnson's novel parallels similar didactic and moral tracts published for children in the nineteenth century. The implicit purpose of the novel was not necessarily to entertain but to promote piety, obedience, refinement, and morality among children and convince them of the virtues of achieving stable middle-class status and sensibility. As in other texts of this type, the central characters are members of the working poor who achieve middle-class status through perseverance and hard work. Clarence and Corinne are energetic, intelligent, hopeful, and ambitious. Clarence wants to attend school, and his adoring sister shares his desire. Like other heroes and heroines, Clarence and Corinne do not abandon their dreams. They experience a series of vicissitudes and victories and ultimately overcome their poverty-stricken beginnings to achieve respect, education, marriage, and middle-class status.

Despite its designation as the first African American children's novel, Clarence and Corinne is not strictly for African American children, nor is it strictly a novel of African American experiences even though the author was African American. Johnson's novel features White characters. For whatever reasons, she chose not to portray African American experiences. Perhaps she was trying to write a "color-blind" novel, yet the sociocultural milieu of her time may have dictated the presentation of White characters. A more suitable candidate for the designation of the first African American children's book is Paul Laurence Dunbar's *Little Brown Baby,* a collection of dialect poems first published in 1895. The poetry is generally of good quality but difficult reading for children because of the orthographic representation of the dialect. An excerpt from the work demonstrates the linguistic facility needed to recite the title poem:

> Little brown baby wif spa'klin' eyes
> Come to yo' pappy an' set on his knee.

> What you been doin', suh-makin' san' pies?
> Look at dat bib-you's ez du'ty ez me. (3)

To his credit, Dunbar's dialect does not resemble the inaccurate language evident in other stories such as Page's *Two Little Confederates*. On the whole, Dunbar's poetry is humorous, nonpolitical, nonreligious, and generally concerned with mundane topics. The collection seems more an appreciation of African American folk culture than an attempt to garner or inspire racial pride, solidarity, or uplift in an overt manner. For some, Dunbar's dialect poetry, with its comical situations and whimsical characters, harkens to the stereotype of the comic Negro. For others, *Little Brown Baby* is a celebration of, or at least a homage to, African American folk culture and a subtle celebration of racial pride.

Arguably, one hesitates to discuss themes and motifs in the African American children's literature of the nineteenth century for the simple fact that only two works qualify.[2] Nevertheless, some themes and motifs appear consistently in both. For example, perseverance, love of family, goodness, and kindness are emphasized. Simple pleasures such as dances, church activities, and picnics rather than elaborate, expensive activities are those deemed to bring joy. However, *Clarence and Corinne*, a text in which religious didacticism dominates, does not radiate the ebullient tone of *Little Brown Baby*.

Dunbar's and Johnson's books both have entertainment, socialization, educational, and aesthetic value, yet to a certain extent that value was limited by the historical period during which the books were published. The majority of African American children during that time were illiterate; few could have encountered the texts in their schooling because major strictures were placed on the funding, curricula, and type of schooling provided for African Americans (Anderson). Given the immense popularity Dunbar enjoyed and the secular nature of his works, it is likely that more African American children were introduced to his work. Nevertheless, both Johnson's and Dunbar's works are notable as antecedents of an alternative literary tradition. The expansion of that tradition occurred as more African Americans became literate and came to view literature as an important element of schooling.

An Emergent Tradition: 1900–1920

The expansion of the new literary tradition awaited the development of an educated African American middle class that demanded culturally authentic literature for African American children. Enhancement of the new tradition also necessitated the emergence of an educated group of people interested in writing as a vocation or avocation. It also depended on the further development of African American publishers and changes in attitudes among White publishers. These necessary preconditions emerged during the early 1900s. In comparison to the previous period, a veritable flood of texts appeared. Some were readers (books used for literacy instruction) such as *Floyd's Flowers* (Floyd) and *The Upward Path* (Pritchard and Ovington). Others were traditional works of fiction.

Many of the texts published during this period can be labeled oppositional texts; that is, they are works that contradict a theme, motif, or stereotype. For instance, Mary White Ovington, a White radical who was associated with the National Association for the Advancement of Colored People (NAACP) for a number of years, wrote two significant oppositional texts: *Hazel* and *Zeke*. Her books were published by the Crisis Publishing Company, an enterprise of the NAACP, and advertised in *The Crisis*, the NAACP's official publication, and in *The Brownies' Book*, a periodical for children published by DuBois in 1920 and 1921.

Hazel details the activities of a middle-class African American child who is pretty, intelligent, cultured, and kind. Hazel, the protagonist, experiences few racial strictures growing up in Boston. She does not encounter racial prejudice until she visits her grandmother in rural Alabama; however, following her grandmother's wisdom, she handles it in a thoughtful manner and decides to dedicate her life to the eradication of prejudice. By contrast, *Zeke* focuses on rural African Americans in the South. Zeke is a poor boy from Alabama who rises to middle-class status and respectability after attending a Tuskegee-like school. A few of the characters from *Hazel* appear in *Zeke* (i.e., Hazel reappears as the refined colored benefactress who aids Zeke and motivates him to achieve).

As forerunners of an emerging tradition, Hazel and Zeke provide more authentic depictions of African Americans but also contain a few stereotypes, some more positive than others. For example, colorism is an aspect of Hazel. While Hazel is depicted as light-skinned with straight hair, her best friend Charity is portrayed as a "pickaninny": dark-skinned, plain, mischievous, and poor. Refinement, restraint, beauty, and moderation are embodied within the character most resembling Whites, and indolence, passion, lack of restraint, and physical plainness are embodied within the darker character. As Brown argues, this dichotomous stereotype was quite extensive in American literature, as evidenced by the number of novels featuring "tragic" mulattoes.

Nonetheless, Ovington attempted to provide African American children with truthful cultural images, entertain them, imbue them with racial pride, and inform them of the achievements of their race. Like earlier writers, she often included didactic asides and vignettes in her novels, and they contain frank discussions about lynching and negative racial attitudes. Quite clearly, Ovington created her work specifically for African American children. She tried to apprise them of the sociocultural realities they faced and attempted to offer them a model of social interaction. The value of Ovington's works is apparent: Her books were among the few alternatives to the stereotyped images of African Americans, and they represent the continued development of an emergent tradition.

Refinement and expansion of the new tradition in the 1920s evolved from the work of W. E. B. DuBois. As evidenced in his powerful essays in *The Souls of Black Folk* and *Dusk of Dawn*, DuBois long held a special interest in children. In the realm of children's literature, DuBois's most important contribution was the formation of the DuBois and Dill Publishing Company with Augustus G. Dill. DuBois and Dill were responsible for three endeavors: *The Brownies' Book* and the publication of two biographies, Elizabeth Ross Haynes's *Unsung Heroes* and Julia Henderson's *A Child's Story of Dunbar*.

The Brownies' Book[3] deserves a special note because it was the premier periodical for African American children until the appearance of *Ebony, Jr.!* in the 1960s. Under the direction of DuBois and literary editor Jessie R. Fauset, *The Brownies' Book* became a beacon of hope, featuring fiction, folktales, biographies, poetry, drama, news stories, and five monthly columns designed to inform, educate, and politicize children and their parents and to showcase the achievements of people of color. Through *The Brownies' Book,* DuBois and Fauset sought to achieve seven goals: to "make colored children realize that being 'colored' is a normal, beautiful thing"; to inform them of the achievements of their race; to teach them a code of honor; to entertain them; to provide them with a model for interacting with Whites; to instill pride in home and family; and to inspire them toward racial uplift and sacrifice. The attainment of these goals, DuBois believed, would result in the creation of a personality Harris (*The Brownies' Book: Challenge to the Selective Tradition in Children's Literature*; "Jessie Fauset's Transference") refers to as "refined colored youth" — young African American counterparts of the "race men" and "race women" of the early years of the twentieth century. Such youngsters revered education, exhibited personal and racial pride, and were committed to racial solidarity and uplift. Several letters published in *The Brownies' Book* from young readers are evidence that some children assimilated the magazine's goals:

> I think colored people are the most wonderful people in the world and when I'm a man, I'm going to write about it, too, so that all people will know the terrible struggles we've had. I don't pay any attention any more to the discouraging things I see in the newspapers. Something just tells me we are no worse than anybody else. (308)

Similarly, Haynes sought to inform African American children of their race's achievements, to inspire racial pride, and to imbue her young readers with a specific ideological view. In the twenty-two biographies of now well-known persons, among them Frederick Douglass, Harriet Tubman, Alexander Pushkin, and Paul Cuffee, she introduced children to African Americans rarely depicted in the school texts of her day. As Haynes writes in the Introduction to *Unsung Heroes*:

This story and the other stories in "Unsung Heroes," telling of the victories in spite of the hardships and struggles of Negroes whom the world has failed to sing about, have so inspired me, even after I am grown, that I pass them on to you, my little friends. May you with all of your years ahead of you be so inspired by them that you will succeed in spite of all odds. (n.p.)

DuBois, his editors, and authors quite unabashedly attempted to imbue children with an ideology that was quite radical in children's literature. Their explicit appeals for racial solidarity, pride, and uplift, and their authentic representations of African American life contrasted sharply with the images in general children's literature. The success of DuBois and his associates, however, is difficult to determine. At least five thousand subscribers received *The Brownies' Book* monthly; however, twelve thousand subscribers were needed to sustain continuous publication (*The Brownies' Book*). The number of copies of Haynes's and Henderson's books sold is as yet undetermined. It is quite conceivable that the imprimatur of DuBois and his association with the NAACP, both considered radical during the period, resulted in reduced sales and distribution. Nonetheless, some children read the texts and the magazine, and it is quite probable that the desired effects were achieved.

The bold objectives and literature developed by DuBois and others were refined further in the period that followed the 1920s. Some changes and advances occurred between 1930 and 1940 that suggested that African American children's literature would have a more promising future. Evidence for that assertion is found in the numbers of books published, the publication of books by major White publishers, and the appearance of many titles in journals or guides directed to librarians.

Strengthening of the Tradition: 1930–1940

While many people contributed to the strengthening of the tradition, the literary efforts of Carter G. Woodson deserve special recognition. Woodson and the authors he published created materials that further expanded the tradition nurtured by DuBois and his associates. Woodson's legacy, at least in children's literature, is as influential as that of DuBois. He established Negro History Week and founded the Associated Publishers and the Association for the Study of Negro Life and History. These three endeavors continue to have direct influences on the education of African American children and on the literature created for them.

In his *The Mis-Education of the Negro*, Woodson articulated a philosophy of education similar to DuBois's, arguing that the education African Americans received in his day had not been devised for, nor did it serve to the benefit of, African Americans. Rather, Woodson claimed, that education was suited mainly for the purpose of maintaining the lowly caste status of African Americans. To ameliorate those conditions, he contended that African American schooling needed to undergo a complete metamorphosis resulting in new texts, new pedagogical techniques, new purposes and goals, and a new kind of teacher unfettered by the internalization of racist ideology. Consequently, Woodson hypothesized, those changes would result in the molding of African American youth educated for individual advancement, skillful in critical thinking, and personally committed to the advancement of their race.

Woodson achieved some of his objectives through the Associated Publishers. This enterprise published a significant number of folklore collections, biographies, poetry anthologies, and histories explicitly designed to educate, entertain, and emancipate. In *African Myths*, for example, Woodson sought to provide children with authentic African folktales. Similarly, the publication of poetry anthologies by Helen Whiting and a reader by Jane D. Schackleford (which depicted the activities of a middle-class African American family) ensured that African American children would have literary choices other than Hugh Lofting's *The Story of Doctor Dolittle* or Hunt's *Little Brown Koko*.

As evidence of Woodson's successes, Associated Publishers continues to exist. During the 1970s many of the titles first published in the 1930s were reissued, most likely as a result of increased demand for authentic African American literature and the general lack of availability of this type of literature from White publishers. Literature published subsequently maintained the gains achieved by Woodson, but a subtle shift in tone and ideology occurred as African American children's literature garnered greater mass acceptance.

The Shift to Assimilation: 1940–1970

Certainly no one person was responsible for the literature of this period, but Arna Bontemps created an extensive body of work over two generations that no doubt helped propel African American children's literature into the mainstream. Bontemps could be characterized as the contemporary "father" of African American children's literature. His body of work — sixteen novels, biographies, poetry anthologies, histories, and folktales — represents the acceptance of African American children's literature among White publishers and readers and the continued expansion of the literature for African American children. Bontemps's *Popo and Fifina*, written with poet Langston Hughes, remained in print for more than twenty years and was translated into several languages (Nicholas). Another text Bontemps edited, the poetry anthology *Golden Slippers*, is notable because it includes poetry by well-regarded and renowned poets such as Dunbar, Countee Cullen, Claude McKay, Langston Hughes, and James Weldon Johnson. *Golden Slippers* deviates from the conventional children's poetry anthology format by not emphasizing didactic poetry, traditional poetic forms, or poetry written especially for children. Moreover, like most of

Bontemps's other work, it was published not by an African American publishing company but by a major White publisher.

The tradition of providing literary models for children to emulate continued with Bontemps, who early on expressed concern about the dearth of biographies for African American children (Alexander). Bontemps himself altered the situation considerably by writing six collective and individual biographies including *The Story of George Washington Carver* and *Frederick Douglass: Slave, Fighter, Freeman*. Bontemps's fiction is notable as well. In addition to his collaboration with Hughes, he collaborated with illustrator and author Jack Conroy on several picture books for children. These books are important because of their genre (tall tales) and because the characters within them are White. Additionally, a tone, albeit a subtle one, celebrating the working class and the working-class perspective runs throughout the books. In his noteworthy singularly composed fiction, books such as *Lonesome Boy* and *You Can't Pet a Possum*, Bontemps celebrates African American folk culture and language patterns. In addition to its literary quality, Bontemps's work is significant because it represents the integration of African American children's literature into the mainstream as well as the shift from explicit racial themes to the more subtle use of race and emphasis on the authentic depiction of African Americans as they engage in typical activities such as attending picnics, hopping trains to the big city, and playing with friends.

Overall, that shift from an emphasis on explicit racial themes and consciousness in literature to a more assimilationist posture using only subtle racial undertones probably corresponds with the changes in the status of African Americans and the increased push for integration that occurred during the period. Bontemps and his contemporaries, writers such as Jessie Jackson (*Call Me Charlie*) and Lorenzo Graham (*North Town*), created works about African American experiences for children of all races. The publication of their work by White publishers resulted in increased sales to schools and libraries as well as increased readership for children's literature by African American authors.

The literature of this period is important because many of the works fall within the category labeled "social conscience literature" by Sims.[4] As Sims notes, the authors of this literature deliberately attempted to develop a "social conscience — mainly in non-Afro-American readers, to encourage them to develop empathy, sympathy, and tolerance for Afro-American children and their problems" (17). She further argues that these books "were created from an ethnocentric, non-Afro-American perspective" (18). Some of the literature fits into another of Sims's categories: the "melting pot" books. These books "ignore all differences except physical ones: skin color and other racially related physical features. The result is that the majority of them are picture books" (33). The guiding principles underlying the creation of such melting pot books are assimilation, universal experiences, and integration, principles that cloak the emphasis on cultural diversity that earlier authors acknowledged, highlighted, and celebrated.

The social conscience and melting pot books served important functions: the amelioration of ignorance about African Americans, the portrayal of African Americans as possessing universal values and sharing universal experiences, and the provision of aesthetic experiences. Although these books were deemed vital during their historical period, the reality of African American life and the continued racial discrimination and retrenchment of the era belied the books' attempts to present a rosier picture. This leads one to question whether the cloaking of cultural differences results in negative or positive consequences.

In the period that followed, several sociocultural factors led to the emergence of a cadre of writers whose avowed purposes for writing and illustrating children's books harkened back to those of DuBois and Woodson. Another category devised by Sims, "culturally conscious" literature, explains the function of this emerging literature and details some of its recurring themes and motifs.

Culturally Conscious Literature: The 1970s and Beyond

Culturally conscious literature, according to Sims, comes nearer to "constituting a body of Afro-American literature for children. They are books that reflect, with varying degrees of success, the social and cultural traditions associated with growing up Black in the United States" (49). Sims argues that the primary intent of these books is "to speak to Afro-American children about themselves and their lives" (49). The elements that distinguish culturally conscious books are major characters who are Afro-American, "a story told from the perspective of Afro-Americans, a setting in an Afro-American community or home, and texts which include some means of identifying the characters as Black — physical descriptions, language, cultural traditions and so forth" (49).

The list of writers who have created culturally conscious literature in this period surpasses the total number of writers in all the previous periods. That list includes Lucille Clifton, Tom Feelings, Eloise Greenfield, Rosa Guy, Virginia Hamilton, Sharon Bell Mathis, Walter Dean Myers, the late John Steptoe, Mildred Taylor, and Brenda Wilkinson. It also includes newer writers of the 1980s such as Angela Johnson, Patricia McKissack, Emily Moore, Joyce Carol Thomas, and Camille Yarbrough. These writers have distinguished themselves because their works are decidedly African American in tone and range of content and because the literary quality of the works equals and, in many cases, surpasses the quality of general children's literature. Some of the writers have received numerous prestigious awards such as the Newbery or Caldecott medals.

Several of these authors have written statements about their aesthetic philosophies reminiscent of Langston Hughes's 1926 manifesto, "The Negro Writer and the Racial Mountain" (Huggins). Virginia Hamilton, arguably the best writer in children's literature today, has written extensively on her craft. Her views are crucial because she has received more awards than any other children's writer (with the possible exception of Katherine Paterson) and because she has written in a variety of genres.⁵ Hamilton encapsulates her aesthetic philosophy thusly:

> I want my books to be read. I want an audience. I struggle daily with literary integrity, black cultural integrity, intellectual honesty, my desire for simplicity in the storytelling, and the wish for strong, original characterization, exceptional concepts for plots ... But when I sit down to write a story, I don't say to myself, now I'm going to write a black story. (12-13)

Other African American writers echo Hamilton's thoughts. Author/ illustrator Tom Feelings articulates his opinions on the aesthetic and ideological functions of art in children's books as follows:

> Books are wonderful tools, and art for children can affect and has the ability to intensify children's perceptions of reality and stimulate their imagination in a certain way. They can also teach racism and reinforce self-hatred and stereotypes. (73)

The works these culturally conscious authors create are not monolithic; they present the range of African American experiences. The images portrayed in their works are culturally and historically authentic. Further, many of the writers capture the orality of Black vernacular English without resorting to inaccurate dialect. The illustrations in many of the books are extraordinary in terms of their artistry and their rendering of the immense variations in physical features among African Americans. An excerpt from the folktale *Mirandy and Brother Wind* demonstrates this fidelity to both truthful portrayal and language:

> First thing, Orlinda come siding up to Mirandy, asking, "Who gon' be yo' partner?" Mirandy tried not to act excited. "He's real special." Then she added, "I wish you and Ezel luck. Y'all gon' need it." "Me and Ezel? Girl, don't be silly." (n.p.)

Just as important, the culturally conscious authors do not hesitate to present historically accurate portrayals of the horrors of the African American experience in the United States. Although the stories are not designed to frighten children or instill in them a sense of hopelessness, their authors portray aspects of the African American experience rarely seen in children's literature. This is especially true for books in this category that depict slavery or racial discrimination. Arguably, the books represent a "storied tradition of resistance";⁶ that is, while accurately portraying historical facts, they do so in ways that highlight African American resistance. For example, in Mildred Taylor's searing novelette set in the South, *The Friendship*, an elderly African American man, Mr. Tom Bee, goes to the local store to purchase tobacco from a White man, John Wallace, whose life he had saved several years previously. Wallace had promised Mr. Bee that he would never disrespect him in front of Whites. However, in an ugly confrontation in Wallace's store one day, Wallace is urged by some other

Whites to put Mr. Bee "in his place," and he shoots Mr. Bee for referring to him as "John." Although wounded, Mr. Bee vows that he will never call Wallace "Mister." The reality and pain of the social dilemmas depicted in this text are rarely approached in children's literature texts generally used in American schools. Thus, in one sense, the culturally conscious books represent the ideal standard for African American children's literature. They provide exceptional aesthetic experiences; they entertain, educate, and inform; and they engender racial pride.

Despite the quality of these works, their full potential has not been met, for a variety of reasons. Since the 1970s, the number of books published by African Americans or others about African American experiences has hovered at about two hundred books per year. Rarely is that number surpassed, and, sadly, many African Americans remain unaware of the existence of these books. Many of these books never reach the hands of African American children. Some have been out of print for significant time periods. Even when the books are available, some teachers are hesitant to use them because they believe that the books depict only bleak ghetto situations, that they might embarrass African American children, or that White children are not interested or may be ill at ease with the books. However, as Harris notes, as recently as 1990, a sixth-grade teacher responded that she was angry that her teacher training failed to expose her to this body of literature; she has since made it available to her students.

What, then, does the future portend for African American children's literature? In some ways, the future looks promising. Several new writers have emerged during the 1980s whose work suggests that African American children's literature will remain a viable, vibrant tradition, albeit one that remains unfairly neglected. From the bedtime story ritual featured in Angela Johnson's *Tell Me a Story, Mama*, to the day-to-day activities of a middle-class African American family related in Emily Moore's *Whose Side Are You On?*, to the frank discussion of the issue of colorism in Camille Yarbrough's *The Shimmershine Queens*, these books present a range of experiences and intimate portrayals of African Americans. They read as if they were written for African American children. Via the language, nicknames, foods, and other aspects and nuances of culture they present, they implicitly inform their readers that the stories are from the African American community, "the 'hood." There is a naturalness about them — these books do not scream messages or didacticism other than those that inherently stem from the affirmation and celebration of African American culture. To their credit, they also justly criticize negative aspects of African American culture, but not in formulaic fashion.

An argument can be made that the culturally conscious books are essential for African American children specifically and for all children generally. Purves and Beach found that children prefer literary works with subject matter related to their personal experiences, that they engage more with materials related to their personal experiences, and that they seek out works with which they can identify or which contain characters whose experiences reflect their own. Further, recent research in cognition supports the notion that familiarity with and interest in a topic or text facilitates comprehension (Fielding et al.). Arguably, reading comprehension among African American children would improve if the literacy materials were more meaningful to them (Kunju; Madhubuti).

If African American children do not see reflections of themselves in school texts or do not perceive any affirmation of their cultural heritage in those texts, then it is quite likely that they will not read or value schooling as much. Children need to understand the languages, beliefs, ways of life, and perspectives of others. White children and other children of color need to read African American literature because notions of cultural pluralism are becoming more important as cultural, economic, and geographical barriers are eradicated. The task confronting educators, then, is to provide all children with opportunities to hear, read, write about, and talk about literature, especially literature that affirms who they are.

Works Cited

Alexander, S. *The Achievement of Arna Bontemps*. 1976, University of Pittsburgh, PhD dissertation.
Anderson, J. *The Education of Blacks in the South, 1860-1935*. U of North Carolina P, 1988.
Baker, A. *Books about Negro Life for Children*. The New York Public Library, 1961.
Broderick, D. *Image of the Black in Children's Fiction*. R. R. Bowker, 1973.
Brown, S. "Negro Character as Seen by White Authors." *Journal of Negro Education*, vol. 2, 1933, pp. 179-203.
DuBois, W. E. B. *The Souls of Black Folk*. 1903. Fawcett, 1961.
DuBois, W. E. B. *Dusk of Dawn*. 1940. Krause International, 1975.
Elson, R. *Guardians of Tradition: American Schoolbooks of the Nineteenth Century*. U of Nebraska P, 1964.
Feelings, T. "Illustration Is My Form, the Black Experience My Story and My Content." *The Advocate*, vol. 4, 1985, pp. 73-83.
Fielding, L., P. Wilson, and R. Anderson. "A New Focus on Free Reading: The Role of Tradebooks in Reading Instruction." *The Contexts of School-Based Literacy*, edited by T. Raphael, Random House, 1984, pp. 149-162.
Fraser, J. "Black Publishing for Black Children." *School Library Journal*, vol. 20, 1973, pp. 19-24.
Greenfield, E. "Something to Shout About." *The Horn Book Magazine*, vol. 51, 1975, pp. 624-26.

Hamilton, V. "The Mind of a Novel: The Heart of a Book." *Children's Literature Quarterly*, vol. 8, 1983, pp. 10-13.

Harper, F. E. W. *Iola Leroy*. 1892. Beacon Press, 1988.

Harris, V. *The Brownies' Book: Challenge to the Selective Tradition in Children's Literature*. 1987, PhD dissertation, University of Georgia,

Harris, V. "Jessie Fauset's Transference of the New Negro Philosophy to Children's Literature." *Langston Hughes Review*, vol. 6, 1987, pp. 36-43.

Huggins, N., editor. *Voices from the Harlem Renaissance*. Oxford UP, 1976.

Kelly, R. *Children's Periodicals of the United States*. Greenwood Press, 1984.

Kunjufu, J. *Developing Positive Self-Images and Discipline in Black Children*. African-American Images, 1984.

Madhubuti, H. *Black Men: Obsolete, Single, Dangerous?* Third World Press, 1989.

Muse, D. "Black Children's Literature: Rebirth of a Neglected Genre." *Black Scholar*, vol. 7, 1975, pp. 11-15.

Nicholas, C., editor. *Arna Bontemps-Langston Hughes Letters, 1925-67*. Dodd, Mead, 1980.

Penn, G. *The Afro-American Press and Its Editors*. Wiley, 1891.

Purves, A., and R. Beach. *Literature and the Reader*. National Council of Teachers of English, 1972.

Taxel, J. *Reclaiming the Voice of Resistance: The Fiction of Mildred Taylor*. Unpublished manuscript presented at the annual meeting of the American Educational Research Association, March 1989, San Francisco, California.

Sims, R. *Shadow and Substance: Afro-American Experience in Contemporary Children's Fiction*. National Council of Teachers of English, 1982.

Vaughn-Roberson, C., and B. Hill. "The *Brownies' Book* and *Ebony, Jr.!*: Literature as a Mirror of the Black experience." *Journal of Negro Education*, vol. 58, 1989, pp. 494-510.

Williams, R. *The Long Revolution*. Oxford UP, 1961.

Williams, R. *Marxism and Literature*. Oxford UP, 1977.

Wilson, H. E. *Our Nig*. 1859. Vintage Books, 1983.

Woodson, C. *The Miseducation of the Negro*. 1933. Associated Publishers, 1969.

Children's Books Cited

Bannerman, H. *The Story of Little Black Sambo*. 1899. Harper and Row, 1923.

Bontemps, A. *You Can't Pet a Possum.* Morrow, 1934.
Bontemps, A. *Golden Slippers.* Harper and Row, 1941.
Bontemps, A. *The Story of George Washington Carver.* Grosset and Dunlap, 1954.
Bontemps, A. *Lonesome Boy.* 1955. Beacon, 1986.
Bontemps, A. *Frederick Douglass: Slave, Fighter, Freeman.* Knopf, 1959.
Bontemps, A., and L. Hughes. *Popo and Fifina: Children of Haiti.* Macmillan, 1932.
Bryant, S. *Epaminondas and His Auntie.* 1907. Houghton Mifflin, 1938.
Caines, J. *Abby.* New York: Harper and Row, 1973.
Dunbar, P. L. *Little Brown Baby.* Dodd, Mead, 1895.
Finley, M. *Elsie Dinsmore.* 1868. Dodd, Mead, 1893.
Floyd, S. *Floyd's Flowers.* Hertel and Jenkins, 1905.
Golding, W. *Lord of the Flies.* Putnam, 1962.
Graham, L. *North Town.* Harper Junior, 1965.
Hamilton, V. *M. C. Higgins, the Great.* Macmillan, 1974.
Hamilton, V. *Paul Robeson: The Life and Times of a Free Black Man.* Harper, 1975.
Hamilton, V. *Willie Bea And The Time The Martians Landed.* Greenwillow, 1983.
Hawthorne, N. *The Scarlet Letter.* Penguin, 1983.
Haynes, E. *Unsung Heroes.* DuBois and Dill, 1921.
Henderson, J. *A Child's Story of Dunbar.* DuBois and Dill, 1921.
Hunt, B. *Little Brown Koko.* American Colortype, 1951.
Jackson, J. *Call Me Charlie.* Harper Junior, 1945.
Johnson, A. *Tell Me a Story, Mama.* Orchard Books, 1989.
Johnson, A. E. *Clarence and Corrine.* American Baptist Publications Society, 1890.
Lofting, A. *The Story of Doctor Dolittle.* J. B. Lippincott, 1948.
McCloskey, R. *Make Way for Ducklings.* Puffin/Penguin, 1941.
McKissack, P. *Mirandy and Brother Wind.* Knopf, 1989.
Ovington, M. *Hazel.* 1913. Books for Libraries, 1972.
Ovington, M. *Zeke.* Harcourt Brace, 1931.
Page, T. *Two Little Confederates.* 1888. Charles Scribner's Sons, 1932.
Paterson, K. *Bridge to Terebithia.* Crowell Junior Books, 1977.
Piper, W. *The Little Engine That Could.* 1954. Putnam, 1980.
Potter, B. *The Tale of Peter Rabbit.* 1902. Fredrick Warne, 1989.
Pritchard, M., and M. Ovington. *The Upward Path.* Harcourt, Brace and Howe, 1920.
Steptoe, J. *Mufaro's Beautiful Daughters.* Lothrop, Lee Shephard, 1987.
Taylor, M. *Roll of Thunder, Hear My Cry.* 1976. Bantam, 1984.

Taylor, M. *The Friendship*. Dial Books for Young Readers, 1987.
Taylor, M. *The Gold Cadillac*. Dial, 1987.
Wilder, L. *Little House on the Prairie*. Harper Junior, 1953.
Yarbrough, C. *The Shimmershine Queens*. G. P. Putnam's Sons, 1989.
White, E. B. *Charlotte's Web*. 1952. Harper Junior Books, 1975.
Woodson, C. *African Myths*. Washington, DC: The Associated Publishers, 1928.

Notes

1. I would tend to label Dunbar's Little Brown Baby the first, though only tentatively. Just as *Iola Leroy* (Harper) previously was believed to be the first published novel by an African American woman until recent research uncovered Harriet Wilson's *Our Nig*, similar shifting circumstances exist with regard to children's literature by and for African Americans.

2. Some researchers (Muse; Vaughn-Roberson and Hill) argue that *The Joy*, published by Mrs. Johnson in the 1880s, could be designated the first work created for African American children during this period.

3. *The Brownies' Book* generally has been designated the first periodical for African American children created by African Americans (see Kelly), but Fraser argues that *The Joy* is the first. A comprehensive examination of *The Brownies' Book* is found in Harris (*The Brownies' Book: Challenge to the Selective Tradition in Children's Literature*).

4. An article by Sims, now Rudine Sims Bishop, also appears in this issue. -ED.

5. Hamilton's *M. C. Higgins, the Great* was the first book written by an African American to win the Newbery Medal. The book also won the National Book Award and the *Boston Globe-Horn Book* Magazine Award, the only book in children's literature ever to do so.

6. The phrase "storied tradition of resistance" was first coined by Susan Cox and appeared in an unpublished manuscript by Taxel.

───── Eight ─────

Critical Indigenous Literacies

SELECTING AND USING CHILDREN'S BOOKS ABOUT INDIGENOUS PEOPLES (REPRINT)
Debbie Reese

Editors' note: Debbie Reese's "Critical Indigenous Literacies: Selecting and Using Children's Books about Indigenous Peoples" first appeared as a column in the journal Language Arts *in 2018. We decided to reprint Reese's column as a chapter here because we value Reese's significant academic contribution to the field of youth literature and because Reese's concept of Critical Indigenous Literacies perfectly aligns with the goals of this book. Reese explains that Critical Indigenous Literacies are about asking critical questions: "Who is telling these stories? How are these stories being represented? Who does this story belong to?" These questions are important questions to ask as we promote Native authors in the classroom year round. These questions are also pertinent to anyone interested in diversity in youth literature. We've positioned Reese's chapter in the Community Frameworks section of this book because scholars working at the intersections of ethnic studies and youth literature often have to gauge harm done while also looking for ways communities have created pathways for empowering through texts and story.*

***

In 1863, President Lincoln issued a proclamation stating that the last Thursday of November would be a national day of thanksgiving. In 1990, President George H. W. Bush issued the first presidential proclamation that designated November as National Native American Heritage Month. With these two proclamations occurring in the same month, many teachers use November as the time to read aloud or assign children's books that feature Native peoples. In this article, I ask teachers to rethink literature used to teach children about Indigenous peoples. In situating the experience of Native peoples across time, I begin with a clarification of terms.

I am tribally enrolled at Nambé Pueblo, which means I am counted on the Nambé census. Most Native people prefer to name their specific tribal nation because being specific helps non-Native people learn that we are far more diverse than what the terms "American Indian" or "Native American" evoke. Historically, "Indian" was commonly used, but over time, more people began using "Native" instead. Most recently, "Indigenous" is emerging as an alternative, as seen in the movements to replace Columbus Day with Indigenous Peoples' Day. I use the terms "Native" and "Indigenous" interchangeably, unless referring to a specific tribal nation.

There are more than five hundred federally recognized tribal nations in the United States today, each with distinct systems of governance, languages, locations, material cultures, religions, and, of course, stories! Some people are taken aback at the word "nation" as applied to Native nations because of the tendency to group Native peoples with other minority groups in the United States. However, that framework fails to encompass our single most important attribute: Native nationhood. Without this recognition, our status as sovereign nations whose people were — and are — Indigenous to this continent are erased. We were not the first *Americans*, because Native nations predate the United States of *America* by hundreds of years. In fact, European and then US leaders entered into diplomatic negotiations with leaders of Native nations who inhabited the lands from the beginning. The outcomes of those negotiations were treaties, much like the ones the US forges with foreign nations today. Nonetheless, depictions of Native peoples as primitive or uncivilized are one of the reasons our nationhood is difficult to accept or understand. In fact, Native peoples had/have distinct cultures passed down from many generations with complex practices and traditions — hardly primitive. Therefore, the larger culture needs to unlearn and rethink how the identities of Indigenous peoples are represented and taught.

Expanding Critical Literacy: Inclusion of Indigenous Peoples

The theoretical term I highlight in this column is *Critical Indigenous Literacies* (Reese). Critical literacy encourages children to read between the lines and ask questions when engaging with literature: Whose story is this? Who benefits from this story? Whose voices are not being heard? While these may seem like difficult questions, Vasquez writes that even in early childhood, children are capable of asking these critical questions when approaching texts. Adding "Indigenous" to critical literacy asks readers to think of those questions when they read stories that have Indigenous characters in them.

Critical Indigenous literacy forefronts the historically marginalized treatment of Native stories — and by extension, Native people. In addition, a critical literacies perspective gives voice to how stories are presented and told about people and their history. For example, our creation stories are just as sacred to us as Genesis is to Christians; we do not view them as folktales. When opening many library catalogs, however, *The Story of the Milky Way: A Cherokee Tale* by Joseph Bruchac and Gayle Ross (1995) is likely to appear under "Cherokee Indians — Folklore." *Beaver Steals Fire: A Salish Coyote Story* by the staff of the Confederated Salish and Kootenai Tribe is most likely categorized as "Salish Indians — Folklore." In fact, both are religious stories explaining some aspect of how the world was created.

In contrast, Peter Spier's *Noah's Ark* is not labeled "folklore," but "Bible stories — O.T." In fact, all three are creation stories, but the Christian story is treated differently. This difference in how Native and Christian creation stories are treated privileges Christianity, perpetuating institutionalized racism that keeps in place the ideologies of a society that is predominantly Christian. One group of creation stories is categorized and treated as fiction while the other group of creation stories is accepted as truth. Despite efforts by Native people to get their stories accurately categorized, there has been little or no movement, which raises critical questions: Whose voice is not heard in the way that stories are categorized? Whose ideologies are implicitly valued by categorical labels?

Another problem is the "myths, legends, and folktales" books that are marketed as Native. They are ubiquitous and mostly written by people who are not, themselves, Native. These authors may not have the knowledge needed to accurately depict aspects of Native traditions, some of which are part of our religious dances. In *Dragonfly's Tale,* for example, Kristina Rodanas shows Pueblo people having a food fight — a misrepresentation of a "throw." During the harvest dance, food items (like ears of corn) are tossed to others as a way to share foods. Rodanas depicted this important community value and spiritual activity as the sort of mischief American kids sometimes engage in. Misrepresentations like these lead to similar critical questions: Who is telling these stories? How are these stories being represented? Whom does this story belong to?

Teachers can make choices that do justice to Native stories by choosing books written by Native writers. Both *The Story of the Milky Way* (Bruchac and Ross) and *Beaver Steals Fire* (Confederated Salish and Kootenai Tribes) are #OwnVoices stories — a hashtag created by Corinne Duyvis to describe a book that is written by someone who is of the particular culture being depicted. The idea is that the quality of a story is improved when the person creating that story is an insider who knows what to share and how to share it with outsiders. As a child, I was taught what can — and cannot — be shared with outsiders. A history of exploitation has made Native writers mindful of what they disclose.

To capture this concept, I have been adding a "curtain" to Bishop's "mirrors, windows, and sliding glass doors" metaphor when I talk or write about Native stories. This is a way to acknowledge and honor the stories behind the curtain — those that are purposefully kept within Native communities. Native communities resisted historical oppression and continue to preserve our culture by cultivating our ways in private spaces — behind the curtain. While Native people share some of our ways publicly in the present day, there is a great deal that we continue to protect from outsiders. Furthermore, it conveys the importance of how #OwnVoices knows what belongs within the community and what knowledge can be shared outside of our communities.

We Can Do Better: Rethinking Native Stories in Classrooms

Let's turn now to Native American Heritage Month and its intersection with Thanksgiving. Many teachers read aloud children's books about the "First Thanksgiving." Some classrooms take part in reenactments, with kids dressing up like Pilgrims and Indians or, perhaps, Wampanoags. Most of these books and activities default to stereotypes where Native people are shown in feathered headdresses and fringed clothing — items worn by Plains Indians rather than anything the Wampanoag people would have worn. When teachers use Thanksgiving as the vehicle for their instruction about Native peoples, they are inadvertently locating Native lives in the past.

There are better ways to bring Native stories and books about Native peoples into classrooms. I focus on Cynthia Leitich Smith's picture book *Jingle Dancer* to illustrate how classroom book collections depicting Native people could be improved. The key ideas are to choose books that are tribally specific (name a specific tribal nation and accurately present that nation), written by Native writers, set in the present day, and relevant all year round, keeping Native peoples visible throughout the school year.

Choose books that are tribally specific. Select books about Native peoples who are/were residents of your specific state. I recommend using websites like the National Congress of American Indians and the Smithsonian's National Museum of the American Indian for information on tribal nations. Smith's picture book is about Jenna, a little girl who is doing the jingle dance for the very first time at an upcoming powwow. In the author's note, Smith shares that Jenna is a citizen of the Muscogee Nation, pertinent to children in Georgia, where the Muscogee people originated, or in Oklahoma, where they are today. Therefore, focusing on the local context empowers tribal nationhood within the states of origin rather than focusing on politically constructed holidays like Thanksgiving.

Use present tense verbs to talk about Native Nations. A teacher in Georgia might say, "Today, the Muscogee Creek Nation is in Oklahoma. Before Europeans arrived on what became known as the North American continent, the Muscogee Creeks were in Georgia." To go even further, use the provocative but accurate word "invaded" instead of "arrived." While reading *Jingle Dancer,* which is set in the present day, show the Muscogee Nation website as a complementary source. Jenna's house is in an everyday neighborhood and she is wearing clothes similar to those of kids in the classroom. She is a person of the present day.

Choose books by Native writers. As noted earlier, Smith is Muscogee Creek. Introducing her as the author is another opportunity to use a present-tense verb.

Because Smith and her character are Muscogee Creek, *Jingle Dancer* is an #OwnVoices story. As such, Smith is writing from her personal knowledge of Muscogee families and communities as they come together to help a child prepare and participate in a ceremonial dance for the first time. Jenna needs specific clothing, learns the steps and music, and understands the meaning of the dance from her tribal community. At one point in the story, Jenna is feeling overwhelmed by all she has to do. In a matter-of-fact way, Jenna's great-aunt tells her about the story of Bat, a Creek creation story. As a result, we learn that Creek families share creation stories with each other to instill strength and as a way to carry on when feeling low or overwhelmed.

Use books by Native writers all year round. *Jingle Dancer* can be used any time of the year. I've focused on it for most of this article, but it is only one of many books available. (A list of recommended books in a range of genres, all written by Native authors and tribally specific, follows the references.) A middle-grade teacher doing a unit on lyrics in pop music might consider using Eric Gansworth's *If I Ever Get Out of Here*. It is tribally specific, set in the present day, and an #OwnVoices story. Every chapter title in the book is the name of a song by the Beatles or Paul McCartney. (If you're a fan of either one, you'll love the discography Gansworth has on his website!) Gansworth's book is about the relationship that develops between Lewis, a Native boy living on the Tuscarora Reservation, and George, a White boy living on a nearby Air Force base.

Each year the market is flooded with problematic books that publishers market to classroom teachers, but there are also gems worth reading. At my website, American Indians in Children's Literature (https://americanindiansinchildrensliterature .blogspot.com), I read as many as I can and create "best of" lists. Visit! See what you'll find for your classroom.

For Further Reading

Hirschfelder, A., , P. F. Molin, and Y. Wakim. *American Indian Stereotypes in the World of Children.* Scarecrow Press, 1999.

This is a very useful text that has eight chapters with several short essays in each one. It also contains an extensive bibliography of books and articles teachers can study to gain a depth of knowledge of the ways Native peoples have been depicted over time.

Jones, G. W., and S. Moomaw. *Lessons from Turtle Island: Native Curriculum in Early Childhood Classrooms.* Redleaf Press, 2002.

Written especially for teachers — by two teachers — each chapter takes a close look at issues in how Native content is taught. It features lesson plans built on children's literature that can provide children with accurate and authentic knowledge.

Children's Literature Cited

Bruchac, J., and G. Ross. *The Story of the Milky Way: A Cherokee Tale*, illustrated by V. A. Stroud, Dial Books, 1995.
Confederated Salish and Kootenai Tribes. *Beaver Steals Fire: A Salish Coyote Story*, illustrated by S. Sandoval, U of Nebraska P, 2005.
Gansworth, E. *If I Ever Get Out of Here*. Arthur A. Levine Books, 2013.
Rodanas, K. *Dragonfly's Tale*. Clarion Books, 1995.
Smith, C, L. *Jingle Dancer*, illustrated by C. Van Wright and Y. Hu, Morrow Junior Books, 2000.
Spier, P. *Noah's Ark*. Doubleday, 1992.

Works Cited

Bishop, R. S. "Mirrors, Windows, and Sliding Glass Doors." *Perspectives*, vol. 6, no. 3, 1990, pp. ix–xi.
Reese, D. "Critical Indigenous Literacies." *The SAGE Handbook of Early Childhood Literacy*, edited by J. Larson and J. Marsh, Sage, 2013, pp. 251-63.
Vasquez, V. *Negotiating Critical Literacies with Young Children*. Routledge, 2014.

Recommended Books

Baker, D. *Kamik Joins The Pack*, illustrated by Q. Leng, Inhabit Media, 2016.
Dimaline, C. *The Marrow Thieves*. Cormorant Publishers, 2017.
Gansworth, E. *If I Ever Get Out Of Here*. Arthur A. Levine Books, 2013.
Herrington, J. *Mission to Space*. White Dog Press, 2016.

Marshall, J., III. *In the Footsteps of Crazy Horse*, illustrated by J. M. Yellowhawk, Harry N. Abrams, 2015.

Minnema, C. K. *Hungry Johnny*, illustrated by W. Ballinger, Historical Society Press, 2014.

Ortiz, S. J. *The People Shall Continue*, illustrated by S. Graves, Lee and Low Books, 2017.

Robertson, D. A. *When We Were Alone*, illustrated by J. Flett, HighWater Press, 2016.

Robertson, J. *The Water Walker*. Second Story Press, 2017.

Robertson, S. *Rock and Roll Highway: The Robbie Robertson Story*, illustrated by A. Gustavson, Henry Holt, 2014.

Smith, M. G. *You Hold Me Up*, illustrated by D. Daniel, Orca Book Publishers, 2017.

——————NINE——————
The Mirror, the Matrix, the Movement

INTELLECTUAL LEGACIES OF THE COUNCIL ON INTERRACIAL BOOKS FOR CHILDREN
Marilisa Jiménez García

> Theories help us to explain, anticipate, interpret, critique, and broaden our worldview. They provide us with a blueprint for understanding a specific phenomenon and encourage us to investigate various elements that influence our studies.
>
> — S. R. Toliver

As the first African American female nominee for Supreme Court Justice, Ketanji Brown Jackson's confirmation hearing featured enduring visuals for the public imagination. Photographers, for example, captured Leila Jackson, Judge Jackson's daughter, admiring her mother. Yet the image of Senator Ted Cruz holding Ibram Kendi's *Antiracist Baby*, a picture-book version of the bestselling *How to be Antiracist*, while grilling Judge Jackson on her political commitments, rather than her legal credentials, illustrates the legacy of children's literature as a political medium. "Do you agree with this book that is taught to kids, that babies are born racist?" Cruz asked Jackson, as cameras turned on the book's illustrations. Cruz underlined the book's use in the Georgetown Day School curriculum, a DC school where Jackson sits on the board of trustees. Jackson said she "believed no child should be made to feel like they are racist or have no value." Her response, though admirable, emphasizes individual feelings rather than the role of literature in upholding and dismantling systemic racism — something the members of the Council on Interracial Books for Children (CIBC) dedicated their careers to exposing unapologetically. As early as 1966, the CIBC boldly confronted the silences around racism and children's books as a national undermining of children of color, the descendants of US-colonized peoples. This chapter examines how the intellectual legacies of the CIBC endure against the challenges of a more racially just literary world. I focus on the CIBC's published works *Human (and Anti-Human)* and *Values in Children's Books* and *Stereotypes, Distortions and Omissions in U.S. History Textbooks* as theoretical texts expositing the organization's intellectual and political commitments and implementation for challenging systemic inequalities in children's texts. Youth literature, according to the CIBC, was key in the battle for intellectual sovereignty and historical literacy, and they identified US imperialism, and the master narrative it inspired, as the root of racism, which they empowered parents and teachers, in addition to authors and librarians, to both research and dismantle.

Scholarship on the CIBC is rare, perhaps because the organization itself functioned as a body of criticism — maybe because the work of youth literature advocates often is not seen as intellectual labor. The CIBC's founders and members, however, included key change markers in literature, the arts, and activism, including Brian Chambers, Piri Thomas, Langston Hughes, Walter Dean Myers, Gwendolyn Brooks, and Nancy Larrick. The CIBC and its publications, such as the recently digitized *The Bulletin,* published between 1966 and 1984, or "Guidelines for Selecting Bias Free Textbooks and Storybooks," are often cited as ideal by contemporary publishers and educators, yet few consider the CIBC as a scholarly forerunner of critical race studies or ethnic studies methodologies. The CIBC's social and literary analysis, offered at little to no cost to the public, intersects and in some cases precedes touchstones and movements credited for transforming the literary and social canon, including ethnic studies, bilingual education, and even Rudine Sims Bishop's "Mirrors, Windows, and Sliding Glass Doors."

The CIBC used the metaphors "the mirror and the matrix" to describe the entrenched world of children's literature years before Sims Bishop. How might the CIBC's mirror and matrix metaphor, for example, differ from and complement Sims Bishop's work and enrich us today? Decades before legal theorist Derrick Bell wrote landmark law articles such as "Who's Afraid of Critical Race Theory?" or Kimberly Crenshaw's "Mapping the Margins" cementing intersectionality as a central tenant, the CIBC developed critical tools for evaluating overlapping oppressions of racism, sexism, ableism, and ageism in youth literature. Furthermore, ten years after *Brown vs. Board of Education* (1956), which made school segregation illegal in the US, the CIBC wrestled with the de facto segregation of the children's literary world through popular texts, textbooks, and readers. The CIBC's intellectual legacy helps us articulate and critically consider how stories on the shelf become stereotypes in and out of the classroom and how youth of color bear the brunt of those consequences. Ultimately, the CIBC offers an opportunity to reclaim liberation frameworks in youth literature rather than depend on terms such as "diversity and representation" as guidelines for progress.

The Mirror: Reflections on the Language, Ideas, and Models for "Diverse" Youth Literature

When it was released in 1976, the Feminist Press called *Human (and Anti-Human) Values in Children's Books* the "first comprehensive guide to a humanistic evaluation of books ... should be used in every children's literature course in the country." In many ways, the CIBC's publications, including its *Bulletins*, are ground zero for scholars of color trying to retrace movements for the desegregation of the children's bookshelf. W. E. B. Dubois's *The Brownies Book* and librarians of color such as Augusta Baker and Pura Belpré established the need for countering injustice and racial maligning in youth literature. However, the CIBC represents a groundbreaking multiracial and transnational solidarity and unified voice for racial justice in youth literature as a direct response to the US Civil Rights Movement of the 1960s. Multicultural scholar and educator Sonia Nieto, for example, writes about her experiences as a teacher at one of the first bilingual education programs in the Bronx and receiving from her principal a copy of *The Bulletin* dedicated solely to Puerto Rican materials as transformative in 1972: "I devoured that issue of *Interracial Books for Children.* It spoke to me in a way that few articles had before then because it seemed to fill a need I had without even knowing it" (Jiménez García ix). Nieto describes an unspoken need for humanizing experiences of learning and belonging to a literary tradition. Such moments spur further knowing, unknowing, and impulse to cultivate transformative learning for others.

Transformative learning is at the heart of ethnic studies, as James A. Banks writes that ethnic studies is "not just a way to integrate ethnic content into the curriculum, but as a vehicle for curriculum transformation and change that will enable students to view events and issues from multiple perspectives, to critically examine structures such as institutional racism and inequality (Sleeter and Zavala viii). Christine Sleeter and Miguel Zavala write, "Ethnic studies seeks to rehumanize experiences, challenge problematic Eurocentric narratives, and build community solidarity across difference" (3). The experiences of Puerto Ricans in children's literature, as colonized subjects in the US, for one, simply would not have been documented without the CIBC, especially during a moment when Boricuas, along with African American, Indigenous, and Asian Americans, were in a struggle for intellectual and political self-determination. The two issues of *Bulletin,* one in 1973 and one in 1983, dedicated to Puerto Rican materials represent perhaps the only critical analysis and realtime documentation of racism and sexism, among other -isms, in children's literature. The CIBC created similar issues dedicated to Asian American, Black American, and Indigenous children's materials, for example. They provided a front seat for parents, teachers, and students to learn about their colleagues in the struggle for ethnic studies curriculum via youth literature, such as the Spring 1970 *Bulletin* that published "A Mexican American Talks about White

Supremacy" by William Martinez of the Mexican American Students Union in Los Angeles, where he boldly described the role of children's books for the Chicano Movement: "Of course, you don't want your lies to show up. So you keep the Chicano child ignorant. You put what you want children to know in your books, and you have left them out of what you don't want them to know" (5). The same *Bulletin* features a front-page story by Byron Williams titled "Notes on Chicano Movement." These texts simultaneously articulate and document the praxis of critical race studies and ethnic studies, including youth voices, for a children's literature community in the thick of these movements.

The CIBC, specifically as an intellectual legacy, matters because it means, long before We Need Diverse Books, for example, a core group of anti-racist scholars, authors, and activists, many of color, resisted the normalizing of sexism and racism in children's books, countering colonial notions of docility and illiteracy of communities of color. Yet the CIBC's main publication, *Human and Anti-Human Values,* rarely shows up in graduate programs for youth literature studies or doctoral exams. Even today, *Human and Anti-Human Values* provides one of the only analyses that honors the nuances in nationalities and ethnicities among colonized communities in the US.

Human and Anti-Human Values opens with a short section on "Terminology," demonstrating the CIBC authors' attention to language and how it connotes political commitments. "Language," they write, "reflecting society, is no more static nor sacred than is anything in the political arena." The authors felt it was important to underline how the language they used to describe racism and sexism in the book may sound dated: "Words which sound 'funny' to us one day, become comfortable in a short time if we are truly determined to rid our language and our society of sexism and racism. But the process must be constant" (viii). They end the section by writing: "In any case, using words as political weapons is a mind stretching exercise. We recommend it." Similarly, in the section "Evaluating Content," which they open with the essay "The Mirror and the Matrix," the CIBC authors remove children's writers from any space of neutrality: "No writer is just a reporter; an artist puts more on paper than their eyes can see" (1). Writing creatively, academically, and for the public was never neutral or simply a product of happenstance, but a reflection of an author's political commitments. In the last ten years, the youth literature field and industry experienced a significant shift, arguably through the public work of networks of women of color writers and practitioners who transformed how scholarly fields, publishers, and practitioners talk about youth literature. Given that "diversity" and perhaps even the more radical "anti-racist" have become marketable words, youth literature advocates and communities should reflect on what (if anything) has changed toward goals such as racial and gender equity in publishing.

One of the projects of *Ethnic Studies and Youth Literature* is to render the institutional barriers in youth literature that prevent equity in our fields as an intellectual problem — not a niceness problem — and to visibilize and credit how US communities of color offer models and solutions that center their intellectual and creative histories. As a beloved organization championed for its work toward equity, the CIBC's writings and goals retrospectively help us reflect on how contemporary conversations on diverse books differ from the interventions they demanded during their existence in the late 1960s and 1970s. For example, the CIBC's various platforms and functions — tracking the publishing industries' numbers on racial, ethnic, gender, and disability difference; awarding authors of color; developing workshops and panels; and reviewing children's books for critical content — live on among various organizations that cite the CIBC as their model, such as the Cooperative Children's Book Center (CCBC), Teaching for Change, and the We Need Diverse Books organization. In our chapter with Alia Jones and Traci Sorell, Jones and Sorell discuss how the CCBC's annual statistics on books published by and about communities of color/ethnicity arrive without much analysis or guidance for industry professionals and practitioners. The CIBC, however, through its strong network of scholars, writers, artists, and activists, did provide contexts and recommendations for the industry on children's texts, which expanded to school readers, while also keying in on content they signaled as reproducing hegemony.

In youth literature, whom we cite and attribute as belonging to a history or tradition provides insights into what we claim as knowledge and whom we see as knowledge contributors. As I wrote in *Side by Side*, the Black Lives Matter and We Need Diverse Books movements in the mid-2010s forced book publishing, in particular, to publicly reconsider the racial makeup of its decision makers, such as reviewers, editors, designers, and administrators. This prompted similar conversations in other children's literature segments, though many might say little institutional or even epistemological change occurred in the research and teaching of children's literature in the anglophone academy. Our humanities/literary studies community only recently began seriously considering systemic racism in the children's literary field, including the exclusion of ethnic studies from children's literature studies at its outset (Jimenez). However, as the CIBC also reminds us, the pursuit of racial justice in children's literature demands our intentional examination of the ideas, models, and terms among all active players, but especially as it pertains to families and students. One question guiding my examination of the CIBC is: How do corporate models of diversity, equity, and inclusion (DEI) differ from models for critical, transnational racial solidarities and epistemologies?

Today, "diverse" youth literature is arguably an industry in itself, as mainstream publishers have rebranded to incorporate diversity in terms of corporate strategy. For example, the Children's Book Council (CBC), the main trade organization in children's book publishing, founded a Diversity Initiative in 2012 that includes awards and recognitions for publishers seen as making significant strides toward "publishing diverse titles, their promotion, diversity in hiring and mentoring, plus efforts that create public awareness about the importance of diverse voices." Large publishing houses such as Candlewick,

Scholastic, Simon and Schuster, Hachette, and Abrams now prominently feature lists of "diverse" titles on their websites, conferences, and press materials. Penguin Publishing, which also began a separate label, Kokila Books, prominently states above its diverse titles list, under the heading "The Conversation": "Let's engage in dialogue and raise our collective consciousness about race and bias. The books and resources found here are meant to help spark discussions across communities, classrooms, book clubs, and workplaces, to raise the next generation of anti-racist children, and to teach us all how to be active allies and participants in shaping a better future."

In the last decade, the We Need Diverse Books movement was a watershed moment in our contemporary reckonings with the whiteness of youth literature. WNDB began as a hashtag and ultimately became a nonprofit organization, and then, in a strategic move resembling the CIBC, began scholarship programs and awards for writers of color. WNDB even partnered with Scholastic Book Club, the primary source for school libraries and materials in the US. In many cases, social media platforms such as X, Instagram, and Facebook have functioned as counter-narratives for librarians, academics, independent scholars, authors, and just plain book nerds to both celebrate and dissect the latest books and the latest numbers from the University of Wisconsin's Cooperative Children's Book Center. The CCBC, formerly led by Kathleen T. Horning, who has cited the CIBC as a source of inspiration, continues one of the CIBC's important former missions of counting the books published in the US. The CCBC then breaks down the numbers by race and ethnicity. However, the CIBC's data studies further broke down systemic barriers including sexism, ageism, and ableism in their purview. In 2015, Lee and Low published the "Diversity Baseline Survey, "which published data on the children's publishing industry, for the first time, visualizing through infographics what many already knew — that publishing decision makers were unbearably white. The study also contributed to critical conversations about access to non-paid publishing internships for communities of color already suffering from housing and food insecurity in metropolitan areas such as New York and Boston.

Professional associations such as the National Association for Teachers of English, American Library Association (ALA), and Children's Literature Association organized panels on diversity, for example, ALA's Day of Diversity programming and ChLA's "Needs of Minority Scholars" in 2015. The ChLA panel was the first time women of color scholars in youth literature openly analyzed the intellectual and institutional barriers in the children's literature field and job market (Nel). The panel featuring Sarah Park Dahlen, Laura Jimenez, Ebony Elizabeth Thomas, and myself later turned into a series of essays, this time including Michelle Martin, a prominent Black woman scholar and former president of the ChLA, for a special edition of *The Lion and the Unicorn* titled "We Need Diverse Scholars.". Arguably, another watershed moment was the founding of the peer-reviewed open-access *Research on Diversity in Youth*

Literature, where we see the influence of the WNDB movement and how the term "diversity" became synonymous with its aspirations and ideals.

Diversity and liberation, however, do not descend from the same ideologies and commitments. Former Young Lord and co-author of the children's picturebook *Vicki and the Summer of Change* Iris Morales has said that "social movements are not just about actions but ideas." Morales, speaking about the third-world liberation movement she formed as part of her activism with the New York City–based Young Lords Organization and documents in in *Vicki*, says, "we were fighting for ideas." The CIBC's formation and ideology intersects with the third-world liberation movement and civil rights movements, also sparking critical race theory (CRT) and ethnic studies. In particular, the advent and struggle for Ethnic Studies provided an intellectual reckoning leading to what Nelson Maldonado-Torres calls "one of the original and influential contributions of the US academy to the array of fields and sciences that constitute the modern Western university" (104-5) If the CIBC is part of our intellectual legacy as a field, then the ideas and actions they were engaged with, such as CRT and ethnic studies, are foundational for understanding the study of youth literature and the praxis of decolonizing its study and industry.

The CIBC and Critical Race and Ethnic Studies Movements: Who's Afraid of the CIBC?

In "Who's Afraid of Critical Race Theory?," Derrick Bell opens his seminal essay by saying that "revolutionizing a culture depends on a radical reassessment of it" (893). Bell, credited as one of the founders of CRT, emphasizes why the legal framework reinvigorates various fields of inquiry while raising the caution of status quo politicians. If CRT and ethnic studies persist today in academic spaces, they do so despite legacies of criminalization and co-opting that should concern any advocate of literature as a tool of social justice. Poststructuralism, postmodernism, psychoanalysis, and even postcolonialism, as critical theories and ideologies, have not been restricted by contemporary state sanctioning. Only a few years before the rise of We Need Diverse Books, in 2010, Arizona famously banned ethnic studies through its restriction of Mexican American studies, a decision that later was deemed racist by a judge. The 2021 book ban in York, Pennsylvania, illustrates how school boards target CRT specifically as a form of analysis, books associated with it, and those perceived as teaching it. Many experts link these bans to the Trump administration's policies on "patriotic" education and — in the wake of the police killings of George Floyd and Breonna Taylor — call for more anti-racist education, a term linked to 1960s activist Angela Davis now popularly associated with Kendi's *How to Be Antiracist*. This newest iteration of criminalizing books for young people differs from simply banning J. D. Salinger's *Catcher in the Rye* for being too risqué for high schoolers. The longer tradition of banning and delegitimizing CRT and ethnic studies demonstrates how normalizing communities of color as foundational in US curriculum policy is met with rage, violence, and possible, if not immediate, criminalization. In other words, it is not just the stories but the people writing and whether the frameworks they use uphold white settler nationalism and patriotism.

CIBC and CRT forerunners were engaged in similar legal and political intellectual conversations in the early 1970s. A glance at the list of contributors of the Content Analysis Instrument in *Stereotypes, Distortions, and Omissions in U.S. History Textbooks* provides a rundown of some of the most influential ethnic studies forerunners, including those who began Ethnic Studies departments in the Northeast and Southwest, such as John Henrik Clarke (Afro American Studies, Hunter College, CUNY), Luis Nieves Falcon (University of Puerto Rico), and Alan Moriyana (Asian American Studies Center, UCLA). Richard Delgado and Jean Stefanic write in *Critical Race Theory: An Introduction* that the "heady advances of the civil rights era of the 1960s had stalled and, in many respects, were being rolled back." Writers, scholars, and activists interested in the law "realized that new theories and strategies were needed to combat the subtler forms of racism that were gaining ground" (27). Responding to new, subtler iterations of racism also marks the rise of the CIBC, which in the late 1960s found it impossible to separate youth literature from public policy. There was an urgency within the organization to articulate and analyze the challenges and solutions for parents and practitioners. Indeed, the CIBC and its critical race contemporaries also share similar approaches to civil rights. For example, Delgado and Stephanic emphasize that, "unlike traditional civil rights, which embraces incrementalism and step-by-step progress, CRT questions the very foundations of the liberal order, including the equality theory, legal reasoning, Enlightenment rationalism, and neutral principles of constitutional law" (26). In 1976, *Human and Anti-Human Values* represented the CIBC's articulation of a crisis of thought and language in youth literature and a reconsideration of the systems and foundation making it possible to create and normalize racist children's texts. They defined racism in *Human and Anti-Human Values* as "the systemic oppression and exploitation of human beings on the basis of their belonging to a particular racial group or people. 'Systemic' indicates that we must look at the status of the group as a whole, and not at those few individuals who may have climbed a 'ladder of success' in the white society. The word 'systemic' also connotes practices and policies which are pervasive, regardless of whether they are intentional or unintentional" (9). This analysis of systemic racism as separate from interpersonal relationships and actions and personal intentionality is one often lost in our more recent conversations using terminology such as DEI in many youth literature communities. Even in teacher and library preparation programs, training and syllabi often incorporate the term diversity as a means of discussing racial and gender justice. And in many cases

DEI engages with interpersonal decisions and additive approaches rather than with systemic policy upholding colonial institutions such as white supremacy.

Oddly, WNDB and the resurgence to describe and undue systemic racism in youth literature in the late 2010s did not, however, include a resurgence in quoting the CIBC's guidelines for approaching US civil rights discourses — though the CIBC is often quoted as an inspiration. For example, the blog *Reading While White*, which started in 2016 during the progress of the WNDB movement, describes its mission as "dismantl[ing] racism," and the collective behind the blog, including librarians Sam Bloom, Allie Jane Bruce, Kathleen T. Horning, Nina Lindsay, Angie Manfredi, and Megan Schliesman, contributes to important content and actions in terms of naming whiteness. I bring up this blog and online community as an exemplar group working to unmask racism in children's literature, but also as a means of examining how our public conversation might go further in naming and analyzing injustice. Ideological terms such as diversity and diverse voices, however, complicate our ability to identify the interrelated systems that create inequities. For example, they write, "In order to do our job, we have to seek out and listen to diverse voices. And those voices are not appearing much in the professional review journals" (*Reading While White*). The authors, as white writers and influencers, "acknowledge the existence of systemic racism and white privilege" as a demarcation in terms of the work they are doing to "advocating for anti-racist policies within our field and beyond." Indeed, this is a call to use white privilege as a driving force for change, yet the CIBC would remind us that combating systemic racism is not a matter of intention. In *Human and AntiHuman Values*, the council, in a move in tandem with critical legal studies, eliminates good intention as an anti-racist ideology or action: "Four hundred years of racism on this continent have left book writing and publishing primarily in the hands of a white, college-educated elite. Four hundred years of racism have left an ethnocentric majority with little knowledge or understanding of other peoples. No matter how good the intent of white authors and artists, they have rarely done a satisfactory job of depicting third world people. And it is the final product that counts — not the intent" (9). Encouraging readers to read and support writers of color matters for social justice, as the writers of *Reading While White* direct their readers. Yet how will readers, or the larger field of youth literature, know how to counter the dominance of whiteness in the field without examining how white dominance is maintained as a matter of policy?

Training in anti-racism, critical race studies, and ethnic studies is sometimes considered a new advent in library science, although the CIBC and other Black librarians, such as Augusta Baker and Pura Belpré, who also form part of the founding of US-based children's library services, created tools to implement such frameworks decades before (Leung; Lugo Vasquez). As Sofia Leung and Jorge Lopez-McKnight write, youth literature studies and publishing tend to "frame […] the race problem as one of diverse representation of racialized bodies, rather than one of racial power, domination, and privilege. David James

Hudson writes, 'Diversity's preoccupation with demographic inclusion and individual behavior competence has ... left little room in the field for substantive engagement with race as a historically contingent phenomenon."

Contemporary preoccupation with diversity manifests as if the exclusion of communities of color and their knowledge systems is ahistorical as opposed to purposeful and deeply rooted in generations of systemic policy. Recent work in youth literature and literacy studies by Ghouldy Muhammed and S. R. Toliver, for example, concerns the reclaiming of Black literacies and storytelling as epistemology and as central to understanding texts, literacies, and learning. In *Cultivating Genius*, Muhammed writes, "In contrast to what is currently found in many schools and classrooms, the historical roots of literacy learning in Black communities were much more expansive and advanced and included the goals of identity meaning-making and criticality" (10). Muhammmed underlines a cycle in which educators simultaneously deny Black excellence while also attempting to "improve and elevate the literacy achievement especially of Black children and other culturally and linguistically diverse populations," which ultimately leads to underserving these communities (9). Toliver emphasizes that her use of Endarkened feminist epistemologies (EFE) and Indigenous story work (ISW) "helped [her] to access alternative truths I had learned to forget. They helped me to explain my need to engage in the work of story and critique traditional qualitative research methods that asked me to leave story outside of my academic work" (167). My work in analyzing the CIBC's tools and ideologies asks us to also consider how generations of scholarship have negated the excellence of communities of color in youth literature, and what applying their frameworks might help us recover.

The CIBC's engagement with CRT — as an analysis of how race impacts access to property and policy in the US — and ethnic studies — as an analysis of reclaiming intellectual autonomy by US colonized peoples — means that the tools they develop also engage historical literacy and recovery, including identifying the historical origins of race-based discrimination as imperialism and colonialism. Indigenous, African American, Chicano, Puerto Rican, and Filipino communities — who were at the heart of the CIBC's tools and materials — represented the US's history of land occupation and interventions. The CIBC actually specified the term "third world peoples" to also connote US communities of color as in solidarity with the struggle against global imperialism (9). Here we see the CIBC engage with the crux of ethnic studies movements as an intellectual project: decoloniality and intellectual sovereignty. CRT is limited by its dependence on US-based jurisprudence and doctrines such as "the one drop rule" leading to what theorists call the Black/white binary (Delgado and Stephanic 67). For example, a critical race analysis might not take into account race-based politics and jurisprudence in Latin America and the Caribbean and the problematic yet foundational racial myth of mestizaje. Terms such as diversity, and indeed many of the statistics on diverse books, for example, treat Black, Asian American, Latinx, and Indigenous or Native as monolithic and do not account for intradiversity among youth and stories. Ultimately, regardless of intention, communities and stories are defined by watered-down terms and concepts in research such as that by the CCBC. Critical liberation frameworks such as CRT and ethnic studies, both complementary to each other and held in tension, assure intragroup nuances and overlapping histories of nationality, race, and ethnicity, figuring into our ways of holding the industry accountable.

The CIBC has always represented, as Bell put it, a "radical reassessment" of society. The section titled "Goals and Targets in *Human and Anti-Human Values* opens with "In an age of great and necessary upheaval, new educational materials — including children's books — must be developed." The CIBC saw its work, which included a Content Analysis Instrument, as transforming children's literature into "a tool for the conscious promotion of human values that will help lead to greater human liberation." The CIBC seemed in concert with Paolo Freire's teachings from *Pedagogy of the Oppressed*, published after the organization's formation, on critical consciousness for education for political liberation. Decoloniality, a key concept in ethnic studies, resists hegemonic, Eurocentric forms of knowledge that specifically erase the sophistication and science of colonized subjects (*Rethinking Ethnic Studies* 72). The right to self-determination of government in ethnic studies mirrors the right to self-determination of knowledge and education materials. The Content Analysis Instrument introduced in *Stereotypes, Distortions and Omissions in U.S. History Textbooks* produced by the CIBC is framed by saying that the struggles of people for independence and/or self-determination are also too varied and widespread to be fully covered in a single volume." The Content Analysis instrument works to demonstrate solidarities among colonized communities of color, "which history texts have traditionally relegated to the background." Moreover, the instrument continues the work of self-determination by monitoring not only inclusion of these communities, but also how history books portray "the relationship between subordination and privilege, powerlessness and power, poverty and affluence" (13).

Contemporary attempts to memorialize the CIBC, however, lose sight of the importance of anti-imperialism and colonialism in the CIBC's terms, goals, and tools. The group's solidarity with the Third World movement meant that it saw the plight of communities of color in the US as a result of US-based land conquest and ongoing colonization and racial capitalism — something that joined with the struggles of liberation of colonized communities across the globe. For example, a glance at the CIBC's recently digitized copies of the *Bulletin* reveals that its writers rarely describe racism without colonialism. Access to the *Bulletin* archive was recently made available through funding by the ALA and the work of scholars such as Nicole Cook, the Augusta Baker Chair of Children's Literature at the University of South Carolina. The keyword index researchers use to search the bulletins, and the site reflect the CIBC's attention to power analysis through words like "racism," "ethnocentrism," and "nationalism." However, the terms "colonialism" and "imperialism" are not key topics in the checkbox filter despite the constant use of these terms in connection with oppression and injustice. The site claims: "In the long-term, this bibliography could aid aspiring authors and illustrators, and publishers seeking to identify trends and gaps in children's literature. As for current initiatives and diversity campaigns, it would behoove them to learn more about the groundbreaking and influential predecessor, the CIBC." The translation of the *Bulletin* into metadata, as opposed to the reading of the text, are clearly two different experiences. Readers would find it impossible to remove colonialism from the power relationships on racism and sexism demonstrated in the *Bulletin*, while the omission of colonialism and imperialism as topics supports an innocence in toward the US as a settler colony (Tuck and Yang; Mignolo). Framing the US as a colonial power and empire in which specific kinds of racism and racial capitalism were enacted on colonial subjects is still something youth literary communities reluctantly, if ever, do.

Yet the CIBC's tools, including critical book reviews in the *Bulletin* and the Content Analysis instrument, were meant to do more than track representation, inclusion, and values such as anti-racism, anti-sexism, and ageism; they were meant to train readers on how literary devices such as character portrayal, setting, and plot could uphold or resist what they called the "colonialist mentality." The colonist mentality, described by CIBC writer Irma Garcia in the 1973 Special Bulletin on Puerto Rican Materials, depended on tropes upholding Eurocentric and US white saviorism that justified invasion. Garcia writes about how this mentality results in writers creating passive characters and negating Indigenous and African heritage. Garcia notes that this sense of passivity even leads to authors' imagination of Puerto Ricans as "illiterate," having no "newspapers, cultural society or political organizations," once again noting the relationship between literacy, history, and political engagement (3). Parents, teachers, and practitioners working with CIBC tools had the knowledge to go beyond representation and analyze how literature could work to uphold or dismantle this colonist mentality. Books including characters of color yet upholding colonial tropes were viewed as ineffective for advancing liberation and allowing communities of color to recover from the dehumanization of the colonial experience.

For example, in the Summer and Spring 1968 issue, Philip Sterling writes about the problems of presenting Harriet Beecher Stowe's *Uncle Tom's Cabin* in urban classrooms, even as critics argued for continuing to teach Uncle Tom's character, in particular, as a "rebel." Sterling takes issue with a Black Washington, DC, school board member, Benjamin H. Alexander, who argued for the teaching of *Uncle Tom* rather than Nat Turner's slave rebellion in classrooms. Sterling writes, "In real life under slavery, Tom's suicidal noblesse was neither characteristic nor effective. It was resistance to the lash, which Tom never offered, that freed tens of thousands of slaves — resistance by sabotage, flight or by striking back when struck" (3). Clearly, the CIBC's goal for texts in the classroom was to educate readers against colonial tropes that were often championed as virtuous forms of resistance. In this particular example, Sterling is clear that it didn't matter if the character was Black, since he was authored by a white woman who failed to show how enslavement was truly resisted by those enslaved. Sterling's example also shows how, even when a person of color submits a text of story for review or inclusion, colonial tropes and character development still matter if the goal of teaching is liberation.

The Mirror and the Matrix: Wrestling with What We See, the Politics of Citation, and Lessons from the CIBC

Youth literature remains a central part of the racial justice movements of the past and present US. Literature and literacy, for communities of color, stand at the center of a humanizing project in which the possibility exists for recovering what imperialism and colonialism took, and continues to take, away. In the CIBC, we see a demonstration and documentation of the most important intellectual movements for racial justice in the last seventy years, along with differences between liberation frameworks and corporate DEI. The history of youth literature for youth of color is marked by resistance and connection to community-based movements. The champions of youth literature writing for the CIBC, among them Sonia Nieto, Piri Thomas, and Walter Dean Myers, were grounded in an epistemology of liberation, for which they created tools to disseminate to practitioners and the reading public. Though not tied directly to the CIBC's work, Rudine Sims Bishop's career underlines deep connection to both multiculturalism, at the height of its influence in US education when she began her career, and youth literature. "Mirrors, Windows, and Sliding Glass Doors," published in *Perspectives: Choosing Books for the Classroom*, by Rudine Sims Bishop is often cited in contemporary conversations by those who know the power and politics of on the lack of diversity in children's books, and rightfully so. Sims Bishop's work in multicultural literature provided a helpful metaphor for unpacking the value and impact of access to culturally relevant literature for young people, including the negative impact of normative white children's texts for both white children and children of color. Sim Bishop writes, "When children cannot find themselves reflected in the books they read, or when the images they see are distorted, negative or laughable, they learn a powerful lesson about how they are devalued in the society of which they are a part" (2). Sims Bishop demonstrates her location in the multicultural movement and sociological theories present by the 1990s in her rejection of the US as an assimilationist melting pot: "Our classrooms need to be places where all the children from all the cultures that make up the salad bowl of society can find their mirrors" (1). Specifically, Sims Bishop supports a central principle of multicultural education — that it benefits white children — when she cites the importance of healthy representations of communities of color for white children:

> Children from dominant social groups have always found their mirrors in books, but they, too, have suffered from a lack of availability of books about others. They need the book as a window onto reality; not just on imaginary worlds. They need that will help them understand the multicultural nature of the world they live in, and their place as a member of just one group, as well as their connections to all other humans. (1)

Here, we see how children's literature forms part of what James A. Banks called "intergroup education" or "when educational reform related to diversity is viewed as essential for all students — and as promoting the broad public interest" (Banks, *"Introduction to Multicultural Education* 10). Indeed, Banks believed the institutionalizing of multicultural education depended on the embracing of it by white communities. This kind of intergroup work is something also in tandem with the tenets of CRT (interest convergence) and ethnic studies (criticality and multiplicity for white students), though a CRT lens perhaps would focus more specifically on race in the US while an ethnic studies lens might engage more transnational solidarities and the role of decoloniality, nationality, language, and sovereignty among representations.

One of my goals in this chapter has been to consider how intellectual predecessors such as the CIBC engaged with the urgent and rigorous frameworks for racial justice in their time. Youth literature as a whole has had a difficult time gaining academic attention and so-called credibility on behalf of communities of color, particularly for those who labor on their behalf (Jiménez Garcia 2017; 2021). The CIBC and Sim Bishop, along with a host of youth literature scholars and advocates, but especially those of color, are de-intellectualized in favor of celebration. For example, Sims Bishop's powerful metaphor was discussed during the creation of one of the most powerful and popular infographics on the lack of people of color in children's books in recent years: "Picture This: Reflecting Diversity in Children's Publishing." Developed by David Huyck, Sarah Park Dahlen, and Molly Beth Griffin, "Picture This" illustrated the CCBC's statistics while demonstrating the power of lack of mirrors. The graphic went viral on social media, demonstrating the urgency of tools for understanding racial justice and youth literature and how contemporary youth literature practitioners receive, disseminate, and debate information in comparison to the CIBC's *Bulletin* and resources, including books such as *Human and Anti-Human Values*. The graphic brought together many past and contemporary youth literature advocates and scholars whose input contributed to the 2018, and still the most recent, iteration of the graphic, which featured cracked mirrors "to indicate what Debbie Reese calls 'funhouse mirrors' and Ebony Elizabeth Thomas calls 'distorted funhouse mirrors of the self.'" Even Dahlen, a strong advocate for youth literature and a Korean-American scholar, adds in a postscript in her blog post about "Picture This" that when she first published the blog post announcing the graphic in 2015 she "failed to cite Rudine Sims Bishop's seminal article 'Mirrors, Windows, and Sliding Glass Doors,' which is clearly the basis for the mirror metaphor in both the 2018 and the 2015 infographic," although Sims Bishop was cited in the postcards printed by Teaching for Change and distributed at many book fairs and conferences around the US. Dahlen writes, "In keeping with #CiteWomen and #CiteBlackWomen, I have added her name in the blog post above ... With apologies for these omissions, Sarah." Throughout this chapter, I have called attention to how the intellectual work of communities of color in youth literature is rarely credited as intellectual. As the CIBC writes in *Human and Anti-Human Values*, the value system in white dominant society is "so powerful that authors can write *totally unaware* of its influence upon them. More often than not, they are unconscious tools of that system" (2). Dahlen's note is symbolic of what the larger community of youth literature must do to reclaim and center the intellectual labor of racial justice forerunners in youth literature. More than just inspiration, our histories serve as models for intellectual and critical engagement with the problems that continue to plague this field and industry.

Sim Bishop's mirror metaphor actually converges in powerful ways with the CIBC, which in 1976 wrote about the role of children's literature as both "a mirror and a matrix." The urgency the CIBC conveys in "The Mirror and the Matrix," written at a critical turn ushering in new critical frameworks tied to racial justice movements, comes to a fever pitch: "The structure of all relations is rattling and creaking, as people of all types challenge the usefulness to humanity." It is at this point in *Human and Anti-Human Values* that the authors distinguish between the two metaphors: "For the mirror flashes with new images. The matrix trembles with change." For the CIBC, the mirror metaphor extended into how the reflections in the mirror would also reflect an intricate, intersecting system that was strong, but also fragile and subject to changing ideas. The authors name children's books as part of the "new educational materials" that "must be developed" to "achieve [a just] society and help prepare children for such a society" (4). Children's books would act as a mirror that revealed the possibilities for change. The CIBC's use of children's books as mirrors and matrixes helps us see how reflections in the mirror go beyond representation and belonging, but also require critical self-reflection. In other words, wrestling with the part of the mirror, even as a writer, scholar, or teacher of color, reveals our complicity in anti-Blackness, sexism, homophobia, and so forth. In 1990, Sims Bishop also wrote about the potential of children's literature and the dangers of how idealism works against racial justice, again, an aspect of her argument that is often left out of contemporary conversations:

> Those of us who are children's literature enthusiasts tend to be somewhat idealistic, believe that some book, some story, some poem can speak to each individual child, and that if we have the

> time and resources, we can find that book and help to change that child's life, if only for a brief time, and only for a tiny bit. On the other hand, we are realistic enough to know that literature, no matter how powerful, has its limits. It won't take the homeless off our streets; it won't feed the starving of the world; it won't stop people from attacking each other because of our racial differences; it won't stamp out the scourge of drugs. (2)

The limits Sims Bishop describes coincides with the CIBC's activist scholarship and with the work of scholars such as Eve Tuck and E. Wayne Yang, who remind us that "decolonization is not a metaphor." Racial justice in youth literature goes beyond representation and into exposing the systemic inequities that have shaped how we tell, write, study, publish, illustrate, read, collect, and prize youth literature — and really have shaped how we tell stories and who is allowed to tell them to the masses. For readers of color, the CIBC reminded that educational materials should support more than just imaginative transformation: "We are advocates of a society in which all human beings have the true, not rhetorical, opportunity to realize their full human potential" (4). Beyond intentions and announcements of certain social justice commitments, youth literary studies as a whole needs to draw on generations of liberation frameworks that help us analyze the outcomes of our decision-making.

Today, as we continue to face legislation on banning CRT and ethnic studies, it is hard to imagine a time where there is no "rattling and creaking" of our society. Our reading publics and practitioners remain in need of rigorous tools — a need that those in corporate DEI efforts claim to answer. Yet the lessons of our intellectual past show that the frameworks we use matter depending on whom they are tied to, and that those who believed in racial justice initiatives also tied those initiatives to community-based movements and actions. Perhaps, in our current climate, which includes being under the scrutiny of bans and legislation, we might be tempted to believe we can continue to do the work of racial justice by simply using words that would seem less threatening to the status quo. But, as the CIBC teaches, words and language matter. How we name certain injustices matters, especially when colonial extraction and land occupation form part of a character's story of displacement. Whom we recognize and serve to equip with tools also matters in terms of who is trained to know the difference between diversity and liberation epistemology — publishers or parents and families who are at the front lines of how young people will respond to a distorted image in a book.

The CIBC also teaches us that our definition of quality children's books should extend beyond the *New York Times* Best Seller list and into the textbooks schools provide to young people as so-called neutral informational instruction. The legacy of the CIBC is also one that asks us to consider how often we see ourselves in youth literature studies as having different schools of thought and traditions. Whom do we cite versus whom do we co-opt? Whom do we recognize as forming our field and legacy as a youth literature field and industry? The

CIBC is as much the legacy of communities of color as it is the entire breadth of youth literature fields and industries.

Works Cited

Bell, Derrick. "Who Is Afraid of Critical Race Theory?" *University of Illinois Law Review* 893, 1995.

Delgado, Richard, and Jean Stefancic. *Critical Race Theory*. 3rd ed., New York UP, 2017.

Council on Interracial Books for Children. "The Mirror and the Matrix." *Human and Anti-Human Values in Children's Books*, CIBC, 1976.

Council on Interracial Books for Children. *The Bulletin.* Spring 1970.

Huyck, David, Sarah Park Dahlen, and Molly Beth Griffin. Diversity in Children's Books 2015 infographic. sarahpark.com blog. 14 Sept. 2016, https://readingspark.wordpress.com/2016/09/14/picture-this-reflecting-diversity-in-childrens-book-publishing/. Statistics compiled by the Cooperative Children's Book Center, School of Education, University of Wisconsin-Madison: https://ccbc.education.wisc.edu/literature-resources/ccbc-diversity-statistics/books-by-about-poc-fnn/. Released for non-commercial use under a Creative Commons BY-NC-SA 4.0 license.

Center for Puerto Rican Studies. "Afternoon Tertulia: Iris Morales ¡Palante, Siempre, Palante!," Oct. 2021, https://www.youtube.com/watch?v=c3od8Bnmt40,

Crenshaw, Kimberlée. "Mapping the Margins: Intersectionality, Identity Politics and Violence against Women of Color. *Stanford Law Review,* vol. 43, no. 6, July 1991, pp. 1241-1299.

Ortiz, Raquel, and Iris Morales. *Vicki and the Summer of Change.* Red Sugarcane Press, 2021.

Nieto, Sonia. "Foreword." *Side by Side: US Empire, Puerto Rico, and the Roots of Youth Literature and Culture*, by Marilisa Jimenez Garcia. UP Mississippi, 2021

Sims Bishop, Rudine. "Mirrors, Windows, and Sliding Glass Doors." *Perspectives: Choosing and Using Books for the Classroom*, vol. 6, no. 3, 1990. Reprinted in *Reading is Fundamental*, 2015.

Toliver, S. R. *Recovering Black Storytelling in Qualitative Research.* Routledge, 2021.

Coda

REFLECTIONS ON STRUGGLE, FREEDOM, AND STORYTELLING

*Marilisa Jiménez García and
Sonia Alejandra Rodríguez*

Storytelling has saved my life a million times over. I (Sonia Alejandra) grew up the oldest daughter in a mixed-status immigrant household where domestic violence and verbal and emotional abuse abounded. My family was poor with limited access to resources and a way out of poverty. My mother, my sister, and I were undocumented, and the systemic violence we experienced should have killed us, and the system tried. I was undocumented before the DREAMers movement, undocumented before "undocumented and unafraid." Silence and isolation were how my family and I dealt with the daily violences we experienced. Books, as Dr. Rudine Sims Bishop reminds us, were my "mirrors, windows, and sliding glass doors" to other worlds, other possibilities. I hid in Ramona Quimby's world, in Clementine's world, in Junie B. Jones's world, in Nancy Drew's world. For a while, all of those worlds worked for me. I felt safe in those worlds because I didn't have to be me but could pretend to be someone else, someone who didn't have to be afraid. The white world of children's books worked for me until it didn't. I grew weary of reading about white girls living their best rebellious lives while my own home life remained chaotic and unsafe. I wouldn't come across a book that spoke about being undocumented or about experiencing domestic violence until I was in college.

Books alone cannot save lives. When there's a demand for diverse books, what we're really demanding is diverse stories that challenge dominant and oppressive narratives. When books are challenged or banned it's because the stories threaten a dominant narrative. I am writing this in a time with the greatest number of book bans and challenges across the US, with LGBTQ+ and BIPOC books being banned and challenged at much higher rates than books with white and heteronormative content. I'm also writing at a time of increased violence against marginalized people around the world. There is no proportional number of books that a child needs to have in order to be rescued from the pain or violence they may be experiencing. One book or a million books would not have changed the fact that I was undocumented and witnessing domestic violence. I am surrounded by books now and am still dealing with PTSD, depression, and anxiety from experiences I had as a young person. Our advocacy for diverse books for young people needs to also include advocacy for accessible health care, for just immigration policies, for prison abolition, for clean breathing air, and for whatever else will keep our children and young people alive.

I suggest a shift in language to loosen the grip conservatives and the publishing industry have around our necks about which stories are acceptable and profitable. The first book I read where I felt seen was Sandra Cisneros's *The House on Mango Street*. Cisneros's stories became a foundation for my career as an English professor and a creative writer. I've memorized characters, lines, images, and feelings from those stories. I have many copies of *Mango Street*, but I don't need the book to retell the stories. When I was an undergraduate, Cisneros's characters made it clear to me that despite having access to one of the largest public libraries in the state, my mother's stories were the ones I needed most. My writing, research, and service around diversity and youth literature isn't about fighting for or protecting books as products of a capitalist system. I write, do research, and do service around books because that's the dominant medium for the stories I want to preserve and share. What I'm passionate about isn't books but storytelling. A slight shift in language about how I write about diversity in youth literature as an appreciation for stories rather than physical books allows me to shift the power from a capitalist industry like publishing to people and communities. Yes, I am fully aware that I am writing this in a book you are reading. But trust that I am also shouting about the importance of storytelling from the rooftops.

***

As we (Marilisa and Sonia Alejandra) conclude this volume, we have in mind the role of struggle, freedom, and storytelling. In our introduction, we talk about the limits of empathy, and, indeed, empathy is sometimes touted as the promise of literature, the arts, and the imagination for the political, social, and moral development of young readers and audiences. Saidiya Hartman, in *Scenes of Subjection*, writes about the dangers of overidentifying with the pain of enslaved African Americans, for example, through literary forms such as the slave narrative and the nineteenth-century American novel. Hartman warns specifically against using pain as a means of "extending humanity to the dispossessed and, in turn, [a remedy for] the indifference of the callous" (18). As Hartman suggests, it is simple to switch from "witness to spectator," from one who affirms and sits with someone else's truth to someone viewing a person's oppression as a vehicle for their own emotions.

After writing this book and reading our contributors' chapters, even reflecting on the current university campus protests against genocide in Gaza, we want to take some time to consider what exactly it is that we want readers, scholars, and creators to do. For example, it is possible to hang up posters of Toni Morrison and Gloria Anzaldúa in a classroom and still show utter disregard for the Black and brown lives coming in and out of our classrooms. It is possible for literature program directors to love books by Virginia Hamilton and quote Rudine Sims Bishop and still fail to retain faculty and students of color who didn't sense that same regard for their words or ideas in the department culture. It is also possible to see diversity and inclusion as books we add or delete from our curriculum at individual or government levels, even as generations of students of color and LGBTQ+ students and readers continue persisting and excelling in various ways in our midst. As Flagler College student Joshua Mast said, "I am born and raised [in Florida]. In the 90s when I was in grade school it [LGBTQ+ stories, history] was something that was not talked about ever. And I still turned out to be me. I exist. So this idea that if we don't talk about it we are just going to go away silently into the night is just pure fantasy." Ethnic studies teaches us that the power in education does not come from authors, book lists, and publishers, but from the students, families, and community members who create knowledge through struggle. Ethnic studies as a framework is simply powerless without centering what writers and communities of color have said about what they are doing and want to see happen.

Lorgia García Peña writes, "to change, we need more than inclusion and diversity; we need revolution and rebirth. We need to start anew from a place in which the lives and experiences of people who have been silenced and excluded are centered" (15). Indeed, this kind of change means much more than seeing the work of the scholars and editors in this volume as "alternatives" to traditional scholarship. A genealogy of intellectual legacies, which can come in multiple forms outside traditional publishing, books, and scripts, provides writers and scholars of color with strength in their community, and, as García Peña implies, this kind of intellectual organizing forms "community as rebellion."

We have also seen how contributors argue for the gathering of more data and nuance of representation in the field. Blessy Sharon Samjose demonstrates the importance of transnationalism when engaging with ethnic studies as a framework for South Asian readings in the US. Jung E. Kim's analysis of Asian American literature, and specifically her work on erasure of queer identities, shows us the dangers of seeing numbers and data on representation as a monolith. This is echoed by the interview with Alia Jones and Traci Sorell, who emphasize the need to access trends and numbers beyond the University of Wisconsin-Madison's Cooperative Children's Book Center and Lee & Low's Diversity Baseline Survey, although these are important sites for data. Sorell, for example, points to how such data might be used in the creation of more policy, from public policy figures to publishing and across the various fields.

We have in mind the struggles of educators, teachers, and students, particularly those serving in public schools, museum education, and libraries. Here, as Leigh Patel writes in *No Study without Struggle: Confronting Settler Colonialism in Higher Education* (2021), "Struggle ... does not mean suffering and pain but people's rigorous engagement with each other and differing ideas of freedom" (2). We have outlined in this book for readers that freedom and liberation rooted in an Ethnic Studies model means countering settler colonialism and its deficit logics as a root of systemic oppression, including racism. However, as Patel also reminds us, shifting our ideas about justice includes seeing students and young readers as so much more than reacting to racism. Struggle and resistance form an integral part of the learning process. Patel writes: "When we limit our understanding of student protest to racism, we overlook both the breadth and depth of how inequities operate through many vehicles in higher education. Moreover, we miss the core of learning, including education for the purposes of struggle, as a profoundly human and humanizing endeavor, defiant and, when necessary, fugitive from the mechanisms of formal education" (14). Part of our work in this book has been to spotlight the transformative and creative ways struggle has shaped the approaches of communities of color to storytelling and youth literatures. Yet, even as we acknowledge the necessity of struggle, we also acknowledge the vulnerability of teachers and students, especially in public pre-K to 12 classrooms and libraries with limited funding for new and trending books and professional development activities. We know our positions in the academy provide us with a certain amount of privilege when it comes to academic freedom in teaching, course design, and access to scholarly materials and books. However, positions in higher education are not created equal, and colleagues at community colleges, junior faculty, adjunct, and graduate students at two- and four-year institutions don't count on the same resources for research and administrative support. For example, in our introduction we call attention to our positionality as graduate students and non–tenure-track faculty when beginning conversations about this project. We worked on this edited collection knowing that this project is a labor of love assembled throughout various institutional battles and lack of support.

Public-school teachers in particular have often been undermined in recent book ban conversations, even for the sake of defending critical race theory (CRT). For example, how many times do we hear proponents of CRT say that this legal theory could not possibly be taught in elementary and secondary schools. Even Randi Weingarten, the director of the American Federation of Teachers, was quoted as saying, "Let's be clear: critical race theory is not taught in elementary schools or high schools. It's a method of examination taught in law school and college that helps analyze whether systemic racism exists — and, in particular, whether it has an effect on law and public policy." While this statement seeks to support teachers, it also problematically sets apart pre-K to 12 teachers and the work they do in their classrooms as not intellectual and non-elite.

K-12 teachers and their classrooms are often romanticized in the academy as the nexus and endgame of what we do as professors and researchers in the pursuit of social justice. Yet there is very little, if any, institutional support for public-school teachers to attend professional development activities beyond those provided by official school district personnel. Teachers in private schools might attend conferences such as NCTE and ALA, and there have been more initiatives to sponsor teachers and educators to attend and nominate them for awards, but the reality is that public-school teachers might be the least likely to be in attendance. Public-school teachers also have little control over the kind of curriculum materials they will have access to and in many cases must provide their own money to purchase and teach youth literature and comics.

In 2021, teachers taking a stand against the book bans in multiple states joined the movement "Teach the Truth" supported by organizations like Teaching for Change in Washington, DC. However, by joining some of the movements and signing petitions, many teachers opened themselves up to conservative groups who then targeted these teachers by name and sometimes even physical address. As academics, we must be careful not to rally anti-racist teachers without realizing that they are the ones putting their bodies and jobs on the line in K-12 classrooms and who risk losing their jobs and having their families targeted. After recent book ban battles, we sometimes hear, "Well, just don't end up in Florida" or "don't work in [insert the battleground state]." But we do not want to advocate for the idea that somehow more liberal-minded states are better places to teach for people of color and/or anti-racist educators. For example, in 2022, New York City's Language Arts curriculum, a city with a 54% student of color classroom population, was recently analyzed by New York University's Metropolitan Center as grossly deficient in diverse literatures and perspectives ("Lessons in Inequity: A Culturally Responsive in Elementary ELA Curriculum"). Indeed, one main takeaway from that report is that the three main curricula used in NYC schools, McGraw Hill *Wonders*, Houghton-Mifflin-Harcourt *IntoReading* and Savvas *myView*, are all mainstays in a majority of states around the US, regardless of districts' cultural and racial makeups. Among the problems cited in the report, all three curricula were found to have deficit language, ahistorical narratives, and "no guidance for teachers on engaging student's prior knowledge, backgrounds, and cultures; or reflecting their own bias, beliefs, and backgrounds." Beyond the whiteness of curriculum materials in a city as diverse as NYC, the New York Public Library, which provides access to new books and often is seen as an intellectual refuge for communities of color, has been defunded by the NYC government — stalling its ability to make acquisitions and provide weekend services and programming. We send a lot of love and support to educators, practitioners, and creatives of color who are constantly being asked to do more with less.

In September 2023, Marilisa attended the Freedom to Teach Conference in St. Augustine, Florida, which convened national and regional stakeholders over the fight for teaching specifically history. In attendance were Regina Gayle Phillips, director, Lincolnville Museum and Cultural Center; Ursula Szczepinska, director of education and research, Florida Holocaust Museum; and Gordon Wareham, director; Cypress Billie, museum educator; and Kim Cunningham, tribal educator, Ah-Tah-Thi-Ki Museum of the Seminole Tribe of Florida. Some of the main takeaways for supporting coalitions of learning from that important dialogue:

1. The importance of public history through museums and local archives emphasizing artifacts, performance, and oral histories as counter-narratives in their own right, especially those by Black and Indigenous communities which provide alternative timelines of local and national histories. For example, St. Augustine's Lincolnville Museum & Cultural Center is housed in an old African American high school, and leads visitors through the history of Black communities in Florida's oldest city-emphasizing Caribbean, Spanish, and US Southern histories. In Queens, New York, Sonia Alejandra underlines the role of the Queens Public Library and its local project on oral histories, the Queens Memory Project. A project that trains community members on conducting oral history interviews from other community members and then live on the library's archives.
2. Assuring that our teaching includes ties to local museums and archives created by marginalized communities and not depending on books solely in the classroom to build historical knowledge. For example, Reanae McNeal, whose chapter centered on AfroIndigenous storytelling and spiritualities, also performs as an Indigenous storyteller in local schools and organizations in Oklahoma. Similarly, in St. Augustine, the Ah-Tah-Thi-Ki Museum on the Big Cypress reservation, places students in conversation with Seminole tribe educators emphasizing the perspective of the Seminole nation in their language, including an exhibit on the disproportionate amount of Indigenous people missing and murdered in the region.
3. The need for action, specifically, local support and engagement in elections and school boards as opposed to engaging only when issues reach national debates or form part of presidential elections.
4. Emphasizing the victories rather than only the challenges. For example, historian Paul Ortiz, president of the University of Florida faculty union and Adreanne L. Martinez, a law student at UF emphasized the power of student and teacher organizing and how the UF faculty and student union was able to overturn some of the restrictions in the "Stop Woke" act on UF's campus.
5. The ways young people, including Black, Latinx, and Indigenous, and LGBTQ+ communities call Florida home, even its the state curricular erasure, and are compelled to stay in their state to create belonging, home, and educational opportunities within and outside traditional academic spaces.

All of these represent ways in which education from the perspective of communities of color, genocide survivors, and LGBTQ+ youth have persisted in a historically contested state such as Florida. However, we believe there is no such thing as uncontested terrain when it comes to the battle for ethnic studies.

***

This collection invites you, dear reader, to witness, to sit with silence, to feel unsettled — these too are signs of solidarity. We opened our collection with an original poem from one of Marilisa's students, Alissa Alina Flores. In some ways, the poem might have been the final push we needed to rearrange our lives to put this collection together. Flores's poem represents the urgency, passion, and need for ethnic studies, diverse literature, and community-centered pedagogy in the classroom. Flores's verses remind us that there is power and healing in who we are and where we come from:

>In *my* curriculum   stories of furrowed brows and
>   big hoops
>   strong curls, red lipstick
>a little *too* aggressive for you
>
>spaces where we unpack and we see ourselves
>we yearn   and yell   and vent
>and I don't know about you, but that's not aggression,
>In my curriculum
>that's what I call healing   *curación*

We have been the narrators of Flores's poem. We have found ourselves in educational spaces demanding to learn more about our histories, our people, and our communities. We are now the educators crafting curricula that we hope do our students justice.

Works Cited

Bishop, Rudine Sims. "Mirrors, Windows, and Sliding Glass Doors." *Perspectives: Choosing and Using Books for the Classroom*, vol. 6, no. 3, (1990, pp. ix–xi.

Garcia Peña, Lorgia. *Community as Rebellion: A Syllabus for Surviving Academia as a Woman of Color.* Haymarket Books, 2022.

Hartman, Saidiya. *Scenes of Subjection: Terror, Slavery, and Self-Making in Nineteenth-Century America.* Oxford UP, 1997.

Khan, Flor, Leah Peoples, and Lindsay Foster. "Lessons in (In)equity: An Evaluation of Culturally Responsiveness in ELA Curriculum." New York University Metropolitan Center, 2022.

Nichols, John. "Randi Weingarten Rips CRT Critics for 'Trying to Stop us from Teaching Students Accurate History." *The Nation.* July 9, 2021.

Patel, Leigh. *No Study without Struggle: Confronting Settler Colonialism in Higher Education.* Beacon Press, 2021.

"Freedom to Teach: Confronting Complex Themes in Contested Space." September 28, 2023–October 1, 2023. Flagler College, St. Augustine.

Contributors

Alissa Alina Flores is a Bronx native dedicated to exploring the intersection between art and activism, deeply informed and inspired by her own experiences within her community and beyond. Currently pursuing a master's of social work degree at Columbia University's School of Social Work, she specializes in advanced clinical practice with a focus on health, mental health, and disabilities. Alissa holds a bachelor of arts degree in sociology and women's, gender, and sexuality studies. Alissa's poetry delves into themes such as Latinx feminisms, the nuances of girlhood, and the critical need for diverse representation in curricula and beyond. She is interested in what it means to foster change through the power of narrative and spoken word. Complementary to her academic and artistic pursuits, Alissa is a case manager at Mosholu Montefiore Community Center, where she guides families through the process of accessing essential resources to meet their specific needs. As a social worker and writer, Alissa hopes to continue this advocacy work to empower the individuals she serves and promote dialogue surrounding social justice issues that impact her community — ultimately striving to bridge the gap between theory and practice in her roles.

Marilisa Jiménez García is an associate professor of children's and youth literary cultures at Rutgers University-Camden department of Childhood Studies. She is the author of *Side by Side: US Empire, Puerto Rico, and the Roots of American Youth Literature and Culture* (University Press of Mississippi, 2021), which won the 2023 Children's Literature Association for Best Book Prize. Her next book takes a look at Florida's colonial past and its Puerto Rican community.

Violet Harris is professor emerita, College of Education, University of Illinois, Urbana-Champaign.

Alia Jones is a master of arts in library and information studies (MLIS) student at the UW Madison Information School. She has experience working in public and academic libraries in Cincinnati, Ohio, and has also worked as a teacher and children's bookseller. Her research interests center on diversity in children's literature, with a focus on Black and Indigenous books and communities. She has served on the 2020 Caldecott Committee and 2022 Coretta Scott King Book Awards Jury and is currently on the 2025 Batchelder Committee. She blogs at www.readitrealgood.com.

Jung E. Kim is an associate professor of literacy at Lewis University. She has co-authored two books on teaching with graphic novels (Rowman and Littlefield; Bloomsbury International) and her third book, on the racialization of

Asian American teachers, is in production with Routledge. She writes about literacy, representation, and issues of equity. Jung is an active member of NCTE, ALAN, AERA, and LRA; believes strongly in the power of representation in literature; and is president of her local school board. She has worked hard to create multiple affinity spaces for Asian Americans in various communities, from the Asian American Caucus at NCTE to a local Facebook group in her town. When not reading, writing, or spending time with her family, you will find her running.

Reanae McNeal is an assistant professor of Africana studies and gender, women's, and sexuality studies at Oklahoma State University. Her research focuses on activist-(her)stories of Afro-Indigenous/African American/Indigenous women, interrelated histories of African Americans and Native Americans, womanist studies/spiritual activism, faith/spirituality, health/healing justice, digital ethnic studies, healing-centered decolonial pedagogies, and colonial/historical/societal/generational trauma. She promotes social healing, advances cross-cultural understanding, cultivates restorative and transformative justice, and fosters the healing of deep wounds through love and transformation. Her work has appeared in books and journals such as *Racial Dimensions of Life Writing in Education, English Leadership Quarterly,* and *Transformation Now!: Toward a Post-Oppositional Politics and Change.* McNeal is currently completing a book on the (her)stories of Afro Indigenous women's survivance.

Debbie Reese is a Nambé Pueblo scholar and educator. Reese founded American Indians in Children's Literature, which analyzes representations of Native and Indigenous peoples in children's literature. She co-edited a young adult adaptation of *An Indigenous Peoples' History of the United States* with Jean Mendoza in 2019.

Sonia Alejandra Rodríguez is a professor in the English Department at LaGuardia Community College (CUNY), where they teach composition, literature, and creative writing. Sonia Alejandra received their PhD in English from the Department of English at the University of California, Riverside. They coedit the journal *Research on Diversity in Youth Literature.* Sonia Alejandra has an MFA in Creative Writing from the City College of New York (CUNY). For more on Sonia Alejandra, visit soniaarodriguez.com.

Lara Saguisag is associate professor and Georgiou Chair in Children's Literature and Literacy in the Department of Teaching and Learning at New York University. Prior to joining NYU, Saguisag taught at the College of Staten Island–City University of New York. Her book *Incorrigibles and Innocents: Constructing Childhood and Citizenship in Progressive Era Comics* (Rutgers, 2018) received the Charles Hatfield Book Prize from the Comics Study Society, the Ray and Pat Browne Award from the Popular Culture Association/

American Culture Association, and an Eisner nomination for Best Academic/ Scholarly Work. She works to advocate energy justice and climate justice through research, teaching, and community service. Her current book project, tentatively titled "When Oil and Childhood Mix," examines the relationships between children's literature and fossil fuels.

Blessy Sharon Samjose has a doctorate in education with a specialization in South Asian Studies from the Ohio State University. She is currently working as an assistant professor of English at VIT (Vellore), India. Her research explores intersections between South Asian Studies and literature for children and young adults, focusing on the scope of social justice through critical readership.

Traci Sorell is a best-selling author who writes inclusive, award-winning historical and contemporary fiction and nonfiction in a variety of formats for young people. She is a two-time Sibert Medal and Orbis Pictus honoree and an award-winning audiobook narrator and producer. Eight of her books have received awards from the American Indian Library Association. A former federal Indigenous law attorney and policy advocate, Traci is a Cherokee Nation citizen and lives within her tribe's reservation in northeastern Oklahoma. tracisorell.com

Index

Abad-Jugo, Cyan, 35
Abantao, Faye, 34
ableism, 16, 79, 101–2, 162, 166
Abrams Books, 166
academy, 2, 4–5, 7–8, 10, 25, 42, 53, 119, 126, 128–29, 153, 164–67, 170, 174, 182–84
activism, 7–8, 10, 12–13, 35–36, 91, 99, 101–8, 111–12, 115, 162, 164, 167–68, 176
Adinkra Dictionary, The (Willis), 99
Adventures of Star Song (Lonewolf and Muhammad), 116
African Myths (Woodson), 144
ageism, 162, 166, 172
agency, 10, 42, 46, 52–53, 69, 92, 107, 122
Aguirre, Aldy C., 34
Ahmed, Leila, 46
Ahmed, Sarah, 63
Ah-Tah-Thi-Ki Museum, 184
Alamillo, Laura, 4–5
Alang, Sirry, 8
Alexander, Benjamin H., 172
Always and Forever, Lara Jean (Han), 84
American exceptionalism, 33, 39n1
American Girl series, 122
American Library Association (ALA), 122, 131, 166, 171
anti-colonialism, 8, 26, 29, 43–44, 46–50, 52, 171
anti-racism, 6, 8, 14, 164, 166–67, 169, 172, 183
anti-sexism, 8, 172
Anzaldúa, Gloria, 59, 104–5, 180
Aquino, Corazon, 30

Araki, Mari, 81
Aru Shah series, 42
Asian American girlhood, 77–92. *See also* girlhood
Asian critical race theory (AsianCrit), 78–79, 81–82, 92
Asian/Pacific American Award for Literature (APALA), 80
Austen, Jane, 19, 86

Bailey, Moya, 112, 113
Baker, Augusta, 163, 169
Banks, James A., 163, 174
Bannerman, Helen, 138
Beach, R., 148
Beatles, 157
Beaver Steals Fire (Confederated Salish and Kootenai Tribe), 155
Bell, Derrick, 162, 167, 171
belonging, 9, 33, 112, 163, 165, 168, 175, 184
Belpré, Pura, 163, 169
Berger, Dan, 7
Billie, Cypress, 184
Birth of a Nation, The (1915), 138
bisexuality, 91
Bishop, Rudine Sims, 108, 122, 135, 145–46, 152n4, 155, 162, 173–76, 179–80
Black Is Brown Is Tan (Adoff), 120
Black Indians (Katz), 116
Black Lives Matter movement, 6, 24, 165
Blackness, 12, 99–116, 122, 130, 175
Bloom, Sam, 122
Blume, Judy, 123
Blumenthal, Karen, 121

Bodyminds Reimagined (Schalk), 72
Bombeck, Erma, 122
Bontemps, Arna, 144–45
Bonus, Rick, 34
book bans, 3, 60, 182–83
"Boondocks, The" (McGruder), 39n4
Boston Globe-Horn Book Magazine Award, 152n5
Bradford, Clare, 2
brahmanical patriarchy, 43–44, 46–50, 52, 57n6. *See also* patriarchy
Bridge to Terebithia (Paterson), 136
British Trading Company, 57n4
Brooks, Gwendolyn, 162
Brown, Mike, 24
Brown, Sterling, 137, 141
Brownies' Book, The, 141–43, 152n3, 163
Brown vs. Board of Education (1956), 162
Bruchac, Joseph, 155
Bryant, Sara Cone, 137
Bulletin, The, 162–64, 171, 172, 174
Bush, George H. W., 153

Cahiles, Weng D., 34
Caldecott medal, 119, 146
Campomanes, Oscar, 27, 32–33
Candlewick Press, 165
canons, 19, 41, 109, 136–37, 162
capitalism, 65, 69, 72, 125, 171–72, 180
Caruth, Cathy, 61
caste. *See* social caste
Catcher in the Rye (Salinger), 167–68
Center for Native American Youth, 100
Chakravarti, Uma, 44, 57n6
Chambers, Brian, 162
Charlotte's Web (White), 136
Chaudri, Amina, 88
Cherokee Nation, 119, 124, 155
child marriage, 41–53, 57n10
Children of the Glades, 129

Children's Book Press, 120
Children's Bookshelf, The, 124
Children's Literature Association, 166
Child's Story of Dunbar, A (Henderson), 142
Chin, Vincent, 82
Choksi, Roshani, 42–43
Cintron-Gonzalez, Edcel, 2
Cisneros, Sandra, 179–80
citizenship, 9, 33, 36, 52, 79, 82, 87, 107, 128
civil rights, 13, 113, 163, 167–69
Clarence and Corinne; or, God's Way (A. E. Johnson), 139–40
Clarke, John Henrik, 168
Cleary, Beverly, 123
Cleveland, Christina, 104, 107
Clifton, Lucille, 146
climate crisis, 2, 63–65, 67, 69, 71–73
Cofer, Judith, 19
colonialism, 2, 4–5, 7–9, 12, 14, 16, 20, 24–27, 29–36, 39n1, 41–46, 51–53, 61, 63, 66, 87, 101, 104, 113, 115, 164, 169–73, 176, 181; British, 43, 51; European, 27; Spanish, 26; US, 162–63
colorism, 101, 141, 148
complicity, 11–12, 15, 33, 48, 70–71, 175
Confederated Salish and Kootenai Tribe, 155
Conroy, Jack, 145
Contemporary Chicana Literature (Herrera), 70
Cook, Nicole, 171
Cooperative Children's Book Center (CCBC), 12, 15–16, 97n1, 127, 165, 166, 181
Coronel, Sheila S., 30
Council on Interracial Books for Children (CIBC), 13–14, 161–77
Courage to Imagine, The (Natov), 60
COVID-19 pandemic, 77, 82, 86

Cox, Susan, 152n6
Creek Nation. *See* Muscogee Creek Nation
Crenshaw, Kimberlé, 45, 87, 162
criminalization, 6, 28, 30, 35, 167, 168
Crisis, The, 141
Crisis Publishing Company, 141
Critical Ethnic Studies (Elia et al.), 7
Critical Indigenous Literacies (Reese), 154
critical race theory (CRT), 6–9, 14–15, 59–60, 78–79, 162, 164, 167–74, 176, 182
Critical Race Theory (Delgado and Stephanic), 14, 59, 168
Crossing Bok Chitto (Tingle), 116
Cruz, Ted, 161
cuentistas, 59–71
Cuffee, Paul, 142
Cullen, Countee, 144
Cultivating Genius (Muhammed), 170
culture, 1–3, 7, 10, 20, 25–27, 32, 34, 42–43, 46–47, 63, 70, 79–80, 83–88, 100–101, 114–16, 136, 140, 145–49, 154–55, 173, 183
Cultures of United States Imperialism (Kaplan and Pease), 27
Cunningham, Kim, 184
Cunningham, Maya, 100

Dahlen, Sarah Park, 126, 166, 174–75
Dandyo, 57n10
DasGupta, Sayantani, 86
Davis, Angela, 167
Debating Darcy (DasGupta), 86
De Burgos, Julia, 19
decoloniality, 11, 25, 34–35, 61, 101, 103, 115–16, 170–71, 174
Decolonializing Methodologies (L. T. Smith), 61
dehumanization, 13, 19, 78, 172
DEI, 12, 14, 165, 168–69, 173, 176

de Jesús, Melinda, 90
Delgado, Richard, 14, 59, 73, 168
delos Santos, Kian Loyd, 23–24, 34
Dill, Augustus G., 142
dis/ability, 12, 92, 99–116, 165
discrimination, 4, 59, 77, 79, 138, 146–47, 170
displacement, 9, 100–101, 116, 176
diversity, 1, 5, 7, 12, 15, 20, 59, 73, 82, 90–92, 103, 108, 113, 115–16, 118n1, 119–20, 127–28, 131, 145, 153–54, 162–68, 170–73, 176, 179–81, 185. *See also* DEI
Doermann, Hannah, 65, 72
Douglass, Frederick, 142
Dragonfly's Tale (Rodanas), 155
Drinnon, Richard, 27
drugs, 23–24, 26, 28, 30, 33, 35, 176
Du Bois, W. E. B., 139, 141–43, 146, 163
Dunbar, Paul Laurence, 139–40, 144, 152n1
Durand, E. Sybil, 101–2, 113
Dusk of Dawn (Du Bois), 142
Duterte, Rodrigo Roa, 23–26, 28–30, 33–35, 39nn2–3
Duterte, Sara, 35
Duyvis, Corinne, 155

Each of Us a Desert (Oshiro), 11, 59–73
Ebony, Jr.!, 142
ecowomanism, 113–15
education and educators, 6–7, 13, 25, 27, 29, 32, 34, 36, 42, 44, 47, 50–53, 57n7, 57n10, 63, 79, 105–7, 109, 119–20, 124, 126, 128–30, 135–36, 139–40, 142–45, 148–49, 155–58, 162–63, 167–68, 170–74, 176, 181–85
Elia, Nadia, 7
Ellis, Amanda, 61–62
Elsie Dinsmore (Finley), 137
Elson, R., 138

empathy, 14–15, 42, 53, 60, 64, 70–71, 73, 145, 180
empire, 6, 23–36, 87; British, 7; US, 4, 7, 12, 16, 24, 26–28, 30–31, 36
Endarkened feminist epistemologies (EFT), 170
Endo, Rachel, 90
environmental justice, 59–73
Environmental Justice in a Moment of Danger (Sze), 65
Epaminondas and His Auntie (Bryant), 137–38
equity, 14, 72–73, 112, 121, 131, 164–65, 183. *See also* DEI
erasure, 2, 5–6, 10, 13, 27, 77, 84–85, 91, 100–101, 110, 114–15, 118n1, 154, 171, 181, 184
exoticism, 41, 53, 89, 137
extrajudicial killings, 23–25, 28–29, 34–35

Falcon, Luis Nieves, 168
Fauset, Jessie R., 142
Feelings, Tom, 146, 147
feminism, 44, 46, 52–53, 78–79, 87, 91–92
Feminism without Borders (Mohanty), 53
Finley, Martha, 137
Flores, Alissa, 11, 185
Florida, 3, 6, 9, 129, 181, 183–85
Floyd, George, 6, 167
Floyd's Flowers (S. Floyd), 141
folklore, 42, 86, 140, 144–45, 147, 154–55
Fraser, J., 152n3
Frederick Douglass (Bontemps), 145
Freire, Paolo, 171
Friendship, The (M. D. Taylor), 147–48

Gadget Girl (Kamata), 80
Gandhi, Mahatma, 49, 50–52
Gansworth, Eric, 157

Garcia, Irma, 172
Garcia-Peña, Lorgia, 181
gender, 2, 8, 10–12, 41–47, 49, 53, 63, 70–72, 78–79, 87, 90, 99–116, 130, 164–65, 168
Gendering Caste (Chakravarti), 57n6
genocide, 6, 66, 180, 185
girlhood, 11–12, 41–53, 77–92
Givens, Jarvis R., 105, 107
globalization, 82
Golden, Arthur, 78
Golden Slippers (Bontemps), 144
Golding, William, 136
Gonzalez, Ann, 2
Graham, Lorenzo, 145
Greenfield, Eloise, 146
Grief Keeper, The (Villasante), 69
Griffin, Molly Beth, 174
Guy, Rosa, 146

Hachette Book Group, 166
Hallmarks of Ethnic Studies Infographic, 10–11
Hamer, Fannie Lou, 112
Hamilton, Virginia, 136, 146–47, 152n5, 180
Han, Jenny, 81, 85–86, 89–90
Harris, Melanie, 104
Harris, Violet J., 13, 113, 115, 135, 142, 148, 152n3
Hartman, Saidiya, 180
haunting, 5–6
Hawthorne, Nathaniel, 136
Haynes, Elizabeth Ross, 142–43
Hazel and Zeke (Ovington), 141
healing, 4, 11, 13, 20, 59–73, 81, 83, 103–4, 110, 113–15, 185
Henderson, Julia, 142–43
Hernandez, David, 7
Herrerra, Cristina, 4, 68, 70–71
heterosexuality, 15, 90–91, 131
Ho, Joanna, 86
homelands, 24, 26, 81, 83, 85, 100–101, 116, 128

homophobia, 16, 175
homosexuality, 90–91
hooks, bell, 49, 100–101
Horizon, The, 139
Horning, Kathleen T., 166
House on Mango Street, The (Cisneros), 179–80
How to be Antiracist (Kendi), 161, 167
How to Hide an Empire (Immarwahr), 2
Hudson, David James, 169–70
Hughes, Langston, 144–46, 162
Human (and Anti-Human) Values in Children's Books (Council on Interracial Books for Children), 14, 162–64, 168–69, 171, 174–75
human rights, 23, 25, 29
Hunt, Blanche Seale, 138, 144
Huyck, David, 174
hypermasculinity, 45
hypersexualization, 78, 89, 92

identity, 1, 31–34, 46, 49, 79, 81, 87, 89, 100–102, 104, 110–16, 128, 131, 154, 170; AsAm, 82, 84–88, 92; Asian, 85; cultural, 10, 86; ethnic, 53; imperial, 27; intersectional, 113; Japanese, 84; Korean, 85; Korean American, 85; monolithic, 5, 102; multiracial, 87–89; national, 2; queer, 181; transnational, 34; US, 34
If I Ever Get Out of Here (Gansworth), 157
Iftikar, Jon S., 79
I'll Be the One (L. Lee), 12
Immerwahr, Daniel, 2, 6, 27
immigrants and immigration, 2–4, 31–34, 36, 63, 77, 82–87, 91–92, 97n2, 179
imperialism, 14, 46, 170–73; British, 2; US, 2, 5, 6–7, 11, 23–36, 41, 162

incarceration of ethnic groups, 27, 39n1, 77, 82
inclusion, 5, 9, 12, 60, 111, 116, 131, 154–56, 170–73, 180–81. *See also* DEI
India, 41–53, 87
Indigeneity, 12, 13, 100–102, 104, 106, 113–16, 128, 130
Indigenous story work (ISW), 170
Institute on Critical Race and Ethnic Studies (ICRES), 6, 7–8, 10
Interracial Books for Children, 163
intersectionality, 10–12, 45, 79, 81, 87, 102, 111–13, 116, 127, 130–31, 162
IntoReading, 183
Iola Leroy (Harper), 152n1
It's Not Like It's a Secret (Sugiura), 80, 82, 91

Jackson, Jessie, 145
Jackson, Ketanji, 161
Jackson, Leila, 161
Japan, 26, 80–84, 86–91
Jet Black and the Ninja Wind (Lowitz and Oketani), 80–84, 87–89
Jimenez, Laura, 166
Jiménez García, Marilisa, 1–8, 10, 13, 25, 101–2, 113, 135, 166, 180, 183, 185
Jingle Dancer (C. L. Smith), 156–57
Johnson, A. E., 139–40, 152n2
Johnson, Angela, 146, 148
Johnson, James Weldon, 144
Jones, Alia, 13, 119–31, 165, 181
Journal of Negro Education, 135
Joy, The (A. E. Johnson), 152nn2–3
Jung, Moon-Ho, 33

Kakatok-katok sa Bahay ni Benok (Knocking on Benok's House) (Sy and Abantao), 34–35
Kaplan, Amy, 27
Kashyap, Keshni, 81

Katz, William Loren, 116
Keeping Corner (Sheth), 11, 41–53, 57n8
Keller, Tae, 85
Kendi, Ibram, 161, 167
Kim, Jodi, 7
Kim, Jung E., 12, 181
Kokila Books, 166
Korea, 84–86

land occupation, 8–9, 170, 176
language, 2, 9, 83–86, 97n2, 107, 113–14, 130, 140, 145–49, 154, 163–68, 174, 176, 179–80, 183–84
Lara, Irene, 108
Larrick, Nancy, 162
Latinx Environmentalisms (Wald et al.), 66
Lee, Gabriela, 2
Lee, Lyla, 12
Lee and Low's Diversity Baseline Survey, 12, 15, 127, 166, 181
Letras y Limpias (Ellis), 61
Leung, Sofia, 169
LGBTQIA: authors, 8; books, 179; characters, 90, 91; readers, 181; rights, 73; students, 181; youth, 184–85
libraries, 10, 13–14, 119–21, 123–24, 126, 128–31, 136, 145, 162–63, 166, 168–69, 180–81
Lincoln, Abraham, 153
Lincolnville Museum, 184
Lion and the Unicorn, The, 1, 65, 166
literacies, 2–3, 13, 42, 47, 52–53, 101, 105–6, 135–36, 141, 149, 153–58, 162, 164, 170, 172–73
Little Brown Baby (Dunbar), 139–40, 152n1
Little Brown Koko (Hunt), 138, 144
Little Engine That Could, The (Piper), 136
Little House on the Prairie (Wilder), 136

Lofting, Hugh, 144
Lonesome Boy (Bontemps), 145
Lonewolf, YoNasda, 116
Lopez-McKnight, Jorge, 169
Lorde, Audre, 19
Lord of the Flies (Golding), 136
Lowitz, Leza, 81
Lugo, Sujei, 122

Mahabharatha (Vyasa), 42
Make Way for Ducklings (McCloskey), 136
Maldonado-Torres, Nelson, 31, 167
Maparyan, Layli, 102–3, 105, 108
Marcos, Ferdinand, 29–30, 35, 39n3
Marcos, Ferdinand "Bongbong," Jr., 35
marginalization, 1, 6, 35–36, 72, 78, 87, 100–102, 105, 108, 113–15, 154, 179, 184
marriage, 11, 41–53, 57n6, 57n10, 86, 91, 139
Martin, Jocelyn S., 35
Martin, Michelle, 166
Martin, Trayvon, 24
Martinez, Adreanne L., 184
Martinez, William, 164
Marx, John, 41
Mast, Joshua, 181
Mathis, Sharon Bell, 146
Matthews-Alvarado, Kevelis, 8
Mays, Kyle, 100, 114
McCall, Guadalupe García, 68
McCartney, Paul, 157
McCloskey, Robert, 136
McCoy, Alfred, 30
McGruder, Aaron, 39n4
M. C. Higgins, the Great (Hamilton), 136, 152n5
McKay, Claude, 144
McKissack, Patricia, 146
McNeal, Reanae, 12–13, 184
Memoirs of a Geisha (Golden), 78
Mercado-López, Larissa M., 4

microaggressions, 59, 86, 90–91
migrants and migration, 2, 29, 32–33, 64, 67, 69, 71, 82, 101
Mirandy and Brother, 147
Mis-Education of the Negro, The (Woodson), 143
Mobley, Izetta Autumn, 112, 113
model minority myth (MMM), 12, 77, 79
Mohanty, Chandra Talpade, 53
Moore, Emily, 146, 148
Moraga, Cherríe, 100
Morales, Iris, 167
More Happy Than Not (Silvera), 69
Moriyana, Alan, 168
Morrison, Toni, 19, 180
Moses (Weatherford), 13, 99–116
mothers and motherhood, 11, 31–32, 42, 44, 46–48, 70–71, 80–86, 88–91, 122, 161, 179–80
Mufaro's Beautiful Daughters (Steptoe), 122
Muhammad, Safiyyah, 116
Muhammed, Ghouldy, 170
Mukherjee, Ayantika, 2
Multicultural Children's Literature in the K-8 Classroom (V. J. Harris), 135
Muratov, Dmitry, 39n2
Muscogee Creek Nation, 156–57
museums, 26, 28, 120, 184. See also individual museums.
Museus, Samuel D., 79
Myers, Walter Dean, 146, 162, 173
myths and mythology, 18, 33, 35–36, 42–43, 85, 107, 144, 155, 170
myView, 183

Nankani, Sandhya, 41
Narmad, 49, 51
National Association for Teachers of English, 166
National Association for the Advancement of Colored People (NAACP), 141, 143
National Book Award, 152n5
National Congress of American Indians, 156
National Council for Teachers of English Cultivating New Voices Among Scholars of Color Fellowship, 135
nationalism, 45–47, 168, 171
National Museum of the American Indian, 156
National Native American Heritage Month, 153, 156
Native Nations, 128, 154, 156. See also individual Nations.
Natov, Roni, 60
Navrange, Kashibai, 50
Naylor, Gloria, 19
Netflix, 90
Newbery medal, 146, 152n5
New York City, NY, 183
New York Public Library, 183
Nieto, Sonia, 135, 163, 173
Noah's Ark (Spier), 155
Nobel Peace Prize, 39n2
No Study without Struggle (Patel), 181

Obama, Barack, 28
Oketani, Shogo, 81
Omvedt, Gail, 56n1
oppression, 1, 4, 7, 11, 13, 15, 25, 29, 31, 42–49, 51–53, 59–60, 62–63, 65–67, 70–72, 77, 79, 87, 101, 103, 106, 109, 111–15, 155, 162, 168, 172, 179–81
Orchards (Thompson), 80–84, 87–89
Ortiz, Paul, 184
Oshiro, Mark, 11
otherness, 7, 14, 16, 24, 60, 77, 82, 163
Our Nig (Wilson), 152n1

Ovington, Mary White, 141
Owens, Deirdre Cooper, 107, 111–12
#OwnVoices stories, 155–57
Oziewicz, Marck, 65, 72

Page, T., 140
Pandey, Iswari, 42
Patel, Leigh, 53, 181–82
Paterson, Katherine, 136, 147
Patil, Vrushali, 45
patriarchy, 41–48, 51, 70, 107, 112. See also brahmanical patriarchy
Patron Saints of Nothing, The (Ribay), 11, 23–36
Pedagogy of the Oppressed (Freire), 171
Penguin Publishing, 166
Perspectives (Bishop), 173
Pew Research Center, 85
Philippines, 2, 11, 23–36, 39n1
Philippines National Police (PNP), 23, 29–31
Phillips, Regina Gayle, 183
picture books, 3, 10, 119, 129–30, 145
Piper, Watty, 136
police, 2, 15, 23–24, 29–31, 33, 35, 167
politics, 2, 9, 19, 25, 26, 33, 87, 125, 127–28, 161–62, 164, 167–68, 171–77, 180
Popo and Fifina (Bontemps), 144
postcolonialism, 2, 25, 41–42, 167
Potter, Beatrix, 136
poverty, 41, 88, 139, 171, 179
power, 7, 16, 29–31, 36, 42, 44, 46, 52–53, 63–64, 66, 68, 70, 72, 85, 107, 130, 137, 169, 171–74, 181, 184–85
Pride and Prejudice (Austen), 86
prisons, 24, 179
privilege, 16, 29–30, 32, 34, 43, 44, 46–52, 108, 155, 169, 171, 182
prostitution, 78, 90
P.S. I Still Love You (Han), 81, 84–90

Publishers Weekly, 124
publishing, 1, 3, 5, 12–13, 15, 16, 25, 35, 78, 124–29, 131, 136, 140, 143–45, 157, 162, 164–65, 169, 172, 176, 179–81
Puerto Rico, 2, 3, 9, 163, 172
Purves, A., 148
Pushkin, Alexander, 142

Queens Memory Project, 184
Queens Public Library, 184
queerness, 11–12, 69, 71–73, 86–87, 91, 181

race and ethnicity, 1–12, 33, 77, 79, 81, 86–92, 101, 104, 107, 109, 111–12, 138, 140–48, 162–66, 168–71, 174, 176, 183; African, 99–100, 104–6, 108–13, 115–16, 172; African American, 9, 12, 99–116, 135–49, 152nn1–3, 152n5, 161, 163, 170, 180; Afro-Cuban, 19; Afro-Indigenous, 12–13, 101, 115–16, 118n1, 130, 184; Afro Latinx, 12; Afro Native, 100; Asian, 91–92, 97n1; Asian American, 3, 9, 12, 27, 77–92, 97n1, 163, 166, 170, 181; Asian/Pacific Islander American, 80, 86; BIPOC, 3, 6–8, 16, 101–2, 105, 111–13, 115, 124–25, 131, 164–65, 179; Black, 3, 12, 19, 24, 99–116, 135, 147, 163, 166, 170, 173, 180, 184; Black-Indigenous, 101, 102–4, 106, 114–16, 118n1; Brown, 19, 46, 180; Chicanx, 4–5, 9, 70, 164, 170; Filipino, 170; Indian, 86, 90–91; Indigenous, 2, 27, 99–116, 127–28, 130–31, 153–58, 163, 170, 172, 184; Iranian American, 91; Japanese, 86, 88–89, 91; Japanese American, 89, 97n2; Korean American, 84–86, 88; Latinx, 3, 4–5, 7, 12, 19, 113, 170, 184; Mexican American,

163–64, 167; Native American, 8, 13, 88, 90, 100, 113, 116, 119–31, 153–58, 170; Pacific Islander, 92; people and communities of color, 1, 4, 8–10, 12, 14–15, 44, 60, 73, 87, 101, 119, 122, 125, 127, 136, 166, 168–77, 180–83, 185; Puerto Rican, 9, 163, 170; white, 9, 12, 14, 16, 32, 39n4, 44, 46, 79–80, 83–85, 87–88, 90–92, 104, 108, 124–25, 131, 136–45, 147–49, 157, 166, 168–70, 172–75, 179
racial justice, 1, 4, 7, 9, 10, 12, 16, 65, 72, 163, 165, 168, 173–76
racism, 1, 3–4, 9, 15–16, 39n1, 45–46, 77, 79, 82, 89–91, 127, 130, 137, 144, 147, 155, 161–65, 167–69, 171–72, 181–82
Ramayana (Valmiki), 42
Ramona series, 123
Rappler news site, 26, 34, 39n2
Rayaprol, Aparna, 42
Reading While White, 169
Real and Imagined Woman (Sunder Rajan), 46
Redmond, Shana L., 7
Reese, Debbie, 13, 135, 174
religion, 41–42, 45, 104, 113, 137, 139, 154–55; Catholicism, 61; Christianity, 99, 155; Hinduism, 47; Judaism, 83
removal, 101, 116
representation, 10, 16, 77–92, 114–15, 125, 130, 143, 162, 172, 174, 176, 181
Research on Diversity in Youth Literature, 1, 166–67
resistance, 10–11, 35, 42–43, 46–47, 49–50, 52–53, 59–73, 77, 90, 101–2, 105, 107, 109, 115, 147, 152n6, 172–73, 181
Ressa, Maria, 39n2
Reynolds, Nancy Thalia, 88
Rhodes, Cristina, 69

Ribay, Randy, 11, 23, 25–26, 34
Rice, Tamir, 24
Rizal, Jose, 26
Rodanas, Kristina, 155
Rodriguez, Robyn Magalit, 32
Rodríguez, Sonia Alejandra, 1, 3–5, 7–8, 11, 179–80
Roll of Thunder, Hear My Cry (M. D. Taylor), 136
Ross, Gayle, 155

Saguisag, Lara, 2, 5, 11, 65, 72
Salesses, Matthew, 15–16
Salinger, J. D., 167
Samjose, Blessy Sharon, 11, 181
Sanchez-Eppler, Karen, 10
Sankofa, 99, 102
Sartre, Jean-Paul, 81
sati, 45–46, 56n3
satyagraha, 43–44, 50–52, 57n11
Scarlet Letter, The (Hawthorne), 136
Scenes of Subjection (Hartman), 180
Schackleford, Jane D., 144
Schalk, Sami, 72, 110–12
Scholastic Corporation, 166
segregation and desegregation, 162–63
Seminole Nation, 184
Severino, Allan, 30
sexism, 16, 46–49, 79, 163–64, 166, 172, 175
sexuality, 12, 45, 47–48, 57n6, 78, 80–81, 86, 89–92, 130
Shakespeare, William, 19
sheroes, 99, 101–3, 106, 110–13
Sheth, Kashmira, 11, 41–53
Shimmershine Queens, The (Yarbrough), 148
Side by Side (Jiménez García), 2, 165
Si Kian (This is Kian) (Cahiles and Aguirre), 34
Silence that Binds Us, The (Ho), 86
Silvera, Adam, 69
Simon and Schuster, 166

Sims, Rudine. *See* Bishop, Rudine Sims
Sixteen Candles (1984), 90
slavery, 2, 6, 99–100, 102–5, 107, 109–14, 122, 137, 147, 172–73, 180
Sleeter, Christine, 5, 9, 10, 163
Smith, Cynthia Leitich, 156–57
Smith, Linda Tuhiwai, 61
social caste, 41–53, 56n1, 56n3, 57n5, 57n11, 144
social class, 2, 23–24, 44, 47, 77, 87, 107; middle-class, 85, 87, 139–41, 144, 148; working-class, 7, 8, 139, 145
social justice, 3, 7–8, 12–14, 42–43, 53, 65, 72, 79, 99, 101–3, 105–6, 108, 167, 169, 176, 182
social media, 1, 24, 122, 123, 166, 174; Bookstagram, 129; Facebook, 166, 188; Instagram, 129, 166; X, 166
social reform, 46, 48–50, 57n10
Society of Children's Book Writers and Illustrators (SCBWI), 121
Sorensen, Sam, 8
Sorell, Traci, 9, 13, 119–31, 165, 181
Souls of Black Folk, The (Du Bois), 142
South Asia, 41–48, 52–53, 181
Spier, Peter, 155
spiritual activism, 101–2, 104–7, 112
spirituality, 12–13, 99, 101–13, 115, 155, 184
Srikanth, Rajini, 53
Stephanic, Jean, 14, 59, 73, 168
Steptoe, John, 122, 146
stereotypes, 10, 46, 52–53, 78, 86, 88–92, 123, 125, 130, 136–38, 140–41, 147, 156, 162
Stereotypes, Distortions and Omissions in U.S. History Textbooks (CIBC), 162, 168, 171
Sterling, Philip, 172–73

"Stop Woke" bill, 9, 184
Story of Doctor Dolittle, The (Lofting), 144
Story of George Washington Carver, The (Bontemps), 145
Story of Little Black Sambo, The (Bannerman), 138
Story of the Milky Way, The (Bruchac and Ross), 154–55
storytelling, 2, 4, 7, 8, 11–12, 15, 42, 59–73, 99, 105, 120, 122, 129, 147, 170, 179–85
Stowe, Harriet Beecher, 172
subjectivity, 2, 10, 70
Sugiura, Misa, 80
suicide, 81, 83, 89
Sunder Rajan, Rajeswari, 46
suppression, 36, 46, 100
Sy, Mon, 34
Szczepinska, Ursula, 183
Sze, Julie, 65, 69, 73

Tale of Peter Rabbit, The (Potter), 136
Tales of a Fourth Grade Nothing (Blume), 123
Taxel, J., 152n6
Taylor, Breonna, 6, 167
Taylor, Dorceta E., 65
Taylor, Mildred D., 136, 146, 147
Teaching for Change, 165, 175, 183
Tell Me a Story, Mama (A. Johnson), 148
Thanksgiving, 153, 156
Thapar-Björkert, Suruchi, 44, 47
This Bridge Called My Back (Moraga and Anzaldúa), 4
Thomas, Ebony Elizabeth, 113, 126, 166, 174
Thomas, Joyce Carol, 146
Thomas, Piri, 162, 173
Thompson, Holly, 81
Tina's Mouth (Kashyap and Araki), 81–82, 86–87, 90–91
Tingle, Tim, 116

Toliver, S. R., 161
Transformative Ethnic Studies in Schools (Sleeter and Zavala), 9, 10–11
transnational contexts, 79, 81–82
transnationalism, 8–9, 34, 41, 43, 52–53, 82, 163, 165, 174, 181
trauma, 26, 36, 59, 61–65, 67, 69, 72–73, 91
Triggered (J. Martin and Abad-Jugo), 35
Trump, Donald, 6, 167
Tubman, Harriet, 13, 99–116, 142
Tuck, Eve, 5–6, 176
Turner, Nat, 172
Tuscarora Nation, 157
Two Little Confederates (Page), 140

Uncle Tom's Cabin (Stowe), 172
Under the Mesquite (McCall), 68
UNSPEAKABLE (Weatherford), 116
Unsung Heroes (Haynes), 142–43
uplift, 43, 50–51, 140, 142–43
Upward Path, The (Pritchard and Ovington), 141

Vasquez, V., 154
Vicki and the Summer of Change (Morales and Ortiz), 167
victims and victimhood, 46, 49, 52, 92, 137
Villasante, Alexandra, 69
violence, 2, 6, 24–25, 28, 36, 50–51, 65–67, 73, 77, 101, 105, 110–12, 168, 179
Viramontes, Helena Maria, 66
Voices of Resistance (Alamillo et al.), 4–5

Wald, Sarah, 66
Wareham, Gordon, 183
Weatherford, Carole Boston, 13, 99, 101–16
Webb, Adele, 29

Weingarten, Randi, 182
We Need Diverse Books movement, 1, 164–67, 169
White, E. B., 136
whiteness, 1, 12, 16, 32, 78, 88, 124, 131, 166, 169, 183
white supremacy, 60, 90, 100–102, 104, 114, 163–64, 169
Whiting, Helen, 144
Whose Side Are You On? (Moore), 148
widowhood, 41–53, 57n8, 57n10
Wilder, Laura Ingalls, 136
Wilkinson, Brenda, 146
Willful Subjects (S. Ahmed), 63
Williams, Byron, 164
Willis, W. Bruce, 99
Wilson, Harriet, 152n1
womanhood, 11–13, 48, 52–53
womanism, 99–116
women, 19, 42–46, 49, 51–53, 57n6, 57n10, 63, 78, 87; African American, 106, 152n1, 161; Asian, 89; Asian American, 78, 86, 89–90; BIPOC, 105, 108–9, 112, 164, 166; Black, 99–116, 166; Indigenous, 100; Japanese American, 90; Latin, 19; white, 173
Women's Union of Nigeria, 19
Wonders, 183
Wong, Anna May, 78
Woodson, Carter G., 143–44, 146

Yamada, Mitsuye, 77
Yang, E. Wayne, 176
Yarbrough, Camille, 146, 148
Yenika-Agbaw, Vivian, 2
You Can't Pet a Possum (Bontemps), 145
Young Lords Party, 19, 167
Young Set, The, 139

Zaidi, Annie, 44
Zavala, Wayne Miguel, 5, 9, 10, 163

www.ingramcontent.com/pod-product-compliance
Lightning Source LLC
Chambersburg PA
CBHW022020220426
43663CB00007B/1151